Embodied Acting

"A focus on the body, its actions, and its cognitive mechanisms identifies ... foundational principles of activity that link the three elements of theatre: story, space, and time. The three meet in, are defined by, and expressed through the actor's body." – *from the Introduction*

Embodied Acting is an essential, pragmatic intervention in the study of how recent discoveries within cognitive science can – and should – be applied to performance. For too long, a conceptual separation of mind and body has dominated actor training in the West. Cognitive science has shown this binary to be illusory, shattering the traditional boundaries between mind and body, reason and emotion, knowledge and imagination. This revolutionary new volume explores the impact that a more holistic approach to the "bodymind" can have on the acting process.

Drawing on his experience as an actor, director, and scholar, Rick Kemp interrogates the key cognitive activities involved in performance, including:

- non-verbal communication
- the relationship between thought, speech, and gesture
- the relationship between self and character
- empathy, imagination, and emotion.

New perspectives on the work of Stanislavski, Michael Chekhov, and Jacques Lecoq – as well as contemporary practitioners including Daniel Day-Lewis and Katie Mitchell – are explored through practical exercises and accessible explanations. Blending theory, practice, and cutting-edge neuroscience, Kemp presents a radical re-examination of the unconscious activities engaged in creating, and presenting, a role.

Rick Kemp (aka Rick Zoltowski) has worked as an actor and director with companies such as the Almeida, Complicite, Commotion, Quantum, and Squonk Opera. He holds an MA from Oxford University, UK, an MFA and a PhD from the University of Pittsburgh, USA, and teaches at Indiana University of Pennsylvania, USA.

Embodied Acting

What neuroscience tells us about performance

Rick Kemp

Routledge
Taylor & Francis Group

LONDON AND NEW YORK

First published 2012
by Routledge
2 Park Square, Milton Park, Abingdon, Oxon OX14 4RN

Simultaneously published in the USA and Canada
by Routledge
711 Third Avenue, New York, NY 10017

Routledge is an imprint of the Taylor & Francis Group, an informa business

British Library Cataloguing in Publication Data
A catalogue record for this book is available from the British Library

Library of Congress Cataloguing in Publication Data
Kemp, Rick, 1958-
Embodied acting : what neuroscience tells us about performance / by
Rick Kemp.
p. cm.
Includes bibliographical references and index.
1. Acting–Psychological aspects. 2. Actors–Psychology. 3. Cognitive
neuroscience. I. Title.
PN2058.K46 2012
792.02'8–dc23
2012007101

ISBN: 978-0-415-50787-5 (hbk)
ISBN: 978-0-415-50788-2 (pbk)
ISBN: 978-0-203-12611-0 (ebk)

Typeset in Goudy
by Taylor & Francis Books

Printed and bound in Great Britain by the MPG Books Group

For Diane, Emil, and Stefan.

Contents

Figures

Tables

Acknowledgements

This book is based on experiences that go back a long way, so the acknowledgements do also …

Thanks to: David Lewis, Dennis Johnstone, Anthony Gee, and especially Sean Moore from St. Benedict's; John Batchelor and Anne Barton at New College; Monika Pagneux and Philippe Gaulier in Paris; all the dear friends with whom I've made shows, too numerous to mention; Buck Favorini and Bruce McConachie at the University of Pittsburgh; Dan Jemmett and the Strandies; Brian Jones, Michael Hood, and other friends, colleagues, and students at Indiana University of Pennsylvania; and Talia Rodgers and Sam Kinchin-Smith at Routledge.

Preface

The germ of the idea for this book appeared when I was studying English literature at Oxford. At that time in England, training in acting was considered a vocational activity, and didn't merit a degree of any sort. Inspired by Peter Brook's *The Ik* and Tadeusz Kantor's *The Dead Class*, the Marx Brothers, Max Wall, and Morecambe and Wise, I was sure at that point that my future lay in theatre, but I had been persuaded by my teachers and parents to take up my Oxford place instead of going to drama school. Oxford didn't have a theatre program, and the study of drama was considered a component of literature. The prevailing attitude towards live performance was that it offered an interesting perspective on a written text, but wasn't worthy of study in its own right. Although I was heavily involved in university dramatic societies, performing and directing both contemporary and classic plays, I felt dissatisfied with my studies, and didn't really know why.

I had a sort of theatrical epiphany when I saw a performance by a group called Moving Picture Mime Show. They performed three long mime pieces, one with full-face "larval" masks, and two in a cartoon mime style. I was thrilled to see what could be done without words, costumes, or props, and had a vision of what could happen if this level of physical expertise could be applied to scripts. Following urgent but inchoate intuitions, I steadfastly ignored missives from the careers office about a future in publishing or the Foreign Office, and, on graduating, started to work as an actor.

In the four years following my graduation I was involved in a wide range of performance styles, gaining a practical apprenticeship. I performed in a street clown trio with Simon McBurney, who was then studying at Lecoq's school in Paris, and later started Complicite, and Neil Bartlett, who later went on to run the Lyric Theatre, Hammersmith. This was a crash course in physical communication: we learned what worked by counting up our takings at the end of the day. We toured around the UK in an ailing Alfa Romeo and got picked up to be the opening act for a gothic punk band called Bauhaus. Which was the end of us as a trio! I performed in the first show by the new Almeida theatre company, played percussion in a pop band called Havana Let's Go! and did a year-long tour of an agitprop piece about unemployment. I joined the 1982 Theatre Company, which had been set up by Neil Bartlett and Latvian writer and director Banuta Rubess to exist for one year. We performed Brecht's *In the Jungle of Cities* and *The Silver Veil* by Latvian poetess Aspazije in an imagistic and deconstructionist way, touring the UK, Europe, Canada, and the USA. The intent to disband after one year dissolved in the face of an offer to present Shakespeare plays as a company in residence at the University of Essex.

During this period I attended a workshop run by Dario Fo, and as a result went to train at his summer school in Italy, subsequently being invited back to teach. Through my association with Fo, the 1982 Company was invited to present the English-language premiere of his solo show *Mistero Buffo*. This was based on the historical figure of the *giulare* – a minstrel clown who performed comic versions of stories from the Bible. I adapted the show for ensemble performance, performed in it and directed it. The show premiered at the Riverside Studios, and then transferred to the Tricycle Theatre before touring the UK. Doing many performances of the same piece alerted me to my limitations as a performer. I felt as though my gestures were bound in the same patterns, and had a physical sensation of encountering invisible confines. I realized that I needed to get a thorough physical training.

Fortunately, I won an award from the Institut Français that allowed me to go and study in Paris. I trained with Philippe Gaulier and Monika Pagneux, two teachers who had just left Lecoq's school and set up their own studio. The course was structured as a sequence of "Stages" focusing on topics such as clown, commedia, melodrama, and tragedy. Each day started with physical training and was followed by improvisatory exercises in the relevant style. This training was revelatory, liberating, and foundational for me. I discovered the value of play and fundamental rules of physical performance – Lecoq's principle that everything moves, that one's body changes according to factors such as physical environment, levels of emotion, degree of will, and that, in a reflexive relationship, the skilled actor can use his or her body to create the illusion of these elements for the audience. I learnt that physical principles inform different styles of performance, and that stillness, rhythm, and tempo create dramatic shape. Monika was at that time Peter Brook's Movement Director, and relayed many of his working practices to us as well as the key principle that she learnt from him – that theatre is the art of making the invisible visible. All of this wonderful information fed into the conviction that I had formed at Oxford, that the body is central to the communication of meaning in performance.

On my return to London from Paris, I created a solo clown show about a Polish Count who lived in a cupboard, which I performed in England, Europe, North Africa, and the Middle East over a period of three years. I did more Shakespeare, and worked with Theatre de Complicite, which by this time was established enough to be invited to mount a season at the Almeida theatre, and to bring a production of Durrenmatt's *The Visit* to the National Theatre. In 1991 I founded Commotion with Gerry Flanagan, who had also trained with Philippe Gaulier. Over the course of seven years we created seven theatrical clown shows, devising scripts through improvisations based on archetypal stories such as Don Quixote, Don Juan, and the Fall of Lucifer. With support from the Arts Council, regional Arts Associations, and the Foundation for Sport and the Arts, we were able to create a new show each year and tour it in the UK before runs in London and at the Edinburgh Festival. During this period I also had the opportunity to train with Yoshi Oida and Master Nakamura in Noh theatre, Keith Johnstone in improvisation, Antonio Fava in Commedia, and Augusto Boal in the format that he called The Rainbow of Desire.

Throughout these different experiences, I was looking for ways to make theatre vital and accessible, to discover how words could be credibly expressed and integrated with movement to create visceral responses in audiences. Concurrently with my professional career, I had been teaching in a variety of contexts, from impromptu sessions with Moroccan street children to running workshops in conjunction with my company's shows, teaching at colleges in England and Europe, leading masterclasses with Monika Pagneux, training clowns at London's Circus Space, and actors on courses in conservatory programs in London. Moving beyond teaching one-off workshops into longer courses made me reflect on what I was discovering in performances and my own training, and deepened my conviction that there were certain basic principles that underlie multiple styles of performance, and that these could be identified through the activities of the body. For example, it is true of both the Commedia performer and the actor working in the style of psychological realism that particular gestures can be expansive or contractive, their movements direct or indirect, postures closed or open. It is also true that audiences receive information from these physical traits and make meaning from them, sometimes consciously, but generally through an unconscious process.

Moving to the US for the new millennium introduced me to a different world of theatrical knowledge. In the professional realm, I found a great reliance on Stanislavski and Method acting, and this emphasis on mental process helped me to explore the links between thought, feeling, and expression. In the last ten years, I've directed 20 productions, and acted in 14. These pieces have ranged in style and genre from psychological realism through theatrical clown to Shakespeare to multimedia image concerts. Similarly to my experience in Europe, I've recognized common principles that are present in a variety of styles, but also that there is a lack of a common practical vocabulary among practitioners to talk about performance. We don't have common terms to describe elements of, or differentiations in, posture, gesture, tempo, or the use of space, but these features are essential in communicating meaning, and are inextricably linked with the conceptual thought that Stanislavskian analysis deals in. Theatre is, of course, more than just saying the words ... *how* we say them is just as much a communicator of meaning.

This brings me to the knowledge that helps to tie all of this together, and which gives a theoretical structure to the principles of performance that I have been discovering in my practical experience. In my own acting, I've been constantly aware of a reflexive relationship between physicality, thought, and feeling. The first clues that I had that this phenomenon was being addressed by scientists came from reading Daniel Goleman's *Emotional Intelligence* and Antonio Damasio's *The Feeling of What Happens*, but it was not until I was introduced to cognitive studies in my doctoral work at the University of Pittsburgh that I realized the full extent of the potential of cognitive science to illuminate the process of acting. Here at last is a range of empirically-based research that acknowledges the centrality of physical experience in perception, cognition, and expression, and offers insights into the mysterious processes of emotion, empathy, and imagination that an actor engages in when preparing and presenting a role.

Introduction

The goal of this book is to explore the implications that recent findings in cognitive science have for the theory and practice of acting in the West. This information offers a framework for a significant conceptual shift in Western thought about acting. Since at least the eighteenth century, Westerners have thought about acting as something that happens from the "inside-out" or the "outside-in." Many schools characterize acting as either a psychological ("inside-out") process, or as one that is physical in origin ("outside-in"). While many training programs include movement classes, or activities such as Alexander Technique, yoga, or dance, these are generally separate from the "acting" classes, and offer the student little information on how to synthesize the two. On the other hand, physically-based approaches tend to neglect textual analysis, again leaving the student without linking information. Most practitioners and teachers talk about the "internal" and the "external" even when they desire an integration of both. This separation is a conceptual one that does not match subjective experience, and the recent surge of interest in body-based and holistic training practices demonstrates a widespread desire to move beyond dualistic concepts. The idea of experiences that are "internal" or "external" rests on a conceptual separation of the mind and body that is now disproved by cognitive science. A shift to a holistic concept of the bodymind will support practices that embrace the reflexive and integrated relationship between physicality, thought, emotion, and expression.

The last 30 years have seen major changes in the scientific understanding of the brain, the mind, and its mechanisms. These have been prompted by increasing sophistication in brain-scanning technology that has provided a wealth of neurobiological data about the brain at work. This information was simply not available before because the workings of the brain are for the most part unconscious, and therefore not available to conscious inquiry. Findings in fields such as neuroscience, psychology, and linguistics have radically altered ideas about how we think, feel, and express ourselves. These can be summarized in three significant conclusions:

1 The mind is inherently embodied, not just in the sense that the brain operates in a body, but because physical experience shapes conceptual thought, and thought operates through many of the same neuronal pathways as physical action. (The term "bodymind" is increasingly being used to describe this phenomenon.)
2 Thought is mostly unconscious, a rule of thumb being that we are consciously aware of only about five percent of the brain's activity.
3 Abstract concepts are largely metaphorical, with the sources of the metaphors originating in our kinesthetic and perceptual experiences of the material world. These experiences generate cognitive systems that reflect our physical environments and form patterns for higher cognitive activity. This means that many of the words and phrases used to describe these concepts have a latent gesture or movement in them.

The implications of this research for theatre practitioners and scholars are wide-ranging and profound. The notion of the embodied mind allows us to move beyond concepts of "psychological" or "physical" approaches to acting. All acting is embodied. The actor's bodymind experiences, formulates, and communicates meaning. This is accomplished through physical experience and activity, imagination, language, non-verbal communication (nvc), and by neuronal mirror mechanisms that support empathy, imagination, and emotion. These features are intertwined in ways that are more holistic than is acknowledged in the current Western dualities of mind/body, self/character, reason/emotion, and knowledge/imagination. Currently, the notion that meaning is primarily expressed through language is predominant, and influences both training approaches and theatrical styles. However, recent research shows that much meaning in inter-personal interaction is communicated non-verbally. A focus on the body, its actions, and its cognitive mechanisms identifies principles that underlie a variety of training methods and performance styles, be they linguistic or imagistic. When this understanding is allied to the perspective of cognitive science on the way that the body and its activities shape abstract thought and conceptual meaning, it is possible to identify foundational principles of activity that link the three elements of theatre: story, space, and time. The three meet in, are defined by, and expressed through the actor's body.

I draw on work by researchers such as neuroscientists Antonio Damasio, Joseph LeDoux, and Vittorio Gallese, psychologist Paul Ekman, and linguist David McNeill that describe phenomena such as the neurobiology of emotion, the sense of self gained from movement, mirror neurons, the reflexive relationship between facial expressions and emotion, and idea units. Combining my experience as an actor, director, teacher, and scholar, I apply these and other findings in cognitive science to the practices of Stanislavski, Michael Chekhov, Jerzy Grotowski, and Jacques Lecoq. These practitioners have been chosen primarily because each has focused on physical activity as a means of exploring and expressing dramatic action – both improvised and textual. As practitioners who have independently formulated a process of actor training, they have each created a body of work that is illustrated by practical exercises.

I also consider the work of contemporary actors and directors such as Anna Deavere Smith, Daniel Day-Lewis, Dan Jemmett, Mike Alfreds, and Katie Mitchell. Despite the wide range of styles associated with these practitioners, I hope to show that, when examined through the lens of cognitive studies, certain foundational principles underlie their practices, and that they fit into a coherent process that can be described by crisscrossing the border between the lore of the studio and the world of theory. This illuminates key features of the actor's process: non-verbal communication; the relationship between thought, speech, and gesture; the relationship between self and character; empathy; imagination; and emotion.

Significant conclusions arise that challenge many common assumptions about acting:

- The brain processes written language in a different way than speech. This specifies the challenge that actors face in converting the words of a script to apparently spontaneous action.
- Much linguistic expression has innate movement tendencies. Identifying these helps the actor to move from written language to action.
- Gesture, posture, and physical behavior communicate conceptual thought.
- Approximately 50 percent (depending on context) of meaning in interpersonal interaction is communicated non-verbally. This means that we should pay equal attention to training an actor's non-verbal communication skills as to training their linguistic skills.
- The formation of new ideas while an individual speaks can be identified through the timing of gestures. This knowledge assists

the actor in communicating a character's shift of mental focus (often called a "beat change").

- Empathy, emotion, and imagination use many of the same neuronal pathways in response to fiction as they do to daily life. This means that concepts of "real" or "truthful" behavior in acting are better understood and described by concepts such as context, stimulus, intent, intensity, and duration.

- The embodiment of a fictional character is the creation of a temporary "situational self." The idea of creating authenticity by complete identification with the character is mistaken.

- Imaginative projection is involved in much mental activity, including memory. This reframes the distinction between the use of autobiographical memory and transformative imagination in the creation of a role, since both approaches involve imaginative activity.

- What we commonly call emotion is, in fact, the conscious awareness of physical symptoms. Neuroscientists make a distinction between Emotions – physiological responses to stimuli – and Feelings – the affective states that arise from conscious awareness of those physiological responses. (To distinguish between the everyday use of the words and their neurobiological definition, the latter are capitalized.)

- There are nine pathways to emotion, three of which are significantly more easily controlled by the actor than the other six.

- Consciously chosen muscular activity can generate the affective states of different emotions. These are no less or more "real" than those generated through mental exercises such as "emotion memory."

- The imagination is more easily stimulated through physical activity than by thought alone.

- Both "internal" and "external" approaches to embodying a character work through physiological processes to stimulate the imagination.

In all of these areas, cognitive science shows that dualistic concepts of process are inaccurate. Approaches to acting that are based on those dualistic concepts reduce the potential of the actor rather than expanding it, and narrow the possible scope of meaning in performance. An approach that acknowledges the holistic and interrelated nature of meaning supports the actor in integrating all the cognitive and expressive features of the bodymind. This information is especially timely in the twenty-first century, as theatre in the West is in a unique historical period where multiple styles jostle with one another and are increasingly combined or juxtaposed in performance. Training programs have to prepare actors to face a wide range of challenges: the linguistic intricacies of classical text; the hyper-naturalism of most screen drama; the bold physical expression of the musical; the abstraction of non-narrative imagistic work; the improvisational spontaneity needed to create devised theatre. This situation makes it all the more important for actors to develop skills that enable them to move from one style to another.

Chapter overview

Acting is a holistic bundle of simultaneous activities. Separation of these activities is necessary for any in-depth study, but is inevitably artificial and suggests an apparent prioritization of elements. The information in each of these chapters is equally as important as the rest, and deals with cognitive activities that are intertwined with one another. Cognitive science gives us the ability to metaphorically "see" processes that are invisible because they happen below the level of consciousness. In this book, rather than attempting a comprehensive analysis, I've focused on key areas in which cognitive science significantly alters or adds to the current understanding of acting. The trajectory of the book starts with a historical and conceptual context for the information, and then, following the metaphor of seeing, addresses the most visible part of the psychophysical process; non-verbal communication (nvc). Although it is visible, much of it is overlooked, as we tend to execute it and assimilate it unconsciously. The next chapter considers some of the invisible mental processes that give rise to this communication, and the relationship between them. A consideration of the cognitive activities involved in creating a character delves further into "invisible" processes, as does an examination of identification between self and character. These are followed by an account of the current cognitive understanding of emotion, in which unseen biological processes provoke visible communication. The conclusion considers some of the implications of this information for the training and practice of acting. The purpose is not to create an acting manual – practical exercises are included to embody the concepts, but these are illustrative examples and not intended to be a comprehensive approach. The chapters are organized around cognitive components such as thought units, imagination, proprioception, empathy, and the ways in which they relate to particular aspects of acting.

Chapter 1 Why should theatre people be interested in cognitive studies?

This begins with a brief history of some of the significant ideas about acting in the West that have a bearing on the "inside-out/outside-in" debate, and places Stanislavski, Michael Chekhov, Grotowski, and Lecoq in context. This brief bit of history is followed by a cognitive perspective on the separation of mind and body, which highlights the centrality of the body in making and communicating meaning, and describes how cognitive science relates to the theory and practice of acting.

Chapter 2 How does the actor communicate meaning non-verbally?

In this chapter I demonstrate the equality of physical behavior to language in communicating meaning. That there is a need to do this exposes another duality within contemporary Western theatre. This reflects the traditional view within psychology that language and non-verbal communication are two separate systems, devoted to different subject matters. Recent research shows that this view is limited and inaccurate. I'll refer to the work of experimental psychologist Adam Kendon and others that demonstrates the close relationship between language and non-verbal behavior. Their findings suggest that gestures are closely linked to speech and are equal conveyors of meaning in many contexts. I'll investigate the way in which psychologists analyze and codify communicative physical behavior and show how this applies to theatrical performance. A description of the neural process of metaphorical conceptualization is then linked to the work of Stanislavski, Michael Chekhov, and Rudolf Laban. The chapter includes some exercises that demonstrate how nvc skills can be honed.

Chapter 3 What is the relationship between thought, physical action, and language?

The difference between the way that the brain processes written and spoken language is at the heart of the challenge that actors face in bringing a script to life. Current research sheds light on what has previously been an unconscious process for actors – that of converting thought to expression. First I describe cognitive linguist David McNeill's findings, which show that although language and gesture are one mental system they operate in fundamentally different ways to complement one another. This analysis rests on his development of a new conception of language, viewing it as an imagery-language dialectic, in which gestures provide imagery. Features of this conception are then applied to textual analysis, with examples from the play *I.D.* This is followed by a biography of Jacques Lecoq and a demonstration of how closely his stated principles correspond to a cognitive understanding of the bodymind. His fascination with, and analysis of, movement enabled him to develop a highly sophisticated repertoire of physical exercises. Given the foundational nature of sensorimotor experience outlined by Lakoff and Johnson, it is evident that such a repertoire is more than a simply physical experience for the actor, and provides a rich resource for the embodied expression of thought. Examples of Lecoq's exercises are then described with relation to the cognitive principles that they embody. These include exercises in heightening awareness of fundamental sensorimotor experiences, work with the neutral mask, embodying the rhythms of natural elements, and embodying poetic metaphor. This demonstrates how their physical nature parallels cognitive processes, and extends the range of the actor by establishing neuronal patterning that is beyond the normal everyday range of behavior.

Chapter 4 How does the actor create a character?

In this chapter I investigate the relationship between the actor's concepts of self and of character, and how the two interrelate. I'll first review some examples of the prevailing "inside/outside" dichotomy in acting discourse, and then describe some areas of cognitive research that relate to this issue. The first of these is a description of the connectionist view of the brain, which models mental activity as a series of neural networks. This model of the brain's operation offers us a way of understanding how abstract concepts are linked to motor activity, a fundamental feature of the bodymind concept. These concepts are metaphorically formed from physical experience in the world, and I focus on one that is particularly significant for this topic, the "mind as container" metaphor. From here, I describe Lakoff and Johnson's analysis of the metaphorical construction of the concepts of self and different selves. This leads on to an examination of the idea of the "essential self" in acting discourse, which is followed by a summary of neuroscientist Joseph LeDoux's concept of the synaptic self, in which consciousness depends on unconscious cognitive processes.

I describe some of the cognitive research that relates to imagination and its relationship to written language, which are, of course, significant features of an actor's approach to creating a character. This is also true of proprioception, a faculty that is partially described by the term "kinesthetic awareness" familiar to many actors. I also summarize Merlin Donald's description of the way in which mimesis is central to cognition and precedes language in human evolution. After a brief biography of Michael Chekhov and a description of his process, I turn to Fauconnier and Turner's theory of conceptual blending to offer a description of how the model of "mental spaces" can be used to understand the way in which we can combine different concepts while maintaining an awareness of their differences – something that explains how we can simultaneously be aware of actor and character while performing. This information is interwoven with more information about Chekhov and his exercises.

Chapter 5 How does the actor identify with the character?

This chapter investigates the ways in which actors discover a sense of identification with the characters that they embody, considering the supposed distinctions between "persona" acting, and "transformational" acting. I talk about how the process of cognitive melding operates in the preparation of a role for performance as the actor combines his or her experience with that of the character. In theatre parlance, this tends to get called "identification with the role," and sometimes "investing," although this term is also used to mean "to make emotionally significant." American actress Anna Deavere Smith's writings on her own process offer an intriguing insight into the creation of character through imitation, which I investigate in a case study. I then define the difference between narrative action and behavioral actions, and describe how this distinction can create greater clarity about how we define character. This is followed by descriptions of proprioception and body schema and body image – cognitive mechanisms that participate in the sense of self. I go on to give an account of the way that mirror neurons provide the neural circuitry of motor activity involved in empathy, emotion, and responses to fiction. This information also relates to the way that the brain processes words and images. I also refer to the work of experimental psychologist Jonathan Schooler who has identified a phenomenon that he calls "verbal overshadowing" in which verbal descriptions of visual stimuli compromise visual memory, and apply this to a consideration of script analysis. I then trace Stanislavski's progression from linguistic analysis of a script to the "active analysis" that he used in the later stage of his life, proposing that the cognitive research that I've described validates the effectiveness of his Method of Physical Actions. This is followed by case studies of Vasili Toporkov, who acted in the last production that Stanislavski directed, and of contemporary actor Daniel Day-Lewis. The chapter concludes with a cognitive definition of character in acting that underlies a variety of different approaches, normally considered to be distinct from one another.

Chapter 6 How does the actor embody emotion in fictional circumstances?

In this chapter, I'll look at Stanislavski's development of emotion memory, and the way his ideas about generating emotion changed over the course of his career. I'll then consider the implications this has for Lee Strasberg's insistence on emotion memory as the actor's central tool, and describe the current cognitive understanding of memory. This is followed by a summary of analyses of emotion by neuroscientists Antonio Damasio and Joseph LeDoux, and a description of psychologist Paul Ekman's discovery of the reflexive relationship between facial expression and specific emotions, along with his identification of the nine pathways to emotion. Further cognitive research demonstrates the way in which physical activity intensifies the imaginative stimulus of emotion, and is applied to an examination of Stanislavski's Method of Physical Actions. This is followed by a description of the different phases of Jerzy Grotowski's work, and how they can be understood in cognitive terms. The final part of the chapter looks at how cognitive information can be integrated into the studio, describing Susana Bloch's Alba emoting, and a sequence of exercises that I've developed that uses the voluntary control of eye movements to stimulate affective change in performers in improvisations and open scenes.

Conclusion

In the conclusion I look at the ways in which cognitive principles can be identified in the work of three contemporary directors: Katie Mitchell, Mike Alfreds, and Dan Jemmett. I point out some of the exciting implications for theatre and for actor training of the research that I have described. I draw on this information to propose a model of the theatrical act, and suggest possible ways in which a cognitive perspective could be integrated into actor training, and inform the creation of a holistic vocabulary of performance that acknowledges the embodied nature of meaning, and links the theatrical elements of time, space, and story.

Chapter 1

Why should theatre people be interested in cognitive studies?

... imagination bodies forth / The form of things unknown ...
A Midsummer Night's Dream V:1:14

Our sense of what is real begins with and depends crucially on our bodies ...
George Lakoff and Mark Johnson, *Philosophy in the Flesh*

It all happens at once. It has to. The impulse, the breath, the speech, the gesture, the walk, the awareness of the guy in the second row who's nodding off, so I punch the end of the line that bit harder. And because I punched harder, my partner is surprised and jolted into her response with that extra calorie of spontaneity, which crackles the air, and the audience almost imperceptibly sits up, drawn in, more alert.

It all happens at once.

And then it's gone.

It's the nature of live performance. Beautiful, ugly, embodied, ephemeral, frustrating, blissful, gone ... but living in people's memories (when we've done our jobs well). And we hope that the memories are strong enough to get us the next job. Naturally, we want to do the best we can, but even more perplexing than the nature of performance itself is the question of training for it. How on earth does one train in a process that simultaneously combines all the features of living real life? Even thought? The obvious answer would be to live life, but the vast majority of people placed in front of an audience and asked to "be themselves" have the utmost difficulty in communicating. They stammer and mumble, their muscles stiffen, they move awkwardly. Clearly, the ability to perform is a specialized one, incorporating skills beyond those used to live everyday life. What are those skills? And how can we train them when they seem to arise from unconscious impulses?

In this book, I'm going to describe how cognitive science offers answers to these questions by analyzing the work of some twentieth-century practitioners from a cognitive perspective. In order to understand what they were striving for, and what they were reacting against, this chapter starts with a brief history of their approaches. This section is a thumbnail sketch of some of the significant ideas about acting in the West that have a bearing on the "inside-out/outside-in" debate, and places Stanislavski, Michael Chekhov, Grotowski, and Lecoq in context. This brief bit of history is followed by a cognitive perspective on the separation of mind and body, which highlights the centrality of the body in making and communicating meaning, and describes how cognitive science relates to the theory and practice of acting.

A brief historical context

The conceptual separation of mind and body in the West was formulated by philosopher René Descartes in the seventeenth century, and is frequently referred to as Cartesian dualism. Descartes was the first modern philosopher to identify the mind with consciousness and self-awareness, and to distinguish it from the material substance of the body. A century later, another French philosopher, Denis Diderot, applied this concept to acting in *Paradoxe sur le Comédien* (written in 1773, but not published till 1830). It was Diderot who crystallized the idea that emotion was separate from physical activity to characterize the ways in which the actor creates the appearance of being affected by emotion. Puzzling over the issue of whether the actor has to be moved in order to move an audience, Diderot described seeing the famous English actor David Garrick do a party trick in which he rapidly altered his facial expression to convey a wide range of emotions: "Can his soul have experienced all these feelings, and played this kind of scale in concert with his face? I don't believe it, nor do you."[1]

Diderot defined the two possible approaches available to an actor as "sensibility" (the capacity to feel "genuine" emotion), or the use of technique (the conscious control of the musculature of expression). Although Garrick himself considered that he used a combination of both, Diderot decided that it must be the case that the actor uses physical technique to affect an audience. Although much of Diderot's analysis was prescient when viewed in the context of cognitive science, the conceptual division of "internal" and "external" approaches to actor training continues to this day. As many actors have acknowledged, it is not an "either/or" phenomenon, and cognitive science now provides the empirical research that supports a holistic understanding. Of course, Diderot is not solely responsible for the conceptual division – the tendency to differentiate "internal" from "external" processes results from a fundamental feature of human perception known as the "recessive body," which I will talk about later on.

Gesture and Commedia in the seventeenth century

Despite the current tendency to separate psychology and physicality, there has long been a widespread recognition that the actor's body is central to any consideration of the acting process. It is both instrument and medium. For example, in the same period that Descartes was writing *Meditations on First Philosophy* (the mid-seventeenth century), English physician John Bulwer published four volumes exploring the human body as a medium of communication, proposing that gesticulation was a natural human language. The best known of these are the *Chironomia* and the *Chirologia*, which identify and describe the meaning of hand gestures. Also current at this time was the highly physical performance style of Commedia dell'arte, in which stock characters were identified by characteristic postures, gestures, and half masks. In the early days of this style, Commedia troupes toured through different regions of Italy and, because of the widely varying regional dialects, performed in an improvised gibberish called *grammelot*. Even after the development of recognizable dialogue, and of written plays that drew on the stock characters and scenarios, physical activity equaled language in communicating meaning.

Declamatory acting

A century later, a contemporary of Garrick's, theatre critic Aaron Hill, published *The Art of Acting*, which included descriptions of the expression of "Ten Major Emotions for Actors." A taste of the period's acting style can be gained from the following extract:

> Rage or Anger expresses itself with rapidity, interruption, rant, harshness and trepidation. The neck is stretched out, the head forward, often nodding and shaking in a menacing manner against the object of the passion … the feet often stamping, the right arm thrown out menacingly, with the clenched fist shaken and a general and violent agitation of the whole body.[2]

A standardized repertoire of gestures was passed on not only through such descriptions and illustrations in manuals and handbooks, but also through an "oral" tradition of stock company training in which apprentice actors learned by imitation. Most European, British, and American actors performed in a consciously declamatory style, ostentatiously displaying their rhetorical skill. The cast stood in a semi-circle center stage, as close to the footlights as possible, stepping forward to "make points," speaking directly to the audience and often encoring favorite speeches. The predominant understanding of theatre was as an artificial construct in which language and physical behavior communicated meaning, but not in a way that mimicked daily life.

Delsarte and physical expression

In the second half of the nineteenth century, however, the development of pictorial realism in scenic design encouraged behavior that would suit its visual environment. French director Adolphe Montigny is credited with starting the trend in 1853 by placing a table downstage center, seating the actors around it and encouraging them to address one another, rather than the audience. Montigny's contemporary, François Delsarte, responded to the scientific spirit of the nineteenth century by seeking to analyze emotions and ideas and how they are expressed. His work was to become internationally known and enthusiastically, if misguidedly, followed. Delsarte divided human experience and behavior into three categories; mental, physical, and spiritual, and linked these to thought, action, and emotion. The body was also divided into parts and related to these three categories. Through this process, Delsarte created a system that described how every part of the body is used in communicating specific emotions, ideas, and attitudes. While Delsarte himself sought to create a connection between "real life" and what was portrayed on stage, the wide dissemination of his ideas in manuals that prescribed "correct" postures and gestures led to a mechanization of his system, leading to further artificiality on stage. Delsarte's intuitive recognition of the connections between thought, emotion, and behavior anticipates many of the findings of cognitive science. However, the assumption that the same postures and gestures would express the same emotions for every actor that used them led to a uniformity that inhibited individual expression and variety.

Realism and the unconscious

These features of an actor's performance became more valued with the development of realism as a style in the late nineteenth and early twentieth centuries, and as psychology gained recognition as a discipline. A key link between emerging psychological thought and theatrical realism was the idea of the unconscious – that people thought and felt things that they were not consciously aware of. Prior to this, the melodramas that were popular in the early nineteenth century involved explicit statements by characters about their thoughts and feelings as they encountered one sensational incident after another. As Anton Chekhov said:

> In real life people do not spend every minute shooting each other, hanging themselves or making declarations of love. They don't spend every minute saying clever things. Rather, they eat, drink, flirt, talk nonsense. And that is what should be seen on the stage.[3]

Chekhov's plays, of course, became internationally celebrated for their realism and psychological nuance, and forever associated with The Moscow Art Theatre and its co-founder, Russian actor and director Konstantin Stanislavski.

Stanislavski and the System

In directing and performing Chekhov's work, Stanislavski recognized that the everyday behavior of the characters expressed an implicit narrative – that they "often feel and think things which they do not express in words."[4] This was the foundation of what became identified as "subtext" – unspoken thoughts and feelings that may be unconscious or conscious, and which have to be communicated through behavior. Given the rudimentary knowledge of the mind at the time, and the exaggerated posturing and gesticulation of the predominant acting style, it is unsurprising that Stanislavski framed his ideas about subtext in terms of "internal" and "external." He acknowledged that Chekhov's writing was a significant influence in this:

> Chekhov gave that inner truth to the art of the stage which served as the foundation for what was later called the Stanislavski System, which must be approached through Chekhov, or which serves as a bridge to the approach to Chekhov.[5]

The use of the phrase "inner truth" demonstrates that he considers authenticity in acting to come from "internal" qualities, but his early directing focused on prescribing a wealth of "external," physical activities for the actor. Prior to rehearsals for *The Seagull*, the first of Chekhov's plays to be staged by the Moscow Art Theatre, Stanislavski wrote a prompt book filled with minute behavioral details such as the combing of a beard, picking of blades of grass, and flicking cigarette ash. Some commentators felt that he was overloading the production with naturalistic details to make it resemble daily life as much as possible. As he explained in *My Life in Art*, he felt that he had to do this as many of his actors were unprepared for the new style of realism: "Many actors merely followed my direction on the outside since they were not yet ready to understand its emotional sense."[6] Over time, he devised exercises to stimulate his actors to create performances that achieved psychological credibility and emotional authenticity, and these exercises became what is known as the Stanislavski System. In the early part of his career, these focused on what he called "inner" aspects, but towards the end of his life he recognized that physical activity could prompt thought and feeling: "Physical truth, and faith in that truth, call out inner spiritual truth and faith, and these free emotion, which comes from its secret hiding place, and begins to enter into all that takes place on the stage."[7] In this, and many other statements, Stanislavski demonstrated an intuitive prescience of what cognitive science now tells us about the relationship between physical action, thought, and feelings.

An important question arises at this point. If physical action can provoke thought and emotion, why did Stanislavski find the postures and gestures of some actors "empty"? Cognitive science shows us that it is not simply the shape (or "form") of a posture or gesture that is involved in meaning. Factors such as breathing patterns, level of muscular tension and tempo of movement are also critical in the reflexive relationship between thought, Feelings, and expression. Stanislavski sought a synthesis of these elements, and continually experimented with ways to "involve the creative subconscious by indirect, conscious means."[8] He called this a "psychophysical" process and towards the end of his life developed the Method of Physical Actions as a way of achieving a marriage of the "internal" and "external."

The dissemination of Stanislavski's System

A series of historical accidents complicated the communication of his System in the rest of Europe and America. *An Actor's Work on Himself*, originally conceived of as one book, was published in two volumes in Russia, separated by 13 years. The English translator thought that the second volume was a revision, rather than a continuation, of the first. She also often distorted the meanings of Russian words. A highly significant example of this lies in the translation of the Russian word *perezhivanie*. A literal translation would be "living through" or "undergoing" an experience, but this was translated as "emotional identification." This has led to a common misconception that actors should completely identify with the character that they are playing. Stanislavski himself declared that an actor who thought that he was another person was a pathological case.

To further complicate the situation, the dissemination of the System in America was closely linked with Lee Strasberg's "Method," developed at the Actors' Studio, founded with Robert Lewis, Stella Adler, and Elia Kazan. Strasberg based his training on Stanislavski's System, but declared that his own approach was distinct from it. He emphasized the release of emotion, and encouraged actors to recall emotional events from their own lives. A number of successful actors were trained at the Actor's Studio, but many scholars and practitioners now believe that Strasberg's approach distorted Stanislavski's System. They cite the fact that he rejected the Method of Physical Actions when told about it by Stella Adler, and that by defining the actor's autobiography as the source of authenticity in performance, he made the actor more important than the character, thus obscuring the artistic truth of the fictional character. Nevertheless, during the second half of the twentieth century, many people in America and England conflated the Method with Stanislavski's System, and these factors (along with others that I describe in Chapter 5), meant that for a large part of the twentieth century, many directors and actors considered his work a purely "psychological" approach.

England and realism

In England, the style of realism had been growing in acceptance since the 1890s, and translations of Ibsen's plays and the work of George Bernard Shaw required actors to forsake the rhetorical style of the nineteenth century in favor of greater verisimilitude. In his capacity as a theatre critic, Shaw flayed Sir Henry Irving, whose vocal flamboyance and melodramatic excesses as an actor had made him a favorite with London audiences. Shaw called for a new kind of acting to suit a new kind of drama: "The function of the actor is to make the audience imagine for the moment that real things are happening to real people."[9] At the time, there was little consistency of acting style, the apprentice system had broken down with the decline of repertory theatres, and communication of technique was largely conducted on an ad-hoc basis. Shaw recognized:

> ... the general need in England for a school of physical training for the arts of the public life as distinguished from sports. An author who understands acting, and writes for the actor as a composer writes for an instrument, giving it the material suitable to its range, tone, character, agility and mechanism, necessarily assumes a certain technical accomplishment common to all actors; and this requires a school of acting, or at least a tradition.[10]

Interestingly, given Shaw's commitment to realism, he called for physical training, seeing no conflict between the acquiring of technique and an actor's ability to behave naturalistically. His contemporary, the actor-manager Herbert Beerbohm Tree also perceived a need for training, and in 1904 established the school now known as The Royal Academy of Dramatic Art.

By the early twentieth century, a variety of production styles had developed in London and regional centers, including the playing of Shakespeare in modern dress, Expressionism, and Tyrone Guthrie's novel interpretations of canonical plays at the Old Vic, incorporating a great deal of movement on stage. In this context, the arrival of Stanislavski's ideas constituted the first systematic approach to the development of a role. Actors such as Michael Redgrave and John Gielgud welcomed this development, while Laurence Olivier resolutely continued to define himself as an actor who worked from "the outside in." The effect of the Russian approach to realism can be gauged by John Gielgud's reaction to working with one of Stanislavski's colleagues, director Fyodor Komisarjevsky:

> ... I began to feel that I could study a part from the inside, as he taught me, not seizing at once on the obvious showy effects and histrionics, but trying to absorb the atmosphere of the play and the background of the character, and then to build it outwards so that it came to life naturally ... [11]

Once again, this approach is defined in terms of "internal," with the implication that Gielgud's own approach prior to this had been "external."

Meyerhold and Vakhtangov

In Russia, Stanislavski's ideas were carried forward by three practitioners from The Moscow Art Theatre: Vsevolod Meyerhold, Yevgeny

Vakhtangov, and Michael Chekhov, the nephew of the great playwright. While I focus on Chekhov in this book, the work of all three offers an interesting illumination of acting in relation to theatrical style and the issue of physicality. The declamatory posturing of nineteenth-century styles had led to a condemnation of physical excess as lacking in realism, but Stanislavski, ever the experimenter, opened a Studio in 1905 to investigate nonrealistic styles. He appointed Meyerhold to lead it, who explored circus and Commedia techniques and developed a directorial style that involved using scenic elements as an apparatus for acting. After a while Stanislavski discontinued the studio, feeling that Meyerhold's emphasis on directorial concept restricted actors, but Meyerhold continued to experiment, founding his own company and developing his system of Biomechanics. This was based on the notion that particular muscular patterns prompted specific emotions. This is a concept that cognitive science now shows to be valid in both large and small movements, but not in a uniform way. Meyerhold, seeking to replace Stanislavski's focus on "internal" motivation with physical and emotional reflexes, incorporated extreme physical action that was radically nonrealistic, in a style that he called Constructivism. To express joy, for instance, an actor would slide down a chute, or execute a somersault. This employed what we now know is a neuro-physiological principle that movement can generate thought and feeling, much as Stanislavski would do in the Method of Physical Actions, but in support of a radically different theatrical style.

Vakhtangov, director of the Moscow Art Theatre's First Studio, also went on to develop his own approach. He is best known for four productions presented in the early 1920s, creating a style that blended Stanislavski's work with that of Meyerhold. He sustained Stanislavski's emphasis on discovering a character's biography and identifying sub-text, but added heightened movement to create a style close to Expressionism. A useful example is his production of Strindberg's *Erik XIV*, a portrait of a king who was half genius, half psychopath. Intended to criticize the institution of monarchy, the production presented courtiers and bureaucrats as automatons, while the common people were played realistically. Michael Chekhov played the role of Erik to great acclaim.

Michael Chekhov

Chekhov was initially a student of Stanislavski's and went on to become a renowned actor, director, and teacher. At the time of his training, Stanislavski's focus was still very much on the use of autobiographical experience to create credibility in characterization. The direction that Chekhov was to take in his own work is vividly illustrated by an incident that occurred in Stanislavski's studio:

> Asked by the teacher to enact a true-life dramatic situation as an exercise in Affective Memory, Chekhov recreated his wistful presence at his father's funeral. Overwhelmed by its fine detail and sense of truth, Stanislavski embraced Chekhov, thinking that this was yet another proof of the power of real affective memory for the actor. Unfortunately, Stanislavski later discovered that Chekhov's ailing father was, in fact, still alive ... Chekhov was dropped from the class owing to an "overheated imagination."[12]

Cognitive science demonstrates that the distinction between memory and imagination is not hard and fast in the way that Stanislavski, or later Strasberg, believed and that imagination is a significant feature of many of our thought processes. Clearly, as a spectator, Stanislavski experienced an emotional truth in Chekhov's performance, but was stung to discover that Chekhov had arrived at this through a process that was different from the one being taught in class. By the end of his life, the development of the Method of Physical Actions brought his conceptual framework much closer to Chekhov's way of working. Viewed from the perspective of cognitive science, both of these approaches use physical experimentation to stimulate the imagination so as to allow the actor to engage emotionally and mentally with fictional circumstances.

Jerzy Grotowski

This description also applies to the work of Polish director Jerzy Grotowski (1933–99) who had a great influence on experimental theatre and actor training in the second half of the twentieth century. Few people associate the style of his work with the realism that is linked with Stanislavski, but Grotowski acknowledges the significance of Stanislavski's ideas in his training: "When I was a student in the school of dramatic arts, in the faculty for actors, I founded the entire basis of my theatrical knowledge on the principles of Stanislavski."[13] Grotowski was, like Stanislavski, concerned with the discovery of truth in performance and believed that a methodical approach was necessary to master this:

> ... the theatre, and in particular, the technique of the actor, cannot – as Stanislavski maintained – be based solely on

> inspiration or other such unpredictable factors such as talent ...
> unlike other artistic disciplines, the actor's creation is imperative;
> i.e. situated within a determined lapse of time and even at a precise
> moment.[14]

This was to be achieved not by the acquisition of skills, but by the removal of blocks between the actor and his or her impulses; " ... allowing him to reveal one after the other the different layers of his personality, from the biological-instinctive source via the channel of consciousness and thought to that summit which is so difficult to define and in which all becomes unity."[15] Significantly, Grotowski's language avoids "inner/outer" dualism and anticipates the current cognitive understanding of interpersonal communication as a synthesis of unconscious biological impulses and conscious thought.

Grotowski's work can be divided into several phases, which I describe in Chapter 6. Only the first of these involved presenting performances to an audience, but common to all of them was a continuous sense of exploration and a desire to synthesize human experience through rigorous physical activity. As Peter Brook has said of him; " ... no-one else in the world, to my knowledge, no-one since Stanislavski, has investigated the nature of acting, its phenomenon, its meaning, the nature and science of its mental-physical-emotional processes as deeply and completely as Grotowski."[16]

In the second half of the twentieth century, Stanislavski's ideas had thus evolved into at least two very different types of actor training and styles of acting – the realism associated with Strasberg's Method and Grotowski's non-naturalistic "Poor Theatre." Many practitioners and scholars came to see these two as representative of "psychological" and "physical" approaches respectively, with heated debate ensuing about their relative merits. Much of this debate is couched in outdated concepts and vocabulary, with subjective terminology frequently confusing the issues. An example of this is the discussion of emotion, which I address in Chapter 6. Empirically derived information about cognitive processes both clarifies the issues of acting theory and offers practitioners and scholars alike a vocabulary that is congruent with the current understanding of the bodymind. It also identifies foundational principles of performance that underlie differing theatrical styles.

Jacques Lecoq

During the same period, Jacques Lecoq (1921–99) was developing a body-based method of actor training in Paris; one that came from a tradition of movement-oriented work that incorporates Antonin Artaud, Jean-Louis Barrault, and Jacques Copeau. Originally a teacher of physical education, Lecoq became a member of Jean Dasté's theatre company, the "Comédiens de Grenoble." Here he was introduced to Japanese Noh theatre and discovered masks, in particular Dasté's "noble" mask, which was the forerunner of Lecoq's "neutral" mask. The ideas of Copeau, who had been Dasté's teacher, became a reference point for Lecoq's exploration, in particular a desire to create "theatre that spoke simply and directly to unsophisticated audiences."[17] This interest led to an eight-year stint in Italy during which he researched Commedia Dell'Arte, participated in setting up the Piccolo Teatro in Milan, and worked with practitioners such as Dario Fo and Giorgio Strehler.

On his return to Paris in 1956, he opened his School of Mime and Theatre. It is important to note that for Lecoq, the word "mime" did not connote the "pantomime blanche" of Étienne Decroux and Marcel Marceau, but a broader mode of physical expression. This involved rigorous investigation of the principles of human movement, which for Lecoq were synonymous with the principles of theatre: " ... the laws of movement govern all theatrical situations. A piece of writing is a structure in motion. Though themes may vary (they belong to the realm of ideas), the structures of acting remain linked to movement and its immutable laws ... "[18] As with Stanislavski, Michael Chekhov, and Grotowski, this statement bears an extraordinary synchrony with the discoveries of cognitive science. Movement and other physical experiences in the material world are the sources of metaphors that shape our conceptual thought. As thoughts are expressed in language they use the neural mechanisms of the sensorial experience that are the source of the metaphor. I describe this phenomenon in more detail in subsequent chapters.

Like Grotowski, whose company was called the Polish Laboratory Theatre, Lecoq's work was investigative and experimental; "Through teaching I have discovered that the body knows things about which the mind is ignorant."[19] After the student riots of 1968, he gave his students more autonomy in their learning process by instituting *autocours*, sessions in which groups of students worked independently of their teachers to create short performances that they presented to the rest of the school on a regular basis. This was one of the features of his teaching that led to the profusion of devised theatre companies that had their origin in his school. Another significant factor was that Lecoq, in contrast to Grotowski, did not seek to create a signature style. While his approach was rigorous and systematic, and incorporated defined styles such as Commedia and Clown, its purpose, as Lecoq often reminded his students, was to give them the tools to create a theatre that did not yet exist. His success in this goal is evident in the variety and numbers of practitioners who base their work in his teachings: Ariane Mnouchkine, Yasmina Reza, Geoffrey Rush, Simon McBurney, and Julie Taymor, to name a few, and companies such as Moving Picture Mime Show, Footsbarn, Mummenschanz, Complicite, Commotion, Told by an Idiot, Peepolykus, Theatre O, Theatre de la Jeune Lune, and Pig Iron, among many others. These individuals and groups represent a wide range of accomplishments and styles, from playwriting to devised theatre, and from movie naturalism to expressive movement. This suggests that there are elements of Lecoq's work that are foundational to acting and theatre, allowing those who have experienced his training to use it as a springboard for their own creativity.

Physical and holistic approaches

The popularity of Lecoq's school, which shows no sign of waning since his death in 1999, is part of a larger surge of interest in physical training in the last 30 years. The contemporary Western actor can train in practices such as those of Michael Chekhov, Tadashi Suzuki, Viewpoints, Commedia dell'arte, and Laban, and several recent publications reflect this interest: Lecoq's Le Corps Poetique; Zarrilli's Psychophysical Acting; Bogart and Landau's The Viewpoints Book; Potter's Movement for Actors; Yakim and Broadman's Creating a Character: A Physical Approach to Acting; Adrian's Actor Training the Laban Way: An Integrated Approach to Voice, Speech, and Movement; Mitchell's Movement: From Person to Actor to Character; and the American Theatre magazine special issue on Movement Training, January 2011. There is also an evident desire to train for acting in a more unified or holistic way, expressed in books such as Rafael's Telling Stories: A Grand Unifying Theory of Acting Techniques; Zarrilli's Psychophysical Acting; Lugering's The Expressive Actor: Integrated Voice, Movement, and Acting Training; Merlin's Beyond Stanislavsky: The Psycho-Physical Approach to Actor Training; and Wangh's An Acrobat of the Heart.

The slowness to adapt

Despite this activity, the partial understanding of Stanislavski and the atomization of training activities that I described earlier is still a predominant feature of many Western acting programs. Historically, theories of acting have responded to changing conceptions of the body that come from the fields of psychology and physiology. It would be reasonable to expect that the changes in understanding of the mind and brain that have occurred in the last 30 years would have provoked alterations in acting theory and training. This process has, however, been very slow. A detailed consideration of the slowness to adapt would form a book in itself, but briefly, and from my own perspective as a theatre professional who is also a professor, a number of reasons present themselves.

The twentieth century saw the growth of specialized training programs for actors, replacing the ad-hoc apprentice system that had prevailed in earlier centuries. Alongside this, the founding of the Actors' Equity Association in the early part of the century (1913 in America, 1930 in Britain) gave further legitimacy to the idea of acting as a profession with its own lore and traditions. Within that profession, there is considerable suspicion of written theory, probably because so much knowledge about acting is held and communicated in a sort of oral tradition – the lore of the studio. This suspicion is strongly influenced by the tendency towards a kinesthetic learning orientation in actors and is further reinforced by the oft-repeated exhortation of "Show me, don't tell me!" in actor training, which prioritizes embodied experience over narrated information. While this is necessary in realistic acting styles, it can create an unconscious prejudice against theory.

Theory and practice

This prejudice is manifested by the tendency of twentieth-century writing about acting to fall in to one of two categories:

1 practitioners who outline a specific practical approach, generally claiming uniqueness; and
2 theorists who view acting from a cultural, social, historical, or political perspective.[20]

The books that I mentioned earlier fall into the first category. Books in the second category that apply cognitive science to theatre are as yet few: McConachie and Hart's *Performance and Cognition: Theatre Studies and the Cognitive Turn*; McConachie's *Engaging Audiences*; Blair's *The Actor, Image, and Action: Acting and Cognitive Neuroscience*; Cook's *Shakespearean Neuroplay*; Rynell's *Action Reconsidered: Cognitive Aspects of the Relation between Script and Scenic Action*; and Lutterbie's *Towards a General Theory of Acting*.

This book bridges the gap between the categories of theory and practice, by applying some of the most significant discoveries of cognitive science directly to the work of key practitioners of the twentieth century to create a praxis-based understanding of acting. Praxis is sometimes defined as the application of theory to practice, and sometimes as investigation through practice – my definition of it here is one of a reflexive relationship between theory and practice, where each informs the other. Many of the ideas involved in both areas are complex – I've done my best to explain them in ways that are both accurate and accessible, and to provide practical examples. These are not intended to create a training manual, but to give the reader an opportunity to experience some of the phenomena that I describe.

Cognitive studies and theatre

The scientific investigation of the mind and brain offers theatre people better ways of understanding the psychophysical processes involved in performance. Cognitive science also offers us tools with which to describe the distinctions between different approaches as well as to recognize fundamental similarities among them. Not only that, but as theatre scholar Bruce McConachie points out, "the sciences of the mind and brain offer conclusions that are based on years of experimentation and research"[21] and consequently have a validity that rests on an empirical base. Furthermore, the understanding that cognitive science offers us is one that acknowledges the central role of the body, and helps us to better understand the relationship between thought and expression, a subject that is hazily expressed at best in most theories of acting.

The recessive body

Cognitive science also gives us an explanation of the mind/body split through a phenomenon known as the "recessive body." This is a feature of our "commonsense" understanding of ourselves that is based on unconscious concepts. As philosopher Mark Johnson points out: "Mind/body dualism is so deeply embedded in our philosophical and religious traditions, in our shared conceptual systems, and in our language that it can seem to be an inescapable fact about human nature."[22] That this notion of dualism is mistaken might seem to contradict our phenomenological experience, and certainly requires an adventurous mental stance to acknowledge. A useful analogy is our experience of the sun. Our perception shows us that the sun moves in the sky, but we know from the work of astronomers and physicists that it is the earth that is moving. Similarly, our perception of our bodies suggests a split between mind and body, but empirical research in fields such as biology, neuroscience, and psychology show otherwise. Johnson traces this phenomenon to its root in the "many ways in which the successful functioning of our bodies requires that our bodily organs and operations recede and even hide in our acts of experiencing things in the world."[23] Our organs of perception are designed to conceal themselves from consciousness so as not to impede our fluid and instantaneous experience of the material world. For example, we are aware of what we see, but not of our eyes doing the seeing.

Emotion

Another feature of the "recessive body" is the way in which we experience emotion. Much recent research (with neuroscientists Antonio Damasio and Joseph LeDoux prominent) takes a biological rather than psychological approach to emotion, revealing the neural and endocrinal processes that stimulate the physiological symptoms that we interpret as emotion. A part of the brain called the amygdala responds to neural information and releases hormones that result in features such as increased heart rate, perspiration, or changes in breathing patterns. We are sometimes aware of these, but cannot sense the activity of the amygdala or our endocrine system. So it often seems to us that the experience of emotion is something that is part of a disembodied consciousness rather than the processes of the body. Paradoxically, the tendency to separate mind from body is a result of the particular nature of our physical existence. Johnson stresses the difficulty of avoiding dualism in both our thinking and our language: "In short, the idea of a fundamental ontological divide between mind and body – along with the accompanying dichotomies of cognition/emotion, fact/value, knowledge/imagination, and thought/feeling – is so deeply embedded in our Western ways of thinking that we find it almost impossible to avoid framing our understanding of mind and thought dualistically."[24]

Cognitive science and acting

In an earlier work, *Philosophy in the Flesh*, Johnson teamed up with linguist George Lakoff to discuss the implications for philosophy of the discoveries of cognitive science. The study of philosophy may seem an esoteric pursuit for an actor, but Lakoff and Johnson point out that everyday life is composed of activities that are based on unconscious concepts such as causation, the nature of the self, and morality, to name a few – all topics of philosophical inquiry. *As human behavior is the raw material of any acting, understanding the concepts and processes involved in perception, understanding, and the creation of meaning is of great value to the actor.* The recognition of the crucial role of the body in perception and conceptualization leads to the concepts of the embodied mind, the cognitive unconscious, and metaphorical thought, as described in the Introduction.

Proprioception

Another cognitive feature that is extremely significant in understanding the acting process is proprioception. Many actors are familiar with the term "kinesthetic sense" from studio work, but proprioception involves more than the awareness of movement. Initially, proprioception gives us information about muscle tone, effort, and balance. Nerve endings in our muscles, fascia, tendons, ligaments, joints, and skin send signals to the brain about the deformation of tissue. This includes information about a number of features: the degree of pressure, which indicates stretching and placement; the speed of movement, and the rate at which the speed is changing; the direction of movement; and, in cases of extreme tissue deformation, pain. Large amounts of information from sensory nerves embedded in muscles and joints are carried through the spinal cord to the subcortical and cortical parts of the brain. This information is integrated through many neural pathways that synapse at various levels of the nervous system to give us a sense of where we are and how we are moving, both at a conscious and unconscious level. It is proprioception that enables us to move in the dark, that is involved as we learn and execute a dance step or tennis stroke, and also allows us to walk or run without exerting conscious control over the activity. Beyond these features, however, proprioception is also involved in gesture, posture, speech, emotion, and the sense of self, features that I will examine in detail in subsequent chapters.

Conclusion

The concept of the embodied mind is one that fundamentally alters the mind/body split on which twentieth-century approaches to actor training are based. The mainstream view of training that is primarily physically oriented, such as that of Grotowski and Lecoq, is that it is exotic and tied to a particular style of non-realist performance. Training methods that stress psychology tend to neglect the mechanics of expression beyond vocal work in the belief that these will take care of themselves, and that "technical" training will lead to non-naturalistic behavior in performance. I propose that the two approaches, rather than being mutually exclusive or necessarily oppositional, are more like two parts of the same river that flow into one another. Training that foregrounds the body does not necessarily neglect the mental activities generally termed "psychological." Instead, it grounds them in action. Physically-based work can stimulate the imagination to create performances of subtlety and nuance in both behavioral and linguistic expression. Training that focuses on mental processes also incorporates physical processes, but often without explicitly acknowledging them. Many practitioners have been working psychophysically – but the concepts and terms that they use to describe this work have been bound by the "internal/external" dichotomy. Creating a cognitive vocabulary for theatrical activities would support a language of theatre that applies to a variety of styles because it is based on foundational cognitive activities.

The empirically-based concept of the embodied mind provides a foundation that explains the effectiveness of approaches to training and rehearsal that consciously link physicality and environment in the expression of meaning. This feature is shared by all the practical exercises that I investigate. While some of the material is necessarily historical, the intent is forward-looking. I hope that the information in this book will be part of a significant shift in the understanding, theory, and practice of acting. I know that this is an ambitious goal – I feel that it is justified by the magnitude of the changes in the understanding of the human mind that have led to the concept of the embodied mind.

These changes reframe the debate about the nature of acting by going beyond dualities such as body/mind or emotion/reason or even truth/ technique to describe acting in a holistic sense, a sense that recognizes the way that meaning is both made and expressed in movement as well as language in an environment defined by space and time. The use of science is not intended to make acting into a science, or to prescribe a formula. Rather, it is intended to better identify the elements of the medium and the skills required to play the instrument. Cognitive science provides an empirically derived theoretical basis for the description of the psychophysiological activities involved in acting. It supports a coherent account of the actor's activity that applies to different styles of theatre, suggesting a vocabulary that can be used equally well for styles such as devised theatre and improvisation as for scripted work. The benefits are wide-ranging; teachers will have a sound conceptual structure for their work, practitioners a more precise vocabulary for communicating with one another. Scholars will have more reliable tools for talking about authorship through action, or distinguishing between styles of acting in relation to genre and period, or screen and stage. Closest to my heart are the benefits to actors. So much of what we do is intuitive, with success hard to repeat, and the reasons for failure difficult to define, and this information will enable us to peer in to the mystery with greater focus.

Key points

- Philosopher René Descartes formulated the conceptual separation of mind and body in the seventeenth century.
- In the eighteenth century Denis Diderot applied the concept to acting and separated "genuine" emotion from physical activity.
- The nineteenth century saw the rise of a more realistic style of acting that encouraged attempts to create the illusion of daily life on stage.
- François Delsarte sought to analyze emotions and how they are expressed, creating a system of postures and gestures that supposedly communicated specific emotions.
- The idea of the unconscious was a key link between the emerging discipline of psychology and theatrical realism, and supported the idea of "subtext," further confirming the "inside/outside" conceptualization.
- Konstantin Stanislavski developed a systematic approach to creating a role that sought to integrate physical action, thought, and Feelings.
- A number of historical accidents, including mistranslations, complicated the communication of Stanislavski's System in the rest of Europe and America.
- In Russia, Stanislavski's ideas were carried forward by practitioners working in a variety of theatrical styles, while in America his system became synonymous with psychological realism.
- In the second half of the twentieth century, Michael Chekhov in Russia and Jerzy Grotowski in Poland developed physical approaches that were founded in Stanislavski's System.
- In the same period in France, Jacques Lecoq independently created a physical approach to actor training from his interest in sports and popular theatre.

- The last 30 years have seen a growth of interest in physical and holistic actor training.
- Cognitive science offers an empirically based foundation for the examination of acting, which highlights the centrality of the body in making and communicating meaning.
- The "recessive body" phenomenon, in which the mechanisms of perception operate below the level of consciousness, is one of the factors that give rise to mind/body dualism.
- Physical and mental starting points for acting processes are not in themselves mutually exclusive or necessarily oppositional, but are often perceived this way by practitioners and teachers.
- The changes in the understanding of the mind that have occurred in the last 30 years propose a radical shift in the understanding, theory, and practice of acting.

Chapter 2

How does the actor communicate meaning non-verbally?

This chapter deals with what actors don't say, how they don't say it, and how this communicates meaning to an audience. I realize that this may sound perverse – after all, the majority of theatrical presentations originate with a script, which is comprised mostly of dialogue. Theatre practitioners, however, recognize that *how* one says the dialogue is vitally important, since the "how" also communicates. In a novel the author can describe the unspoken thoughts, feelings, and motivations of a character. The playwright, however, is restricted largely to the words that a character says, and it is up to the actor to contextualize those words by deciding on the intent that drives the words, to create facial expressions and physical behavior, to make the speech sound life-like through the use of vocal tone, varied emphases, tempo, and cadence of speech. Artists who create material through improvisation are using all these aspects spontaneously, sometimes with conscious intent, sometimes unconsciously.

In theatre, these features of expression are usually called "behavior," or sometimes "body language." I'll use the term non-verbal communication (nvc) that is current in social psychology. The increasing sophistication of this field and the development of audio and video technology have resulted in an empirically derived analysis and codification of nvc. Additionally, findings from experiments conducted by linguistic psychologists into the feature of gesture provide us with important information about communication, thought, and feeling:

- social psychologists have defined activities and categories of behavior to create a taxonomy of nvc
- gesture is equal to language in communicating meaning, but operates in a fundamentally different way

- physical experience shapes much conceptual thought through metaphor
- gesture operates reflexively, integrating expression, thought, and feeling.

This information can be of great benefit to actors; it is much easier to practice a skill when you have a definition of its components and a corresponding vocabulary. In most current training programs, the development of skill in using nvc occurs tangentially to other subjects, without definition as a topic in its own right. An understanding of the equality of nvc to language in communicating meaning makes for more expressive and defined performances. Additionally, the identification and practice of metaphorical actions enables the actor to make conscious choices to link impulse with expression. Finally, developing sensitivity to the way in which physicality, thought, and feeling are intertwined increases the actor's range. There is, however, an obstacle in translating this information for use in performance, which is the fact that psychologists define nvc from the point of view of observers and are not generally engaged with the issue of how to teach people to create it. Actors, of course, are primarily concerned with generating nvc.

This chapter demonstrates how theatre practitioners can use this scientific information. First, I describe how the current understanding of nvc arose, and then consider the integration of nvc into training approaches, giving an example of a practical training exercise. Following this is an account of experimental psychologist Adam Kendon's research into the relationship between gesture and language, and an analysis of the use of nvc in a scene from *The Importance of Being Earnest*. A description of the neural process of metaphorical conceptualization is then linked to the work of Stanislavski, Michael Chekhov, and Rudolf Laban. The chapter concludes with another practical exercise that assists actors in integrating impulse with expression through the use of Primary Actions – metaphors that have their root in specific physical activities.

The development of nvc analysis

The codification of nvc in the field of psychology is comparatively recent. The modern concept of nvc originates in the 1940s, as developments in audio-visual technology allowed for the recording and study of movement as meaning. The films of Gregory Bateson, an ethnographic consultant, alerted psychiatrists to the way in which interpersonal communication uses far more than words: "It was soon realized that

tones of voice, modes of hesitation, styles of talking, patterns of into-
nation, vocal quality, bodily posture, bodily movements of all sorts,
glances, facial expressions, were all playing a very important role ... "[1]

However, this period of analysis of nvc was characterized by the
now contested belief that nvc used devices quite different from
speech and dealt with different areas of meaning, specifically, that it
was concerned *only with interpersonal relationships*, and that language was
the only form of communication that could convey abstract ideas and
complex information. This position is typified by Bateson's observation
that " ... nonverbal communication is precisely concerned with matters
of relationship ... From an adaptive point of view, it is therefore
important that this discourse be carried only by techniques which are
relatively unconscious and only imperfectly subject to voluntary
control."[2] This attitude persists even as late as 1978, as this quote
demonstrates: "In human social behavior it looks as if the nonverbal
channel is used for negotiating interpersonal attitudes while the
verbal channel is used primarily for conveying information."[3] However, recent research shows that this understanding is misguided and
incomplete, both regarding everyday communication and also by
extension, performance. The current understanding of the bodymind
offers a more holistic account of the way in which speech and nvc
complement each other in communicating meaning.

Expressive behavior in actor training

The understanding of nvc that prevailed among psychologists from
the 1940s to the early 1980s still seems to hold sway in many training
approaches, such as Strasberg's Method, that focus on a "psychological" approach and avoid conscious use of the body for fear that this
will be somehow inauthentic. This is typified by a story told to
American director Tina Landau about the Steppenwolf Theatre
Company in Chicago:

> a young director was working with the ensemble on a new play and
> gave them an exercise relating to gesture, and there they were work-
> ing, when suddenly one of the Steppenwolf ensemble members
> threw down her notebook and started screaming, "We don't do
> gesture work here! We don't do gesture work ANYWHERE! In
> fact, we don't DO gesture work! In fact, I don't DO gestures!!!"[4]

The relevance to Landau was that she was about to go and work with
Steppenwolf, and was being warned that her body-based Viewpoints

system might not sit well with company members. Fortunately, the story ends well – after successfully working together on a production, the actress in question tells Landau "[o]f course I do gestures – we all do, every day, onstage and off – but not when it *takes away from* rather than *adds* to my life onstage."[5]

The assumptions that underlie the story tie into a view of theatre as a medium that communicates mainly through language, with behavior arising as an unconscious by-product. In most script-based productions, a process that derives from Stanislavski's early work is used to analyze the text. In rehearsal the actor and director investigate the dialogue in the context of the given circumstances and the narrative to determine what each character wants – their "objective" or "motivation" – recognizing that these wants may not be explicitly stated. (Recent scholarship has shown that the Russian word "zadacha" that Stanislavski used, which was translated as "objective," is better understood as "task" or "problem," but the term "objective" is still widely used.) These can be long-term wants – over the course of the play as a whole – or short-term, the length of a scene, or a unit within a scene. The next step is to decide what the character does in order to achieve his or her goal – their "actions." This process is usually called "table work" or analysis and leads to linguistically expressed decisions that then have to be converted into embodied action.

In Stanislavski's time, the concept of body language as we think of it was still unknown, and he had rejected Delsarte's attempts to codify posture and gesture in favor of an "internal" realism. Actors were encouraged to "live through" the given circumstances, imagining themselves in the character's situation. This imaginative identification would supposedly trigger appropriate behavior in an unconscious way. It is, of course, this behavior, or non-verbal communication (nvc), that we focus on when rehearsing. In a scripted production, the words, after all, already exist – it is our job to make them come alive through behavioral and vocal choices. In improvisation, or in creating devised pieces, speech and behavior are already unified, but it's generally recognized that the behavior is vitally communicative.

Nvc and language

Given that nvc is so central to the practice of making theatre, it is a curious paradox that we don't have a comprehensive vocabulary for behavioral communication. In addition to the factors mentioned above regarding psychologists' understanding of nvc, this reflects the fact that we absorb communication from nvc in daily life almost subliminally; it is visible if we consciously look for it, but is generally assimilated unconsciously. However, several studies show that adults rely more heavily on non-verbal than verbal cues in determining meaning in personal interaction, and also that non-verbal cues are *trusted more than linguistic meaning if the two are in conflict*.[6] Nvc can *confirm*, *modify*, or *contradict* the explicit meaning of the words of the script. In a realistic performance style, if an actor does not attend to the behavioral choices that he or she is making, they run the risk of *unintentionally* confirming, modifying, or contradicting the script's verbal content, leaving the audience unconvinced or confused. If the performance is non-realist, it is generally through behavior that the actor has to communicate the style. A great example of this lies in the period style of Restoration comedy, in which a code of postures and gestures expresses battles of status alongside the verbal wit. In contemporary theatre, actors often have to move from realistic characters to the embodiment of qualities, or even other beings. For example, in the American experimental theatre company Pig Iron's recent show *Chekhov Lizardbrain*, the cast alternated between naturalistically playing family members dealing with the death of a parent, and embodying brain neurons that behaved like lizards. All of these examples present the actor with the challenge of communicating through behavior.

Behavioral communication

Different training approaches have set about dealing with this challenge in different ways. The four practitioners who are the main focus of this book all arrived intuitively at physical solutions. As we'll see later, physical action is not only expressive, but can trigger feeling and conceptual thought in the actor. Towards the end of his career, Stanislavski had grown frustrated with the table analysis described above: " … after long discussions 'at the table' and individual visualizations, 'the actor comes on stage with a stuffed head and an empty heart, and can act nothing.'"[7] This frustration led him to develop a system called "active analysis" and the use of physical actions, which are more easily controlled by the actor (there's more information about this in Chapter 5). His contemporary, Michael Chekhov, was from an early age a proponent of a psychophysical approach, as the quotes from him later in this chapter demonstrate. Grotowski saw his own work as a continuation of the Method of Physical Actions, and developed a unique style of physical expression that was far from naturalistic, but had a great emotional impact on his audiences.

Lecoq's work with the neutral mask, which I'll describe in the next chapter, involves the embodiment of the movement rhythms of animals, elements, and materials.

A systematic vocabulary of nvc offers a cognitive framework for these methods and for more recent analyses of movement, such as Laban (in its application to acting) and Viewpoints, and adds a greater level of detail in communicative behavioral features such as facial expressions and eye movements. Current research on the different systems at play in nvc can be used to create training in nvc that is equivalent in detail and scope to vocal training. This offers theatre practitioners a vocabulary for the ways in which we express thoughts and feelings that are implicit in a situation, but not explicitly expressed in language. In current theatre practice this is commonly called subtext, but since that term depends on the concept of reading lines of text I use the term "non-verbal meaning" as one that offers more scope and is more sensitive to the current understanding of communication.

The social psychology model of nvc

The identification of the components of nvc allows for targeted training activities. This not only improves the actor's expressive abilities, but can also stimulate the imagination and affective states through the reflexive neural patterning of proprioception – a sort of multi-directional neural feedback system. This phenomenon, which I described in Chapter 1, gives the brain information about bodily position and states, and participates in features such as learning a dance step, one's level of well-being, and even the sense of self. For example, one study found that people felt more confident with a posture that included a straight back and chest out than they did with a curved back in a slouched posture.[8] Another study demonstrated that people duplicating the muscular activity of smiling by holding a pen between their teeth enjoyed watching cartoons more than people who were prevented from smiling by holding a pen between their lips.[9]

Psychologist Dale Leathers offers a useful overview of the different categories that are now used in analyzing nvc.[10] While these categories are based on the observation of behavior, they can be used as a framework for the creation of communication when combined with acting studio exercises. The benefits of applying this analysis to acting are:

- it is empirically derived from common human experience and is therefore applicable to a wide range of styles

- it is objective, and therefore avoids the confusion that derives from the use of the varied subjective terminology of different practitioners, or vocabularies that are tied to particular styles
- it is comprehensive and coherent, providing a framework for existing practices, and identifying gaps in those practices.

The systems that Leathers identifies generally interact with verbal communication, but can operate in the absence of speech, or even assume a dominant role in certain situations. He defines three non-verbal systems; the Visual, which includes Kinesic, Proxemic, and Artifactual subsystems; the Auditory; and the Invisible, which includes Tactile, Olfactory, and Chronemic subsystems. For the purposes of this discussion, I will be selective, and focus on those elements that are in the actor's control in a performance, and communicable to an audience in the majority of situations. Smell, for example, is not often used as a communicative device in theatre, and Artifactual communication (the information that is conveyed by the overall appearance of face and body) is more in the purview of costume and make-up design.

The Visual system is the major source of nvc, followed by the Auditory, and then the Invisible. In the Visual system, Kinesic communication is made up of facial expression, eye behavior, gesture, and posture. Proxemics consists of the use of space, distance between individuals, and the idea of territory (the "ownership" of spatial areas). The Auditory system is composed of nine different attributes that can be consciously controlled by the communicator: loudness, pitch, rate, duration, quality, regularity, articulation, pronunciation, and silence. In the intriguingly named Invisible system, the Tactile subsystem, while experienced by an individual as touch in daily life, becomes visible to an audience in performance, and is closely related to gesture. Chronemics deals with the use of time in interpersonal

Table 2.1 The three systems of nvc

Visual	*Auditory*	*Invisible*
2 subsystems	**9 components**	**3 subsystems**
Kinesic communication: facial expression, eye behavior, gesture, and posture.	Loudness, pitch, rate, duration, quality, regularity, articulation, pronunciation, and silence.	**Tactile**: use of touch. **Olfactory**: use of smell. **Chronemics**: use of time in interpersonal interaction.
Proxemics: the use of space, distance between individuals, and the idea of territory.		

interaction. In Western culture, this is closely associated with status – the scheduling of meetings, for instance, often reflects the relative hierarchical positions of those involved, and lack of punctuality from lower status individuals is often considered an affront to the established pecking order. Conversely, high status individuals sometimes use lateness as a way of demonstrating their power.

In performance, time is generally considered in terms of rhythm, tempo, and pace. Rhythm can be understood not only in its musical sense, but more widely as a pattern of iterations over time. These can be iterations of visual or audible elements, as in rhythms of movement or speech, but also of narrative events. For example, "rising action" in a climactically structured play can be defined rhythmically by the decreasing duration between significant narrative events, leading to a sense of acceleration. An important distinction needs to be made between tempo and pace. Tempo is the speed at which lines are delivered and actions occur, while pace is the rate at which the audience receives new information. An actor could use a fast tempo of speech, but if this does not communicate information to the audience, there is no genuine pace. Chronemics also includes the phenomenon known as "timing" in a performance, which describes the temporal interplay between actors. In this context, the unit most relevant to the actor is the second, or even the microsecond. At this level, the manipulation of time becomes intuitive rather than mechanical, a matter of feel.

As the categories used by social psychologists are formulated from the point of view of the observer, it makes sense to make some adjustments in order to apply the analysis of nvc to acting. The changes that I propose below mean that categories can be used for both the observation *and* the creation of behavior. Additionally, the adjustments mean that conceptual connections can be made across categories, acknowledge the degree of control that the actor can exert, and make links with familiar concepts and existing terminology. The following table lists nvc terms on the left, theatre terms on the right.

In most contemporary actor training programs, vocal training is well catered for, reflecting the systematic investigation of the voice by practitioners such as Edith Skinner, Kristin Linklater, Cicely Berry, and Catherine Fitzmaurice. Movement, also, is often addressed by Alexander Technique, or yoga, Laban, or Viewpoints classes. Few programs, however, deal in an explicit way with facial expressions, eye behavior, posture, or gesture. The information in this book points the way to how these gaps can be addressed. For example, psychologist Paul Ekman has codified facial expressions – these are described in Chapter 6. Jacques Lecoq's neutral mask work (which I

Table 2.2 Nvc categories and theatre terms

Nvc categories	Theatre terms
Facial expressions	Facial expressions
Eye behavior	Eye behavior
Posture	Posture
Gesture	Gesture
Space, territory, closeness	Spatial dynamics and movement; rhythm and tempo of movement and action
Vocal loudness	Volume, projection
Vocal rate	Tempo of speech
Duration, regularity, silence	Rhythm and cadence of speech and sound
Pitch	Pitch, inflexion
Quality	Timbre
Articulation	Vocal production, enunciation
Pronunciation	Accent and dialect

describe in the next chapter) offers the actor imaginative and rigorous ways of discovering the expressive qualities of posture and gesture. An adaptation of choreographer Rudolf Laban's work, of which I give an example at the end of this chapter, helps the actor to define the metaphorical qualities of gestures.

The following exercise is one example of how a component of behavioral expression can be simply identified and practiced. This sort of work is rarely done in actor training programs because it doesn't fit with the prevailing concepts of authenticity and naturalness as "internal" qualities that would be contaminated by "technical" exercises.

Exercise: eye movements and imagination

The eyes are significant communicators in interpersonal interactions, as well as indicators of thought and feeling. They occupy a unique position in the body's cognitive systems. As psychologists Daniel Richardson, Rick Dale, and Michael Spivey describe: "Eye movements are uniquely poised between perception and cognition. They are central to the function of the visual system, but for such scanning to be efficient, it cannot be simply a random sample of the visual world. To be useful, eye movements must be related to an organism's memories, expectations and goals."[11] Richardson and his colleagues refer to a number of experiments that demonstrate how we create a form of spatial indexing of information, whether that information is present in the physical environment or not. Since eye movements are generally the result of unconscious impulses, but are also subject to conscious control, the actor can use them both to communicate thought to an audience through spatial indexing, and also to stimulate his or her own imagination through proprioception. The foundation for this ability lies in defining different types of eye movement in order to make conscious choices. The following exercise defines these types, using a verb that begins with "S" for each one to create a mnemonic of "The Five S's."[12]

Step 1 Sit comfortably upright in a location without distractions. Lengthen the muscles in the back of the neck to encourage a neutral posture. Take a few moments to let the muscles of the face relax.

Step 2 "Search." For 30 seconds, move the eyes constantly around your visual field, keeping the head still, and not resting on any one location any longer than another. Avoid creating any patterns of movement. After 30 seconds, stop and notice how you feel. Students frequently report a sense of disorientation, sometimes even nausea. Take a minute to regain a sense of neutrality through even and sustained breathing.

Step 3 "Select." In this movement, the eyes come to a rest on one particular point. Repeat the "search" activity for 30 seconds, but this time, intersperse it with moments of "select." What happens to your thoughts each time you select? At the end of the 30 seconds, reflect on what seem to have been the mental processes that were stimulated by the activity. When the activity of "search" is not related to the external environment, it feels as though one is searching one's own thoughts, and that each "select" is a moment where one thinks one has found information.

Step 4 "Shift." This involves moving the eyes directly from one selected point to another, without any intervening searching. Try this for 30 seconds, using different locations for each selected point, and varying their height and lateral placement. You can also experiment with the tempo of the eye movement. At the end of 30 seconds, reflect on the experience. Did it feel like you were weighing different options of action? Now think of an imaginary context in which this might occur and repeat the exercise for 10 seconds, making the final "select" directly in front of you. What character came to mind? Was a decision made?

Step 5 "Sustain." Here, the eyes sustain their focus on one point. For 30 seconds, try the following sequence; search, select, shift, sustain. Hold the sustain on the point that you arrive at after switch until you need to blink, then begin the sequence again. If you can hold the sustain until the end of the 30 seconds, then do so. What sense of self do you experience when maintaining your visual focus in this way? Students often report a sense of deter-mination, or mental focus. Did you notice your facial expres-sion altering during the sustain? If so, this demonstrates the way in which neurological pathways operate reflexively, and how the conscious control of one feature can affect others.

Step 6 "Shut." In this activity, the eyelids close briefly. The duration can vary from a blink to several seconds. Try blinking rapidly while searching. Do thoughts and Feelings arise? Then try the sequence described in Step 5, and shut after three seconds of sustain, holding for three seconds. The action tends to emphasize whatever feeling has arisen from the previous activity. Often, students describe the experience of this activity as expressing the thought "I can't believe my eyes."

This solo exercise is designed to identify types of eye move-ment and to practice consciously controlling them, while notic-ing the effect on the imagination and one's affective state. In Chapter 6, I give examples of how this information can be used in ensemble work.

Much nvc is involuntary and unconscious, and so the challenge for the actor is to make consciously-chosen nvc appear credible. For example, in the category of facial expressions, psychologist Geoffrey Beattie observes:

> Voluntary or deliberate facial movements, like false smiles, are controlled by the cerebral hemispheres and show an asymmetry in their expression on the face as a result of this. Involuntary facial movements that reflect real emotion, such as genuine smiles, are controlled by lower, more primitive areas of the brain, and are essentially symmetrical on both sides of the face.[13]

Clearly, the difference between apparently genuine and false displays of emotion will provoke a response in audiences. Observant audience members might find the difference discernible at a conscious level, and would probably identify false displays of emotion as "bad acting," unless such a false display was appropriate in the fictional cir-cumstances. Other, less observant members might feel vaguely unsat-isfied or subliminally unconvinced by the acting, without being able to identify why. Later on, I'll talk about the neural mechanisms that operate unconsciously in empathy and emotion, but for now the focus is on observable features of communication. Like a pianist practicing scales, it makes sense for the actor to work at practicing the mechanics of physical expression, to understand and control how features such as posture, gesture, and facial expression communicate, and how to make voluntary actions in these areas *appear* involuntary and therefore spontaneous. Like any other skill, this takes practice and needs to be assimilated to the point where its mechanics are engaged unconsciously.

The "conscious competency" model of assimilation is useful in demonstrating the process by which this can happen.[14] This model is a useful reminder of the need to learn, and train others, in sequential stages. According to this model, the learner always begins at Stage 1 – "unconscious incompetence," and if successful in their training, will end at Stage 4 – "unconscious competence," having passed through Stage 2 – "conscious incompetence," and Stage 3 – "conscious competence." In Stage 1, the student has no awareness of, or ability in the skill being taught. In Stage 2, the student is aware of the skill, but has not yet developed any ability. In Stage 3, the student is able to perform the skill, but needs to consciously think about it to execute it, while in Stage 4, the skill has become integrated to the point where it can be performed without conscious thought. These stages are easily recognized by anyone who has learned a skill such as riding a bike or driving a car: a non-driver is at the level of unconscious incompetence; a beginner would be at the level of conscious incompetence; someone who has just passed his or her driving test is at the level of conscious competence; the driver who gets to work without remembering the drive is unconsciously competent.

It is worth reminding ourselves of this process in order to counter the still active tendency in many theatre programs to resist "technical" training in the misguided assumption that it will produce "technical" performances. This mistrust is based on a phenomenon that is easily recognized from an experiential point of view. If an actor is thinking of technique while performing in a realist style, they are not focusing on the fictional circumstances of the play, and from the point of view of people who mistrust technique, this inevitably compromises "truth."[15] This stance ignores the concept of "dual consciousness" expressed by Michael Chekhov, which describes the phenomenon of being simultaneously aware of self and character. I'll explore this more fully later in the chapters on character, but for now, it's a useful example of how an understanding of acting as a psychophysical activity rather than a purely mental one leads to concepts that sit well with the current cognitive understanding of the bodymind. This understanding includes research that focuses on the use of gesture that accompanies speech.

Gesture and speech in nvc

The feature of nvc that has the most connection with specific conceptual meaning is that of gesture. Gestures generally have three phases: the preparation, where the arms move from their resting position; the "stroke" where the main action occurs; and the retraction, where the arms return to their resting position. Timing is important; in spontaneous gestures that accompany speech, the stroke coincides with the significant word or phrase.

This means that the preparatory phase normally precedes the noun or verb most closely associated with the gesture, so that this can be synchronous with the stroke. Contrived gesturing often looks "wrong" because the timing is off. Observers quickly detect forced gestures by their unnatural timing, and the executor of a gesture can feel the difference between appropriate and inappropriate timing. This simple experiential exercise illustrates the phenomenon.

Exercise: Gesture timing

Read the following sentence: "I will NOT accept that."

Now, speak it out loud with a gesture.

Where did you find yourself placing the stroke of the gesture? Probably on the "NOT." Now try saying the phrase again a few times, placing the stroke on a different word each time. Do these versions feel as natural as the first?

Try the same exercise with "It's GREAT to see you."

What gesture arises spontaneously on "GREAT?"

Notice the different nuances of meaning that arise when you place the stroke on different words. Did some of these make you think of unwelcome guests?

Social psychologists identify several different types of gesture:

- **Emblems** are specific and culturally defined, consciously used, and consciously understood. Examples are "thumbs up," and the tips of the thumb and forefinger meeting to make a circle, suggesting "perfect" or "ok."
- **Iconic gestures** describe physical, concrete items and illustrate what is being said, for example, showing size or shape. These are

related to **mimetic gestures**, which do the same thing, but can be used without accompanying speech. These can be generated consciously or unconsciously.

- **Deictic gestures** point at significant objects, which may be specific (one object), general (a class of objects), or functional (e.g. opening a hand towards a door to communicate "you go first"). These can be generated consciously or unconsciously.

- **Metaphoric gestures** are closely related to concepts and can be abstract (such as the rolling of hands around one another to suggest uncertainty) or specific (placing the palms of the hands together in a prayer position to suggest "plead" or "beg"). I describe these in more detail later in this chapter. These are more likely to be generated unconsciously than consciously in everyday behavior.

- **Arbitrary gestures** are those in which a specific code has to be learned, such as baseball signs or the Sign Language used by deaf people. The learning of the code is evidently a conscious activity. Once the code has been assimilated the user is at the level of unconscious competence.

- **Regulators** indicate turn taking in conversation, like a person lifting a hand with forefinger raised to show that they are about to speak. These can be generated consciously or unconsciously.

- **Affect displays** show emotion, from the anger that is apparent in the tightening of a fist, to the anxiety indicated by hand-wringing. These are more likely to be generated unconsciously than consciously in everyday behavior.

- **Beat gestures** can be executed by a finger, hand, or arm. A single beat is a strike that creates emphasis and draws attention to a single piece of information. Repeated beats can accompany the expression of a package of significant information. Rapid tapping of the foot or fingers generally suggests impatience. These can be generated consciously or unconsciously.

Despite the potential for conscious control of gesture, the vast majority of gestures in everyday speech are unconsciously generated, produced alongside words (rather than substituting for them) and *almost impossible to inhibit*. This last feature probably explains the fact that most people, when confronted with a discrepancy in meaning between verbal and non-verbal communication, will trust the non-verbal. Spontaneously occurring gestures that accompany speech generally fall into the categories of iconic and metaphoric.

Iconic gestures are generally pictorial representations that show the speaker's mental image and point of view. Their particular form often shows a close relationship to the meaning of the accompanying speech, and can sometimes add information to what is said. In an example from cognitive linguist David McNeill's *Hand and Mind*, a speaker describes a cartoon figure bending back a tree, saying "he bent it way back" and accompanying this by the physical action of grasping and pulling back. The gesture shows that the tree was attached to the ground – information not explicitly mentioned in the verbal portion of the utterance.

Metaphoric gestures are also essentially pictorial, but the content is an abstract idea rather than a concrete object or event – an image of an abstraction. This occurs because metaphoric gestures frequently represent abstract concepts that have been metaphorically formed from sensorimotor experience:

> Metaphor allows conventional mental imagery from sensorimotor domains to be used for domains of subjective experience. For example, we may form an image of something going by us or over our heads (sensorimotor experience) when we fail to understand (subjective experience). A gesture tracing the path of something going past us or over our heads can indicate vividly a failure to understand.[16]

Because of this, *work with metaphoric gestures offers the actor one of the most accessible ways to develop their facility with expressing abstract concepts.* I'll talk about this in more detail at the end of this chapter.

The understanding of the way in which gesture operates has become increasingly refined, and research has begun to create a holistic context for the types of gesture described above. Psychologist Adam Kendon's experiments are part of a growing body of evidence that shows that gestures are closely linked to speech, but present meaning in a form that is fundamentally different, and that through hand movements, people (often unconsciously) communicate thoughts:

> Gesture contributes in many different ways [to meaning]. In some cases it may seem as if a gesture provides an expression parallel to the meaning that is provided in words. In other cases gesture appears to refine, qualify or make more restricted the meaning conveyed verbally, and sometimes we encounter the reverse of this. In yet other cases gesture provides aspects of reference that are not present at all in the verbal component. In other cases again, gesture may serve to create an image of the object that is the topic of the spoken component.[17]

Clearly, understanding the different ways in which gesture communicates meaning can be extremely useful for the actor. While Kendon's focus is on hand and arm movements, *actors can extend his analysis to other features of non-verbal communication*. For example, while listening to another person speak, a rapid lateral eye "switch" in synchrony with a sharp exhale of breath can vividly communicate disbelief or disdain. While not a gesture in the sense that it is executed by the hand and arm, it is gestural in that it communicates meaning without language. Kendon's research, together with that of David McNeill (which I address in the next chapter) demonstrates the way in which the physical activity of gesture is part of the process of generating "utterances" – a term for communication that may be linguistic, gestural, or both:

> When a speaker speaks, the speech is organized into a series of packages ... [t]hese packages tend to correspond to units of meaning ... which may be referred to as "idea units." Gesture is also organized into packages of action, ... which coincide with and tend to be semantically coherent with ... the "idea units" ... However, the gestural expression typically takes up just a part of the idea ... For example, it may bring out an aspect of meaning associated with the verb ... or it may add an imagistic dimension to something referred to by a noun. The precise way in which a coincidence is achieved ... appears to be variable. In our interpretation, this means that the speaker can adjust both speech and gesture one to another as if they are two separate expressive resources which can be deployed, each in relation to the other, in different ways according to how the utterance is being fashioned.[18]

The concept of "idea units" offers an intriguing validation of the Stanislavski-inspired process of breaking up a script's action and dialogue into units ("beats"). However, in the light of this information, it may be more useful to use the term "impulse" in script analysis, since this is not as conceptually tied to language as the word "idea," but still implies discrete packages of expression. Impulses can produce words or gestures or both combined. Reading the words of the script becomes a process of reverse engineering to discover the impulses that generated them. These need to be assimilated in rehearsal so as to successfully embody them, and I'll investigate this process more fully in the next chapter. Kendon's analysis also supports the common practice in rehearsing Shakespeare of identifying the "active" word in a line, and consciously executing a gesture to accompany it. This gesture may or may not be carried through to performance, but serves to enrich the actor's physical experience of the text, thus integrating written language with speech and gesture.

Kendon's work demonstrates that speech and gesture are linked, and is part of a growing body of work that disproves the notion that nvc is reserved for interpersonal relationships.[19] For many theatre practitioners, this may seem self-evident from practical experience. After all, the whole concept of non-verbal meaning depends on this notion, but the paradoxical situation that obtains in most theatre training programs is that there is no systematic organization of the elements that communicate non-verbal meaning, or even a comprehensive vocabulary. Now that there is an empirical basis for codifying nvc, it makes sense to use this as a basis for an approach to training actors in physical communication. This does not need to replace existing knowledge or techniques, such as Viewpoints or those of Lecoq and Laban, but offers a framework within which these practices can be understood, and linked more explicitly to textual work.

Case study: nvc and *Earnest*

To demonstrate how this vocabulary can be employed in relation to performance, I'm going to apply it to an extract from Act II of *The Importance of Being Earnest*. This extract demonstrates the way in which Wilde sought to define what actors *do* as well as say, revealing his awareness of the degree to which behavior communicates meaning.

Cecily. May I offer you some tea, Miss Fairfax?
Gwendolen. [With elaborate politeness.] Thank you. [Aside.] Detestable girl! But I require tea!
Cecily. [Sweetly.] Sugar?
Gwendolen. [Superciliously.] No, thank you. Sugar is not fashionable any more. [Cecily looks angrily at her, takes up the tongs and puts four lumps of sugar into the cup.]
Cecily. [Severely.] Cake or bread and butter?
Gwendolen. [In a bored manner.] Bread and butter, please. Cake is rarely seen at the best houses nowadays.
Cecily. [Cuts a very large slice of cake, and puts it on the tray.] Hand that to Miss Fairfax.
[Merriman does so, and goes out with footman. Gwendolen drinks the tea and makes a grimace. Puts down cup at once, reaches out her hand to the bread and butter, looks at it, and finds it is cake. Rises in indignation.]

Gwendolen. You have filled my tea with lumps of sugar, and though I asked most distinctly for bread and butter, you have given me cake. I am known for the gentleness of my disposition, and the extraordinary sweetness of my nature, but I warn you, Miss Cardew, you may go too far.

Cecily. [Rising.] To save my poor, innocent, trusting boy from the machinations of any other girl there are no lengths to which I would not go.

Gwendolen. From the moment I saw you I distrusted you. I felt that you were false and deceitful. I am never deceived in such matters. My first impressions of people are invariably right.[20]

The stage directions are explicit, specific, and detailed in describing the desired physical and vocal behavior of the characters, and make clear the way in which the comedy of the scene arises from the tension between genuine feelings and "the shallow mask of manners." However, to include such a level of detail for all the dialogue in a play becomes unwieldy and restrictive, and even with Wilde's liberal use of adverbs, there are still a significant number of choices to be made by the actor. (There is, of course, considerable variance among playwrights in the extent that they use stage directions that describe behavior, a feature that is affected by many factors, including period, style, and genre.) In the case of this extract, the following analysis shows that the amount of nvc that communicates meaning far exceeds even the stage directions that Wilde has included.

I'll refer to two filmed versions of the play. The first, directed by Anthony Asquith, was released in 1952,[21] and features Joan Greenwood as Gwendolen, and Dorothy Tutin as Cecily. The second, directed by Oliver Parker, was released in 2002,[22] and features Frances O'Connor and Reese Witherspoon respectively in the same roles. Some allowance has to be made for the fact that the second version has cut significant portions of the script, and often intercuts a scene with visual montage shots of action that is only reported in the stage play. Both cinematographers use close-ups to direct attention to the action of placing sugar in the tea, rendering a portion of the actors' behavior invisible, and also cut to reaction shots of Merriman's face on some lines. In the following table, lines and stage directions are in the left hand column, descriptions of behavior in each version in the second and third column respectively.

Table 2.3 Nvc in the *Earnest* tea scene

Script	Asquith 1952	Parker 2002
[original stage direction] {} = cut in Asquith () = cut in Parker		
Cecily. May I offer you some tea, {Miss Fairfax}?	Facial expression not visible, exaggerated rising vocal inflexion at end of sentence.	Neutral facial expression, low vocal timbre, constant pitch, eyes "Shut" at start of line, then narrowed with visual focus avoiding G. and directed downwards.
Gwendolen. [With elaborate politeness.] Thank you. {([Aside.] Detestable girl! But I require tea!} 'Miss Cardew' added in Parker.	Upright posture. Forced smile, followed by angry facial expression (narrowed eyes, muscular tension around mouth), "Sustain" on C. from corners of eyes, "Shifting" to front at end of word in avoidance of eye contact, narrowing of eyes.	Body and face not visible. Descending vocal inflexion.
Cecily. [Sweetly.] Sugar?	Slight lean towards G. hand extended towards sugar bowl, eyes "Shift" down towards hand, then up to G. Head tilted, chin pushed forward.	Downturned mouth, angry expression, eyes "Shut," head tilted down.

Table 2.3 (continued)

Script	Asquith 1952	Parker 2002
Gwendolen. [Superciliously.] No, thank you. Sugar is not fashionable any more.	Eyes widen, head turns towards C, eyes narrow, then "Shut" on 'No,' open on 'thank you.' Eyes "Sustain" on C, then "Shift" downwards. Slight chuckle after 'Sugar,' followed by a sneer and then a smile. Vocal inflexion descends on last three words, as head is turned to front, breaking "Sustain" on C.	Moves into C.'s personal space to sit down, sneers, then smiles, seats herself with torso oriented away from C, posture reclining on back of chair, visual focus in opposite direction from C, tilts head away from C, rests it on hand, eyes "Shut" briefly, then moves hand to chin.
[**Cecily** looks angrily at her, takes up the tongs and puts four lumps of sugar into the cup.]	Eyes "Select" sugar bowl. Frown. Hand grasps sugar cubes, eyes "Shift" to G. Hand places sugar cubes in cup, as eyes "Shift" to cup. Small smile. As cubes are released, eyes "Shift" back to G. Hand emphasizes action of releasing cubes.	Close-up of C.'s hand placing three cubes of sugar in cup, then mid-shot showing chin thrust forward, angry expression, changing to smile as C. "Selects" G, dropping fourth cube in cup. Passes cup to Merriman.
Cecily. [Severely.] Cake or bread and butter?	Not visible. Rising vocal inflexion on 'cake,' then again on 'butter.'	Rising vocal inflexion on 'cake,' slight pause, consistent pitch for rest of line. Head turned to side, away from G. Chin thrust forward, corners of mouth turned down. Eyes "Shift" to side away from G, brief "shut" of eyes on 'bread,' simultaneous with slight shrug of shoulders.

Table 2.3 (continued)

Script	Asquith 1952	Parker 2002
Gwendolen. [In a bored manner.] Bread and butter, please. Cake is rarely seen at the best houses nowadays.	Receives cup from C. Head and visual focus switch to cup. Slow vocal tempo on first sentence, with low pitch. Vocal inflexion descends on 'please.' Head moves front after receiving cup. Eyes "Shut" on 'cake,' open on 'is' and "Shut" again on 'rarely.' This word is drawn out (first vowel sound sustained). Head tilts to side on 'best houses.' Smile follows completion of sentence, with eyes "Shifting" down.	Smiles, sits up, accepts cup of tea from Merriman. Flat vocal pitch on first sentence, slight pitch variation suggesting laughter in second sentence, torso turned away from C., eyes "Sustain" away from C., then "Shift" down to cup.
Cecily. [Cuts a very large slice of cake, and puts it on the tray.] (Hand that to Miss Fairfax.)	Eyes "Sustain" on cake, mouth open with tip of tongue placed on top teeth, as hand takes slice of cake and places it on plate. Eyes "Shift" to plate, then to G. Mouth closes; muscular tension around mouth. Eyes "Shift" to Merriman as plate is handed to him. Eyes "Sustain" on Merriman's eyes as plate is transferred.	Action not shown – cut to facial reaction of Merriman.

Table 2.3 (continued)

Script	Asquith 1952	Parker 2002
[**Merriman** does so, and goes out with footman. **Gwendolen** drinks the tea and makes a grimace. Puts down cup at once, reaches out her hand to the bread and butter, looks at it, and finds it is cake. Rises in indignation.]	Merriman purses lips, eyes "Shift" down and sideways to G. before placing plate on table in front of her.	Upright seated posture. Widening of eyes, slight 'gulp' vocalization as tea is drunk. (Other action not shown. close-up of Merriman's hand placing cake on table.)
	G. head lowered, eyes "Shift" down, sips tea, and then eyes "Shift" up suddenly with open mouth and a slight frown after tasting it. Mouth closes. Muscular tension around mouth as eyes "Shift" down to cup again, then expression of disgust. Eyes "Shift" to C. and "Sustain" for speech.	
Gwendolen. (You have filled my tea with lumps of sugar, and though I asked most distinctly for bread and butter, you have given me cake. I am known for the gentleness of my disposition, and the extraordinary sweetness of my nature, but I warn you, Miss Cardew, you may go too far.)	Eyes narrow. Expression of puzzlement on 'sugar.' Vocal rhythm steady, pitch low, pronunciation smooth, pitch descends on 'cake.' G. stands on 'cake.' Eyes "Sustain" on C. Volume increases on 'gentleness,' 'extraordinary' is emphasized by elongation of central vowel sound, eyes "Shut" simultaneously with this. Vocal tempo increases, volume rises, timbre gets fuller until 'Miss Cardew,' then a quick eye "Shift" to Merriman precedes a sudden softening of timbre and decrease of volume for 'you may go too far.'	(Not included.)

Table 2.3 (continued)

Script	Asquith 1952	Parker 2002
Cecily. [Rising.] (To save my poor, innocent, trusting boy from the machinations of any other girl there are no lengths to which I would not go.)	Eyes "Shift" down and away from G. until 'machinations.' Sideways head movements. Chin thrust forward. Vocal rhythm has slight pauses, vocal tempo increases to 'machinations,' when face assumes aggressive expression; lips pressed together, chin pushed forward, eyes wide. Eyes "Sustain" on G. from this point to end of speech. Stands on 'there are.' Vocal volume increases on 'no lengths,' slight pause after these words, and tempo increases for final phrase. After standing, posture is upright with arms held away from torso, chin raised.	(Not included.)

Table 2.3 (continued)

Script	Asquith 1952	Parker 2002
Gwendolen. From the moment I saw you I distrusted you. I felt that you were false and deceitful. (I am never deceived in such matters. My first impressions of people are invariably right.)	Elongation of words, raised volume, raised pitch in first sentence. Upright posture, raised chin, eyes "Sustain" on C. Increase in vocal tempo in second sentence, sideways movement of the head on 'never,' eyes "Shift" down and to the side, then back to C. Chin raised further on 'My first,' 'invariably' elongated by sustaining of second vowel sound. Final consonant of 'right' emphasized. Considerable pitch variation throughout. Arms drawn back from shoulders in final sentence, breathing rate increases in tempo.	Leans towards C., eyes "Sustain" on C. Low vocal timbre, low volume, exaggerated vocal articulation, consistent pitch. Head inclined towards C., chin thrust forward, muscular tension around mouth.

The close examination of these two different versions raises many interesting points. Most importantly, it makes clear that *the meaning and the comic effect of the scene depend on nvc.* If the scene were played only for the explicit meaning of the language, the disagreement between the two characters would be puzzling and apparently superficial. Perhaps the most surprising feature is the sheer amount of non-verbal information that is present and, by extension, the sheer amount of information that we process unconsciously when interacting with others or watching drama. For reasons of clarity and space, I have only included the nvc of each actor as they are speaking – there is, of course, at least double that information when one considers the nvc that is displayed as characters listen to each other and respond non-verbally.

As one would expect from actors at the top of the profession in their respective periods, there is a high degree of facility and accomplishment with nvc. It is unlikely that the actors in these scenes were consciously thinking about posture, gesture, and vocalics as they were speaking; these depend, of course, on the "unconscious competence" gained by preparation and assimilation through rehearsal. It's intriguing how actors separated by 50 years use very similar aspects of nvc to communicate, for example the chin pushed forward and narrowed eyes that both Tutin and Witherspoon use to communicate Cecily's dislike of Gwendolen. This activity is a vibrant example of the way in which behavior can provide "aspects of reference that are not present at all in the verbal component." Another instance lies in a momentary gestural activity of Greenwood's in the Asquith version. As she says "but I warn you, Miss Cardew, you may go too far" there is a swift eye "shift" to Merriman before she lowers her vocal volume and pitch. This suggests that Gwendolen suddenly recalls the presence of a servant, and reins back the expression of her indignation for propriety's sake. This indicates that Greenwood has a greater awareness of the social mores of the period within which the play is set than is demonstrated in the 2002 version. Another example from the same speech illustrates how one of the "5 S's" components links with speech. On the word "extraordinary," Greenwood employs a "shut" that synchronizes with her elongation of the central vowel. The two factors together contribute to the emphasis that she has chosen to give this word.

From an analytic point of view, the identification of components of nvc makes it possible to use objective criteria to identify differences in style. For example, the 1952 version appears more formal; comparing the elements of nvc show that this impression is generated by a number of factors. Firstly, Tutin and Greenwood maintain upright postures throughout. Neither of them recline as O'Connor does, nor use the inclination of the torso that she does towards the end of the scene. Both actors in the 1952 version have a high degree of vocal articulation; vowel and consonant sounds are clearly distinguished and separated from one another. Vocal tempo is slower overall in the 1952 film, and the rhythm of speech from both actors includes more pauses than in the 2002 version. This sets up the confrontation at the end of the scene to be more forceful, however, than in the 2002 version. Both actors maintain an upright standing posture, "sustain" their visual focus on one another, and increase the volume and tempo of their speech. Consequently, the contrast with the behavior in the earlier part of the scene is more marked than in the confrontation between O'Connor and Witherspoon. This means that there is greater variation in the dramatic tone of the piece, something that might suggest that Asquith's version is closer to a stage tradition of presenting the play in England, while Parker's version seeks to fit the play into the romantic comedy genre of contemporary film-making.

While working on this analysis, it became very evident how the application of technology raises awareness of nvc. Even watching the scenes attentively at normal speed I did not notice facial expressions that appeared when the material was run in slow motion. Psychologist Paul Ekman calls these "micro expressions" – rapidly appearing and disappearing expressions that do not register consciously in the viewer's awareness (I'll address Ekman's work more fully in Chapter 6). Repeatedly experiencing the scenes also alerted me to vocal mannerisms that were not evident in the first viewing. A full analysis of the different ways that the two films contextualize the meaning of Wilde's script would take a book in itself, but I hope that this example demonstrates the validity and usefulness of applying a vocabulary derived from social psychology to analyze the non-verbal aspects of performance. Given that this vocabulary addresses the full range of human expressive behavior, it can be used with other, non-realist styles of drama and therefore successfully address devised, imagistic, and improvised performances.

Metaphorical gesture

As I mentioned earlier, metaphorical gestures offer the actor an accessible way in which to embody abstract concepts. This is because of the metaphorical way in which conceptual thought is shaped by physical experience. Lakoff and Johnson point out that:

> Our abilities to move the way we do and to track the motion of other things give motion a major role in our conceptual system. The fact that we have muscles and use them to apply force in certain ways leads to the structure of our system of causal concepts. What is important is that the peculiar nature of our bodies shapes our very possibilities for conceptualization and categorization.[23]

This is because "[our] brains are structured so as to project activation patterns from sensorimotor areas to higher cortical areas."[24] A simple example of this can be seen in our understanding of time. "There is an area in the visual system of our brains dedicated to the detection of motion. There is no such area for the detection of global time."[25] Motion is directly perceived and is thus available as a source for our metaphor systems to give shape to the abstract concept of time. The neural activity that makes this connection becomes more established with repetition until *a permanent connection is forged in the brain*. This means that metaphor is part of our perceptual apparatus rather than a post-perceptual activity of disembodied reason, as has been thought. Thus, in English, the most basic metaphor for time involves "an observer at the present who is facing toward the future, with the past behind the observer."[26] We conceive of the future as being ahead of us, the past behind, and this becomes a permanent neural connection.

Metaphoric thinking, far from being a feature of expression that is restricted to poetry, literature, and art, actually operates at every level of cognition. Indeed, Lakoff and Johnson state that "[c]onceptual metaphor is pervasive in both thought and language. It is hard to think of a common subjective experience that is not conventionally conceptualized in terms of metaphor."[27]

This has important implications for actors seeking to create vivid embodiments of thought, because it shows that most concepts of subjective experience are metaphorically based on a sensorimotor source domain, and therefore *have embodied movement tendencies*. This understanding of the way in which physical experience in the material world shapes conceptual thought gives an interesting valence to a statement made by Michael Chekhov long before cognitive science was established:

> [T]here are no purely physical exercises in our method ... our primary aim is to penetrate all the parts of the body with fine psychological vibrations. This process makes the physical body more and more sensitive in its ability to receive our inner impulses and to convey them expressively from the stage to the audience.[28]

Chekhov's concept is rooted in the notion of thought and physical activity being inextricably entwined. He proposed that the actor should practice a range of gestures in order to increase sensitivity and expressivity:

> Train yourself to make certain gestures with the utmost expressiveness, as fully and completely as you can. These gestures might express, for instance: drawing, pulling, pressing, lifting, throwing, crumpling, coaxing, separating, tearing, penetrating, touching, brushing away, opening, closing, breaking, taking, giving, supporting, holding back, scratching.[29]

That this is more than a mere technical exercise is supported by Lakoff and Johnson's description of the way in which we create conceptual metaphors through a process of conflation:

> We acquire a large system of primary metaphors automatically and unconsciously simply by functioning in the most ordinary of ways in the everyday world from our earliest years. We have no choice in this. Because of the way neural connections are formed during the period of conflation, we all naturally think using hundreds of primary metaphors.[30]

The authors go on to give examples of the way in which sensorimotor experience is mapped on to conceptual thought. Taking one of these examples that uses one of the words from Chekhov's list enables us to see how the link between physical action and thought occurs. In this example, the primary metaphor is "Help is support," and is derived from the sensorimotor domain of physical support and the primary experience of "Observing that some entities and people require support in order to continue functioning."[31] Through a process known as conflation, "permanent neural connections between the domains develop."[32] This means that Chekhov's exercise of practicing specific gestures *is both a physical and a mental activity*.

This, and many other of Chekhov's exercises, embrace the psychophysical nature of acting, and demonstrate a conception of the body as a *permeable organism* as well as a container with an inside and an outside. This quality is particularly apparent in exercises that relate the actor to his or her spatial environment. Chekhov proposes a sequence of exercises that identify four types of movement in space: molding, floating, flying, and radiating. Molding involves sensing the shapes that one's body makes in space – as if the body creates a series of molds in the air. This helps the actor to develop an awareness of form, and recognize that "vagueness and shapelessness have no place in art."[33] Floating involves imagining that the air supports you like water and, Chekhov states, induces a sense of "calm, poise and psychological warmth."[34] Flying involves imagining that one is soaring like a bird as one moves and, Chekhov suggests, will create a "sensation of joyful lightness and easiness [that] will permeate the entire body."[35] Radiating involves the imaginative projection of rays from the body that both precede and follow any movement that ends in a static position. While Chekhov, like many other Western practitioners, uses an "inner/outer" terminology, it is infused with the sense that communicative energy flows through the corporeal materiality: "While radiating, strive, in a sense, to go out and beyond the boundary of your body ... souls can be made manifest and convincing through powerful *radiation*." He also senses a reflexive relationship that incorporates imagination, physical activity, and affective state: " ... sensations you will experience will be those of freedom, happiness and inner warmth. All these feelings will fill your entire body, permeating it and making it more and more alive, sensitive and responsive."[36] Many contemporary practitioners, myself included, have been inspired by Chekhov's thoughts and exercises, and I investigate them in more detail in Chapter 4. As the examples that I've mentioned demonstrate, there is considerable sympathy between his approach and current cognitive knowledge, but overall it lacks organizational principles that could make it a comprehensive system.

Rudolf Laban's work, however, provides a useful framework for an initial approach to the demonstration and practice of physical actions as metaphorical expressions. Laban was a choreographer who developed a system of notation of human movement in the 1920s. Combined with his book *Effort*, this notation is now known as Labanotation and is widely used in choreography. In recent years, acting teachers have also combined Laban's analysis with exercises developed by one of his students, Irmgard Bartenieff, to develop a sophisticated program of exercises in physical action and movement in space.[37]

Exercise: Laban efforts as primary actions

The following exercise shows the way in which defined physical actions embody metaphorical concepts, and is a useful introduction to the way in which physical action can both stimulate and express conceptual thought. I use the term "primary action" as a link to the cognitive idea of primary metaphors. The exercise combines the cognitive understanding of the metaphoric connection between physical action and conceptual thought with Laban's identification of three components of movement: weight, space, and time. Activities in each component operate in a continuum between two extremes: weight from heavy to light; space from direct to indirect; and time from sudden to sustained. Later, the component of "flow" was added, which operates from bound to free. In this exercise I use the original three categories to maintain clarity about the metaphors that are produced by combining elements from each category. The following chart is derived from my practical experience as an actor in England in the 1980s and 1990s, and represents part of the studio "lore" of that period. The exercise introduces the idea and practice of gestures that both express and define a concept. It also helps actors to make the connection between experiential physical activity and the idea of dramatic "actions" (activities in pursuit of a goal).

Table 2.4 Laban efforts as primary actions

Weight	Space	Time
Heavy (or Strong)	Direct	Sudden (or Quick)
Light	Indirect	Sustained

Selecting one quality from each column gives you eight choices:

1 <u>Heavy</u>–<u>Direct</u>–<u>Sudden</u> describes a **PUNCH** (Figure 2.1)

Figure 2.1 Primary Action: Punch

2 <u>Heavy</u>–<u>Direct</u>–<u>Sustained</u> describes a **PUSH** or **PULL** (Figure 2.2a and Figure 2.2b)

Figure 2.2a Primary Action: Push

Figure 2.2b Primary Action: Pull

3   <u>Heavy</u>–<u>Indirect</u>–<u>Sudden</u> describes a **SLASH** (Figure 2.3)

Figure 2.3 Primary Action: Slash

4   Heavy–Indirect–Sustained describes **WRINGING** (wringing out a cloth) (Figure 2.4)

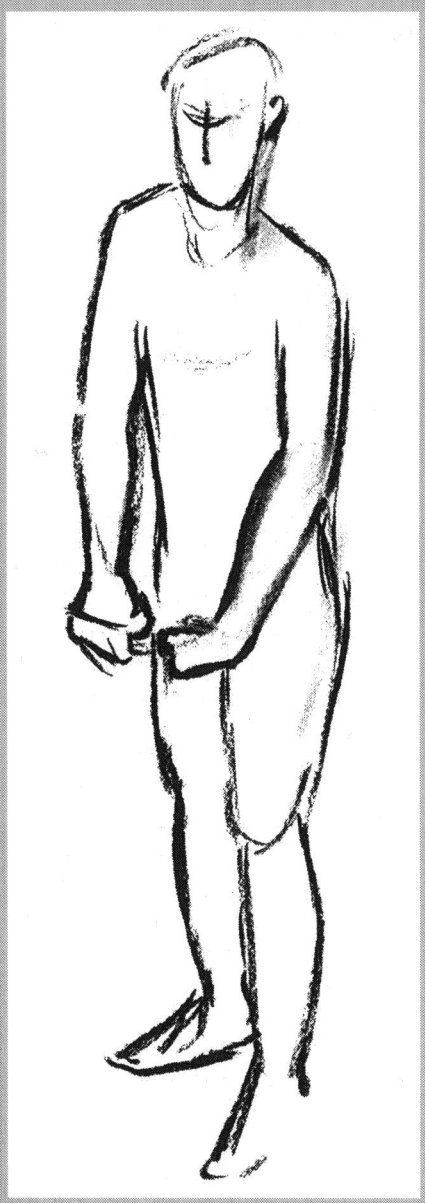

Figure 2.4 Primary Action: Wring

5   <u>Light–Indirect–Sustained</u> describes **STROKING** (like stroking an animal) (Figure 2.5)

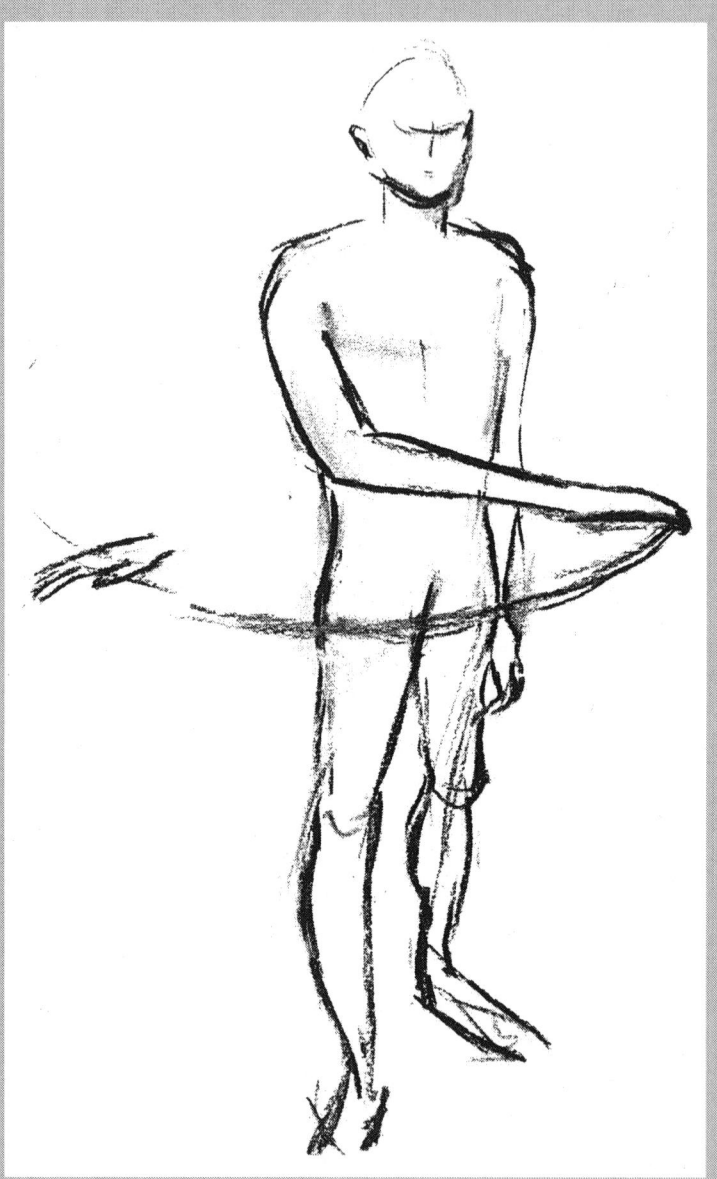

Figure 2.5 Primary Action: Stroke

6 <u>Light–Indirect–Sudden</u> describes **FLITTING** about (also called **FLICKING**) (Figure 2.6)

Figure 2.6 Primary Action: Flit

7 Light–Direct–Sudden describes a **DAB** or **TAP** (Figure 2.7)

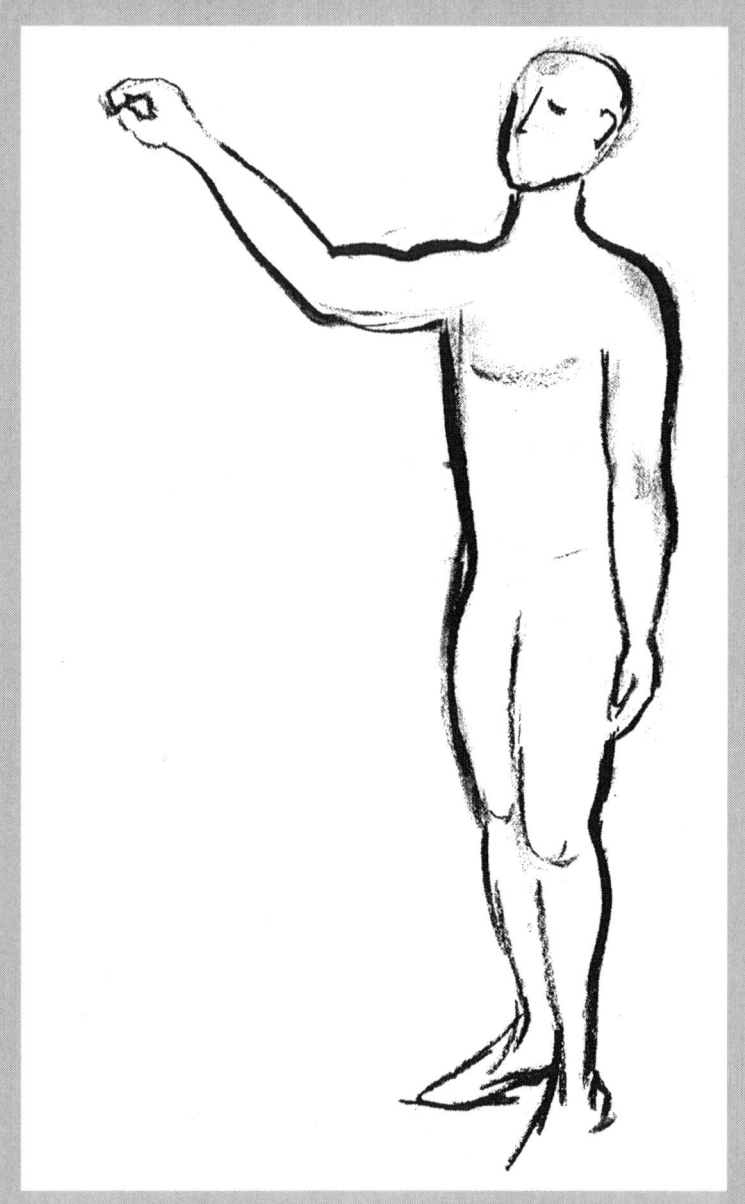

Figure 2.7 Primary Action: Dab or Tap

8   Light–Direct–Sustained describes a **GLIDE** (Figure 2.8)

Figure 2.8 Primary Action: Glide

Step 1

This phase of the activity introduces the metaphorical actions in a playful way that allows the actors to gain defined physical and vocal experience of each one. It's useful for the exercise leader to encourage "size" at this stage – big physical actions, loud vocal expression.

The actors stand in a circle. All repeatedly execute the physical action of "punch," saying the word "punch!" with the stroke of the gesture.

The exercise leader then invites pairs to have simple conversations across the circle. Each phrase that is said must be delivered as a physical and vocal punch (without contact!). Depending on the level of confidence the group has, these can be done simultaneously, or one pair at a time with the rest of the group observing. When done simultaneously, the participants are less self-conscious because they are not being observed. The same process is repeated for each of the actions. This simple and crude application of the actions to speech serves to release inhibitions, and create definition.

Step 2

The actors move individually in the space with the exercise leader calling out each action. The action is repeated physically for one minute, without vocalization or interaction between the actors. After each action, the exercise leader encourages the actors to notice how they feel and what sense of self arises from the action. This alerts them to the affective qualities generated through proprioception.

Step 3

The group now splits into pairs, with one person observing the other as the individual simply "thinks" the metaphoric actions, imaginatively visualizing them without vocalization. He or she is invited to allow the body to respond to the visualization, but to *avoid* consciously demonstrating the action or using large movements. It is helpful if they choose actions in a different sequence than the one used originally. The group is encouraged to identify factors such as eye movements, breathing patterns, changes of tension in the musculature of the face or the body as a whole.

The range of "size" and nuance visible in these activities demonstrates the applicability of these actions to a variety of styles and genres. The behavior in Step 1 would be appropriate in a farce, while Step 3 offers the subtlety needed for naturalistic work on screen. Of course, given the fact that the verbs describe behavior that happens in daily life anyway, they provide a useful vocabulary for a director or instructor to use in giving feedback to the actor. Another significant benefit is the added ease with which instructors, directors, and actors can identify levels of intensity. Because each action has a physical origin, one can talk about the metaphoric range of movement or the relative force of the metaphorical punch in the vocal delivery.

This introduction can be followed by improvisations in which the actions are expressed vocally, with a reduced range of movement in the physical action. Comic improvisations can be set up in which all but one player in a group share the same metaphoric verb of action. We could see the "wringing" family at breakfast, with a "flitting" teenage son, or a group of "punching" workers confronting a "dabbing" boss, with comedy arising from the extreme contrasts. The process of proprioceptive feedback means that the consciously chosen gestural activity provokes ideas – improvisers rarely seem at a loss in this exercise. Following this, greater subtlety and dramatic range can be gained in paired improvisations that give the players freedom to choose actions from the group of eight. The focus on the metaphoric actions often helps actors who otherwise get "stuck" in improvising, either because of "brain-freeze" caused by panic, or because they are thinking on a narrative scale, and not paying attention to their immediate environment or fellow players.

The application of the actions to text can begin with "open" scenes (dialogue with no indication of character or circumstances). The text can be memorized and then the actors can improvise the actions, finding a variety of ways to "behave the text," thus making clear that linguistic meaning can be confirmed, modified, or contradicted by gestural behavior. I have found this approach to be very useful in helping trainee actors to achieve behavioral differentiation of their actions, since primary actions offer definition at a level of detail, and create a variety of expression. This exercise is also an excellent introduction to the Stanislavskian concept of actions in pursuit of a goal. This is often one of the most difficult concepts of his system for students to grasp. The behaviorally specific metaphoric actions make very clear the way in which one person can seek to have an effect on another. This forms a foundation for the definition and use of actions that are less behaviorally specific such as persuade, explain, plead, seduce, command, comfort. The behavioral actions often serve as vehicles for these; a vocal expression of "stroke" could express "comfort," or "slash" could express "command." This level of definition also supports choices that intrigue audiences by their unexpectedness – "glide" expressing "threaten," or "wring" to express "explain." This approach also offers directors a clear and specific vocabulary to use in communicating with their actors, not only in script-based work, but also in improvisation and devising, where coherence is often achieved by elements other than cause and effect narrative. As with other exercises that practice the components of nvc, actors need to progress to unconscious competency to assimilate the application of these defined actions.

Conclusion

Activities such as these enable the actor to link space, time, and story in precise ways, and offer the actor a model of the way in which impulse becomes action that is congruent with the current understanding of the embodied mind. This understanding enables direct actions to synthesize "internal" experiences of psychological and emotional states, and "external" expressions of those states through behavioral activity in a reflexive feedback loop. The next chapter investigates the cognitive processes involved in this process in more detail.

Key points

- Social psychologists have defined activities and categories of behavior to create a taxonomy of nvc that can be applied to theatre.
- Gesture is equal to language in communicating meaning, but operates in a fundamentally different way.
- Non-verbal cues are trusted more than linguistic meaning if the two are in conflict.
- Physical experience shapes much conceptual thought through metaphor.
- Gesture operates reflexively; it can both express and stimulate thought and Feelings.
- Nvc can be consciously employed, and appear spontaneous when unconscious competence is achieved.
- The majority of gestures that spontaneously accompany speech fall in the iconic and metaphoric categories.
- Gestures are closely linked to speech, but present meaning in a form that is fundamentally different.
- Impulses generate "utterances," which can be linguistic, gestural, or both.
- Nvc can *confirm*, *modify*, or *contradict* explicit verbal meaning.
- Movement stimulates imagination and feeling.
- Sensorimotor experience shapes conceptual thought through metaphor.
- Metaphor is part of our perceptual apparatus.
- Concepts have embodied movement tendencies.
- Metaphoric gestures, by expressing concepts, can stimulate channeled imagination and feeling.
- Channeled imagination and feeling can be applied to creating dramatic material or embodying text.

Chapter 3

What is the relationship between thought, physical action, and language?

The previous chapter demonstrated how visible behavior communicates meaning. This chapter investigates the cognitive processes through which this behavior arises. Improvised and devised performances integrate verbal and non-verbal meaning at the moment of creation in a phenomenon that I call "authorship through action." Most performances, however, start with a written text in which authorship of the dialogue and sequence of events has already occurred. Despite some descriptive stage directions (as in *The Importance of Being Earnest*), most of the dialogue in scripts dictates what characters say, while leaving it to the actor and director to create the "how" of its being said. This involves, of course, a psychophysical process that combines thought, imagination, and expression as the actor seeks to embody the fictional content of the script. As described in the previous chapter, the traditional view within psychology has been that language and nvc are two separate systems, devoted to different subject matters, while recent research shows that the two are part of the same system, but operate in radically different ways. The difference between the way that the brain processes written and spoken language is at the heart of the challenge that actors face in bringing a script to life. Current research sheds light on what has previously been a largely unconscious process for actors – that of converting written language to embodied expression.

First, I'll describe cognitive linguist David McNeill's findings, which show that although language and gesture are one mental system, they operate in fundamentally different ways to complement one another. This analysis rests on his development of a new conception of language, viewing it as an imagery-language dialectic, in which gestures provide imagery. Features of this conception are then applied to textual analysis, with examples from the play *I.D.* This is followed by a biography of Jacques Lecoq and a demonstration of how closely his stated principles correspond to a cognitive under-standing of the bodymind. Examples of his exercises are then described with relation to the cognitive principles that they embody. These include exercises in heightening awareness of fundamental sensor-imotor experiences, work with the neutral mask, embodying the rhythms of natural elements, and physicalizing poetic metaphor.

Language and gesture as one system

Cognitive linguist David McNeill has pioneered the recognition that gesture and language are equal communicators of meaning: "[G]estures are an integral part of language as much as are words, phrases and sentences – gesture and language are one system."[1] He points out, however, that gesture and language operate in different ways: "Utter-ances possess two sides, only one of which is speech; the other is imagery, actional and visuo-spatial. To exclude the gesture side, as has been traditional, is tantamount to ignoring half of the message out of the brain."[2] While McNeill is not concerned with theatre or acting in his research, his findings underscore the importance of physicality and image in the actor's process: "If one knows how to read them, the gesture can convey meaning no less than language, but the method used by the gesture for doing this is fundamentally different from language."[3]

The difference between language and gesture

Although McNeill recognizes language and gesture as parts of the same system, he proposes a view of their functions that makes them complementary to one another, and identifies crucial differences between them: "Language has the effect of *segmenting* and *linearizing* meaning. What might be an instantaneous thought is divided up and strung out through time ... the total effect is to present what had been a single instantaneous picture in the form of a string of seg-ments."[4] When an actor speaks from a script, the challenge is to transform this "string of segments" into apparently instantaneous thought. In written language, the segmentation of meaning is unme-diated by any physical action, but when language is spoken, meaning can be complemented or modified by gesture: "Gestures are different in every way. This is because they are themselves multidimensional and present meaning complexes without undergoing segmentation or linearization. Gestures are *global* and *synthetic* and *never hierarchical*."[5]

In McNeill's analysis, the term "hierarchical" arises because the meanings of the words are combined to create the meaning of the sentence. In understanding a sentence, we start with the lower level words, whereas in gestures, we start with the overall concept portrayed by the gesture. It is this concept which gives rise to the meaning of the individual parts. Consequently, a gesture is a symbol – it is global in that the whole is not composed out of separately meaningful parts. Rather, the parts gain meaning because of the meaning of the whole. To illustrate this, McNeill provides the example of a person representing a running cartoon character by moving his hand through space while wiggling his fingers:

> The gesture is a symbol in that it represents something other than itself – the hand is not a hand but a character, the movement is not a hand in motion but the character in motion, the space is not the physical space of the narrator but a narrative space, the wiggling fingers are not fingers but running feet. The gesture is thus a symbol, but the symbol is of a fundamentally different type from the symbols of speech.[6]

A further significant difference between language and gesture is that gestures have no standards of form. These are the linguistic rules that utterances must follow, or be rejected as ungrammatical. Gestures have no such rules and therefore reflect the idiosyncrasies of the speaker: "Precisely because gestures are not obliged to meet standards of form, they are free to present just those aspects of meaning that are relevant and salient to the speaker and leave out those aspects that language may require but are not relevant to the situation."[7] While many of McNeill's experiments focused on the observation of people making iconic gestures (as in the earlier example of a gesture of bending a tree back), the principles that he has identified also apply to other gestures of arm and hand, such as metaphoric gestures. Actors can experiment with the application of these principles not only to gestures of the arm and hand, but also to the other "gestural" elements of nvc at an actor's disposal. This information gives theatre people a valuable way of understanding the notion of "interpretation" of a role. While scripted language remains the same from production to production, each actor's gestural communication brings their own understanding to the text, and communicates that understanding to the audience.[8]

Theatrical application

These findings have important implications for actors and trainers of actors. They identify one of the crucial components involved in transferring written scripts into embodied behavior. Bad acting, I suspect, often arises because the actor hasn't made the mental leap from the linear nature of written language into the gestural imagery of spoken language. *Given that about 90 percent of spoken utterances in daily life are accompanied by gesture, acting that does not incorporate gesture (both physical and vocal) will appear stiff and unexpressive.* In theatre, we often refer to this as a lack of "investment," meaning that the actor doesn't seem to be fully engaged in the character's thought processes. Common responses from instructors and directors include exhortations to "feel it more," or to transpose biographical experience to the fictional circumstances, or to discover analogous situations that might prompt imaginative identification. Following these suggestions often results in the imaginative connection necessary to make the dialogue more expressive, but none of them work directly with the psychophysical process that underlies the phenomenon. However, the exercises of Jacques Lecoq that I describe later in this chapter develop a heightened and defined awareness of the relationship between thought, gesture, and language. This faculty supports the actor in creating varied and distinct material in improvised and devised work, and heightens the ability to respond gesturally to written language. Before looking at his work in detail, there are several more relevant cognitive principles to consider.

Imagery and language

McNeill develops his analysis of the relationship between gesture and speech in *Gesture and Thought* (2005), arguing for a new conception of language, viewing it as an imagery-language dialectic, in which gestures provide imagery. Expanding on an approach introduced by Lev Vygotsky in the 1930s, McNeill proposes that gestures are key ingredients in an "imagery-language dialectic" that fuels both speech *and* thought. Gesture is an integral component of language in this conception, not merely an accompaniment to, or ornament of, speech but synchronous and co-expressive with it. While McNeill's earlier work demonstrated what gestures reveal about thought, here, gestures are shown to be active participants in both speaking and thinking. Gesturing has a dialectical relationship to language, and both participate in formulating meaning, with their opposition creating instability that gets resolved in expression. This analysis is developed from close observation of the synchrony of speech forms and gestures that suggests that they are co-expressive of the same underlying thought unit. The instability of the confrontation of opposites (imagery and language) in the process of thinking for speaking seeks resolution in utterance that can be expressed either as gesture or speech, or both. The smallest element of this dialectic is the Growth Point (GP), a snapshot of an utterance at its beginning psychological stage.

Units of thought and textual analysis

This analysis has exciting implications for actors, since it includes valuable information about the relationship of thought to expression – the core of meaning in a performance. While the analysis uses observed speech and gesture to identify units of thought and their expression, its findings can be reverse-engineered to apply to the reading of a script in preparation for performance. Actors who are familiar with a Stanislavskian form of script analysis think of tasks (or objectives) and actions (or tactics) – identifying what the character wants and what they do to get what they want. As Stanislavski himself realized when he came to creating the Method of Physical Actions, this knowledge on its own doesn't necessarily assist the actor in embodying the character. It can define the architecture of a character's journey, but doesn't provide a process for stimulating the moment-to-moment behavior that communicates that journey. *Often, it can inhibit this process by placing the actor's mental focus on long-term intentions, rather than the immediacy of impulse and response in the fictional environment.* McNeill's empirically derived information can be used to complement the Stanislavski model by offering smaller units of analysis that cumulatively form larger episodes of action. It offers a reliable way of analyzing dialogue that depends on the identification of units of thought, the differentiation between contextual information and new ideas, and the points in a phrase or sentence where a gesture is originated. This happens when new information is added to established context, which gives the actor a useful tool in textual analysis and facilitates the subsequent transformation of written language into embodied speech. When this approach is linked to the understanding of nvc and metaphoric gesture described in the previous chapter, it connects different temporal units in analysis by identifying fleeting impulses, their expression in behavioral action, and "actions" in the way that they are normally understood (contradict, flatter, bully, etc.).

Background and focus

A key feature of McNeill's theory is the differentiation of "background" and "focus" – visual metaphors that distinguish contextual information from information that is "newsworthy." McNeill describes a process whereby we construct meaning as we speak:

> The speaker shapes the background in a certain way, in order to make possible the intended significant contrast within it. Background and contrast are both necessary and are constructed together. A new "meaning" is a fresh differentiation from a constructed background – meaning has this dual character of being both a focal point and an implied background, and both are necessary ...[9]

The GP can be thought of "as an image that is being categorized linguistically-an image with a foot in the door of language, as it were. The combination is called a growth point since it is meant to be the initial form of a thinking-for-speaking unit out of which a dynamic process of organization emerges."[10] A further feature of the GP is that it

> addresses the concept that there is a specific starting point for a thought. Although an idea unit continues out of the preceding context and has ramifications in later speech, it does not exist at all times, and comes into being at some specific moment; the formation of a growth point is this moment, theoretically, and it is made visible in the onset of the gesture ...[11]

In everyday speech, when speakers are mentally focused on the content of their communication, a new idea is generally marked by a gesture. Consequently, when an actor identifies a new idea in a passage of dialogue, he or she knows that this is an appropriate moment for a gesture, and in choosing to use one, helps to clarify meaning for an audience. Most actors, myself included, have until now conducted this process unconsciously, making intuitive choices at this level – after all, most gestures in daily life are generated unconsciously. McNeill's information gives actors a way of consciously approaching this intuitive process, further refining script analysis. In his model, meaning progresses in a stream of contrasts between context and GPs – information communicated by a GP generally forms context for the next new idea. Analyzing a script at this level can be especially useful for plays that do not follow a traditional cause and effect narrative. Without such a narrative, or the "given circumstances" associated with the style of psychological realism, defining tasks and actions can be difficult, and it is often necessary for the actor to assign such features where none are suggested by the text. The following example shows how the traditional approach to analysis can be supplemented by Growth Point identification.

Case study: identifying Growth Points in *I.D.*

I.D. is actor Anthony Sher's play about the 1966 assassination of South African Prime Minister Hendrik Verwoerd, the architect of apartheid. It was developed from the book *A Mouthful of Glass* in a series of workshops at the National Theatre Studio with director Nancy Meckler. The script moves in a non-linear and kaleidoscopic fashion that invites a meta-theatrical and kinetic style of production. The play text includes many "theatricalist" features, such as a talking tapeworm and a "Ballet of the Suitcases," and gives little formal indication of given circumstances, relying on an audience's knowledge of South Africa's recent past, and of Verwoerd as the head of a brutally repressive racist regime.

The following information is drawn from my experience of playing Verwoerd in the US premiere. The chart below shows a brief extract from a long speech of Verwoerd's. The script is in the left-hand column, the "background" (or context) for each utterance in the central column and the "focus" (or newsworthy information) in the right-hand column. The analysis that I give here is retrospective (I did not find out about McNeill's work until after the production) but often synchronizes with the places where I found myself gesturing in performance. Some of what I had discovered in rehearsing the role was intuitive, while some choices were the result of conscious investigation. In places, the current analysis shows me moments where I could have found more detail and nuance than I did. The identification of GPs is not intended to be proscriptive – it is entirely possible that another actor would identify different thought units and different moments of gesture. In rehearsal, I had made an early choice that had a significant psychophysical effect. Although the play's style was non-realist, Verwoerd was a historical figure. I managed to find some audio recordings and worked on precisely imitating not just his accent, but the tempo and cadence of his speech, the timbre of his voice. I began to feel a different sense of self when I adopted these vocal features and I know that this influenced my understanding of the linguistic content as I spoke it, rather than read it.

Verwoerd's first appearance is described like this: "*Tight spot on VERWOERD. A slight smile always on his broad face with its snout-like nose. His manner is very calm, very civil, very persuasive. He manages to be both benign and sinister.*"[12]

There is no indication of fictional location or given circumstances, beyond the acknowledgement of the theatrical device of the focus created by the tight spot. Only at the end of his long monologue (two and a half pages) do the stage directions give more information: *"He is suddenly interrupted by knocking. He sighs. The knocking persists. The lights gradually reveal that he's in a small private dressing room – with a full-length mirror on a stand."*[13] The choice to reveal this location only after the monologue suggests the author's desire to keep the audience guessing about Verwoerd's physical location. In his monologue he talks about the nature of oration, personal recollections, his rationale for apartheid, and his leadership style, among other things. At times he seems to be addressing an audience, at times engaged in an intimate conversation, at times talking to himself. These different modes are retrospectively explained to the audience by the appearance of the mirror, and Verwoerd's explanation to his wife (who's been doing the knocking) that he's practicing a speech. However, to make the monologue dramatically engaging, the task cannot simply be "to perfect a speech," and there are no other characters to provoke tasks and actions. I chose to play the speech directly to the audience, treating it as the audience of Verwoerd's imagination, or a confidant, or an interviewer, or a class being lectured to, as the mode of speech changed. The structure of the speech cleverly mirrors Verwoerd's political manipulation – for example, the concept of apartheid is introduced after Verwoerd has said that there's "no place for hatred in the job of leader. It is not about hatred of others. It is about love of your own people."[14]

Here is the extract of the speech that is analyzed in the table below. It is worth reading it in its original form first, to get a sense of its initial meaning before seeing the analysis. It comes at a point where Verwoerd is speaking about his style of oration:

I will go to any lengths to ensure that my audience absorb my message. I will deliberately modulate my tones – like this – speaking quite softly, quite slowly – almost like a parent might use to lull the little ones into slumber – and I can keep this up – as I'm doing now – for a very, very long time – an hour or so, say – which is actually negligible during some of my longer orations. Now what would you expect the effect to be on my audience? Yes, correct, absolutely correct, the eyelids start to droop, the head to tilt downwards. But it is at this point, this point exactly, that the method becomes most effective. Which of us haven't started to drop off at the wrong moment? At our child's school concert perhaps. Or behind the wheel of a car, say. Think of the panic that grips you. That dual pull. Of sleep and of responsibility. Both such powerful forces. And there you are torn between the two. Not unlike some unfortunate soul on that medieval instrument, the rack. Now it is in this very state, I believe, that my cabinet hears me most clearly.[15]

Table 3.1 Growth Points in Verwoerd's speech

Script / = GP	Background	Focus (gesture stroke)
/I will go to any lengths to ensure that my audience absorb my message. / I will deliberately modulate my tones – like this –	My audience absorbing my message (from speech preceding extract). / The lengths to which I'll go. / Modulating	'any lengths' 'modulate'
/speaking quite softly, quite slowly – / almost like a parent might use to lull the little ones into slumber – /and I can keep this up – /as	my tones. / Speaking softly and slowly / Like a parent / Lull the little ones /	'softly' 'slowly' 'parent' 'lull'
I'm doing now – /for a very, very long time –/an hour or so, say –/which is actually negligible during some of my longer orations. /Now what would you expect the effect to be on my audience?/ Yes, correct, absolutely correct, the eyelids start to droop,/ the head to tilt downwards.	keeping this up/ doing this now/ doing this for an hour/ an hour is negligible/ My long orations/ Effect on my audience/ You are correct/	'keep this up' 'now' 'very, very long time' 'negligible' 'effect' 'correct' 'droop'
/But it is at this point, /this point exactly, /that the method becomes most effective./ Which of us haven't started to /drop off /at the wrong moment? /At our child's school concert perhaps. /Or behind the wheel of a car, say. /Think of	Eyelids are drooping/ Head tilting/ This point At this point/ The method is effective/ Which of us/ Dropping off/ Wrong moment/ Wrong moment/ Dropping off at the wheel	'tilt downwards' 'this point' 'exactly' 'effective' 'Which of us' 'drop off' 'wrong moment' 'child's school concert' 'wheel of a car' 'panic that grips'

Table 3.1 (continued)

Script / = GP	Background	Focus (gesture stroke)
the panic that grips you. /	Panic	'pull'
That dual pull. / Of	Dual pull	'sleep'
sleep and of	Sleep vs.	'responsibility'
responsibility. /Both such	responsibility	'powerful'
powerful forces.		
/And there you are torn	Powerful forces	'torn'
between the two. /Not		
unlike some unfortunate	You are torn	'unfortunate soul'
soul /on that medieval	You are an	'the rack'
instrument, the rack. /	unfortunate soul	
Now it is in this very		
state, I believe, /that my	You are on the rack	'state'
cabinet hears me most	In this very state	'hears'
clearly.	My Cabinet hears me	'clearly'

In general, the GP becomes the next background, or context. There is one exception, where the context of "Dropping off at the wrong moment" serves as background for two focus points, the "child's school concert" and the "wheel of a car." The analysis of this extract reveals two major features of interest. Firstly, the catchment column exposes the structure of ideas in the speech, laying bare the malicious and manipulative skeleton of what is being said beneath the qualifications and modifiers. Verwoerd relates power and control to himself, vulnerability and obedience to the listener, and the speech invites the actor to employ the methods that are described (" ... modulate my tones – like this ... keep this up – as I'm doing now ... ") in a metatheatrical blending of actor and character. Thus the way that Verwoerd exerts control is not only described linguistically but also embodied in performance. This aspect is enhanced by the second feature of interest. At least half of the words or phrases in the focus column have their root in direct physical experience or perception: lengths, modulate, softly, slowly, keep this up, droop, tilt downwards, this point, drop off, panic that grips, pull, sleep, powerful, torn, hears, clearly. This makes the writing lively in stimulating expressive gestures (both iconic and metaphoric), and their accompanying proprioceptive effects.

The way in which gestures communicate meaning is further illuminated by another significant feature of McNeill's model. McNeill's experiments have identified what he has called the "catchment." This is "a kind of thread of consistent dynamic visuospatial imagery running through the discourse segment that provides a gesture-based window into discourse cohesion."[16] It is recognized when two or more gestures in a sequence of discourse display recurring features, such as shape, movement, space, orientation, dynamics, and so on. These indicate *how an individual groups meanings, or separates them.* Again, an understanding of this naturally occurring phenomenon gives the actor a useful tool. Consciously chosen gestures can *show* audience members the links between different ideas, illuminating the implicit meaning of a piece of dialogue. Audience members' perceptions of this can, of course, vary from subliminal to conscious, depending on the way that the actor manipulates their gestures. The concept of the catchment also helps an instructor or a director to define problems in training or a performance; *if we see repetitive gestures when the linguistic content varies in ideas, the actor has not established this variety at an ideational level.*

Case study: catchment and gesture in Verwoerd's speech

The integration of a script's ideas can be enhanced by the use of McNeill's concept of the catchment. In the following extract from Verwoerd's speech, the focus points leading up to the metaphor of "the rack" give an example of how this can be done, by combining intuitive responses with conscious analysis. Actors can experiment with the application of these principles to other gestural communication, such as facial expressions, head position, and posture. In the table below, the gestures that accompany the focus points are not intended to be proscriptive, but illustrate some of the cognitive principles at work in the performance choices that an actor makes.

Table 3.2 Focus point and gesture in Verwoerd's speech

Focus points	Stroke of gesture (Arms and hands return to rest unless otherwise indicated)
'Which of us'	Arms in front of torso. Both hands roll out to sides, showing palms.
'drop off'	Head inclined to left side, slight smile.
'wrong moment'	Eyes widen.
'child's school concert'	Left arm in front of torso. Left hand rolls out to side, showing palm.
'wheel of a car'	Right arm in front of torso. Right hand rolls out to side, showing palm.

Table 3.2 (continued)

Focus points	Stroke of gesture (Arms and hands return to rest unless otherwise indicated)
'panic that grips'	Right arm in front of torso, gripping motion of right hand into clenched fist. (Remains in place for next gesture.)
'pull'	Both arms in front of lower torso, both hands in clenched fists, both pulling out to respective sides. (Remain in place for next gesture.)
'sleep'	Left hand unclenches, rolls out to side to show palm.
'responsibility'	Right hand unclenches, rolls out to side to show palm.
'powerful'	Arms remain in position, both hands close into clenched fist.
'torn'	No physical gesture (see note below).
'unfortunate soul'	Slight sideways inclination and shaking of the head.
'the rack'	No physical gesture (see note below).

As always, the actor's art involves balancing the instinctive with the calculated – this analysis describes a synthesis of psychophysical prompts and more conscious choices. Few of the gestures are iconic; the speech deals more with abstract concepts than physical objects, and to consciously illustrate these would be oddly literal. Most of the gestures are metaphoric, and often give information that is not included in the language. For example, the gesture on "drop off" suggests an indulgence of an unfortunate human trait by the speaker. The bilateral gestures that follow are a very clear demonstration of the concept of the catchment. As the two gestures for "sleep" and "responsibility" mirror each other, their similarity shows that the concepts are balanced in the speaker's mind. Their spatial opposition on the left and right of the body show that they become opposing forces, the increasing power of which is emphasized by the clenching of the fists.

In working on this part of the speech, I was aware that the intuitive gestures progressed from open and expansive to closed and constrictive, with increasing muscular tension until "torn" and "rack" – the two most violent images in this extract.

I noticed, but chose to restrain, an impulse for a tearing gesture on "torn." This conscious choice was made to avoid duplicating verbal and non-verbal information (often called "captioning" by theatre practitioners), and also in the hope that the surprise of neutrality at this point would heighten the impact on the audience. Calmness in Verwoerd as he uses these violent metaphors suggests that he is comfortable with the violence, and in control. It is also a non-verbal reminder of a statement that he made in the speech prior to this extract: "I prefer what I call the Deadly Calm approach. Deadly Calm Approach. Deadly calm. *(Slight pause.)* Now what I was demonstrating there was the use of repetition."[17] This again illustrates the concept of the catchment, extended to postural and vocalic gesturing, and working over a longer duration of time. The stillness on "torn" recalls both the concept, and also the combined verbal and non-verbal expression of "Deadly calm" from earlier in the speech.

Jacques Lecoq

As I mentioned earlier, few, if any, training programs have courses that are dedicated to nvc as it is defined by social psychologists. There are, however, approaches that develop actors' sensitivity to the cognitive impulses that prompt gesture, and refine their ability to express them. While Jacques Lecoq's work largely predates the findings described above, and was developed independently of this scientific research, much of it displays a remarkable concordance with the mechanisms that Lakoff and Johnson and McNeill identify, suggesting that Lecoq's analysis of human behavior was both insightful and thorough.

Lecoq's biography reveals a lifelong fascination with movement and the body, and places him in a tradition of movement oriented work that leads from Copeau through Dasté to his school, and has been expressed in the work of artists such as Dario Fo, Ariane Mnouchkine, Simon McBurney, and Julie Taymor, and companies such as Footsbarn, Mummenschanz, Complicite, Commotion, Peepolykus, Theatre O, Theatre de la Jeune Lune, and Pig Iron among many others. Born in Paris in 1921, Lecoq taught physical education and sport from 1941 to 1945. This brought him into contact with Jean-Marie Conty, a master of physical education and friend of Antonin Artaud and Jean-Louis Barrault. This led to an increasing interest in theatre, and the formation of a theatre group in 1945 that staged large-scale festive events celebrating, for example, the home-coming of prisoners of war. Jean Dasté happened to see one of these events and invited Lecoq to join his theatre company, known as the "Comédiens de Grenoble," where he was put in charge of physical training. Here he was introduced to Japanese Noh theatre, and dis-covered masks, in particular Dasté's "noble" mask, which was the forerunner of the neutral mask. The ideas of Copeau, who had been Dasté's teacher, became a reference point for Lecoq's exploration, in particular the "ambition to take theatre that spoke simply and directly to unsophisticated audiences."[18] In 1948 Lecoq moved to Italy, originally for three months, but stayed for eight years. During this period, he directed at the university theatre in Padua, and researched Commedia dell'arte with the sculptor Amleto Sartori, rediscovering the technique of making leather masks, and developing the neutral mask. He then set up the drama school at the Piccolo Teatro in Milan with Giorgio Strehler and Paolo Grassi, and worked as a director and choreographer with actors such as Dario Fo and Anna Magnani. In 1956 he came back to Paris armed with discoveries about Commedia Dell'Arte, Ancient Greek tragedy and the movement of the chorus, and a set of commedia masks given to him by Sartori. In 1956 he opened his School of Mime and Theatre and later set up his own theatre company, worked at the National Popular Theatre with Jean Vilar, and then on television, writing and directing a series of 26 silent comic films entitled *La Belle Equipe* (The Great Team). Before long the school had expanded and Lecoq decided to devote all his efforts to teaching: "I have always loved teaching, seeing it as a path to my own greater knowledge and understanding of movement. Through teaching I have discovered that the body knows things about which the mind is ignorant. This research into body and movement has been my passion and I still long to share it with others."[19]

Lecoq taught at his school until a few days before his death in 1999. The school continues to flourish today under the direction of Lecoq's wife, Fay, with classes led by former students. The nature of the teaching evolved during Lecoq's lifetime, as he added significant features such as the study of clown in 1962, and the Laboratoire d'Etude du Mouvement (Movement research laboratory) in 1977.[20] At the time of his death, the structure of the course involved a first year with open admission, followed by a second year by invitation only, for approximately a third of the first year students. Lecoq describes the training as taking place along two parallel paths, the study of improvi-sation and its rules, and the investigation of movement technique and its analysis. Concurrently with their classes, students engage in "autocours" – self-directed group work that generates small productions that are shown to the teachers and other students. The first year involves work with the neutral mask, expressive and character masks, movement training and analysis, and creative exploration that links theatre with painting, poetry, and music. Students that graduate to the second year work on five dramatic styles, which Lecoq calls "territories," following the metaphor of "The Journey" that he uses to describe a student's progress through the school. Lecoq describes the styles as follows:

1 Melodrama (grand emotions)
2 Commedia dell'arte (human comedy)
3 *Bouffons* (from grotesque to mystery)
4 Tragedy (chorus and hero)
5 Clowns (burlesque and absurd).[21]

Lecoq's work and cognitive principles

Lecoq's founding principle was *"Tout Bouge"* – everything moves. His fascination with, and analysis of, movement led him to develop a highly sophisticated repertoire of physical exercises. Given the foundational nature of sensorimotor experience in shaping abstract thought outlined by Lakoff and Johnson, it is evident that such a repertoire is more than a simply physical experience for the actor, and provides a rich resource for the embodiment of thought in language. Indeed, in some of his statements, Lecoq foreshadows the statements of principle that Lakoff and Johnson lay out:

> ... the laws of movement govern all theatrical situations. A piece of writing is a structure in motion. Though themes may vary (they belong to the realm of ideas), the structures of acting remain linked to movement and its immutable laws ... Outer movements resemble inner movements, they speak the same language. My main fascination is with the poetics of these permanencies, which give birth to writing.[22]

This focus on movement and its laws as the structure of acting bears an astonishing conceptual resemblance to Lakoff and Johnson's identification of sensorimotor experience as the source domain for conceptual metaphor.

Lecoq's statement also links strongly to Lakoff and Johnson's work on neural modeling and the embodiment of mind. Lakoff and Johnson make a strong argument that "the same neural mechanisms used in perception and movement are also used in abstract reasoning."[23] They focus on models for three kinds of concepts:

1   Spatial relations concepts, for example those named by English words such as *in, on, over, through,* and *under.*
2   Concepts of bodily movement, represented by verbs such as *grasp, pull, lift, tap,* and *punch.*
3   Concepts indicating the structure of actions or events ... such as *starting, stopping, resuming, continuing, finishing,* including those indicated grammatically as in process (in English, *is/are* plus the verb stem plus *-ing: is running*) or completed (*has/have* plus the verb stem plus *-ed: has lifted*).[24]

Lakoff and Johnson make clear the relationship that they see between bodily experience and conceptual thought: "In such models, there is no absolute perceptual/conceptual distinction, that is, the conceptual system makes use of important parts of sensorimotor system that impose crucial conceptual structure."[25] This statement lends credence to Lecoq's observation that "Outer movements resemble inner movements, they speak the same language." Indeed, a significant thread of Lecoq's philosophy of training for the theatre, expressed in *The Moving Body,* repeatedly links a progression of training to the development of the human in learning about the world. As babies our experiences of the physical world are images, touch, movement, before they are language. In writing about his method of improvisation, Lecoq says "The aim of these initial exercises, taken as a whole, is to delay the use of the spoken word. The imposition of silent performance leads the students to discover this basic law of theatre: words are born from silence. At the same time they discover that movement, too, can only come out of immobility."[26] Thus the progress of an actor through Lecoq's training method replicates the processes described by Lakoff and Johnson whereby our physical experience of the world shapes the structure of thought:

> The dynamics underlying my teaching are those of the relationship between rhythm, space and force. The laws of movement have to be understood on the basis of the human body in motion: balance, disequilibrium, opposition, alternation, compensation, action, reaction. These laws may all be discovered in the body of a spectator as well as in that of the actor.[27]

I will examine some of his exercises in detail, linking them to the cognitive processes outlined above, and showing how their physical nature parallels cognitive processes. In particular, I will focus on three areas of his work. First, I will look at exercises in heightening awareness of fundamental sensorimotor experiences such as push/pull. These link to what Lakoff and Johnson call primary metaphors – projections of activation patterns from sensorimotor areas of the brain to higher cortical areas. Second, I will look at Lecoq's work with the neutral mask, where actors develop their range of sensorimotor experience by embodying rhythms such as those of fire and water, different animals, and man-made substances. This work leads to the third area, that of exercises in embodying poetic metaphors, which reverses the direction of the process, starting with a received linguistic stimulus, and translating it into sensorimotor experience. This again links very closely to the cognitive processes relating written language to speech outlined by Lakoff and Johnson and McNeill.

Early work in a student's progression through Lecoq's school involves silent improvisation, and investigation and analysis of movement. To describe the bare bones of the activities cannot hope to replicate the somatic experience, but will at least give the reader a flavor of Lecoq's approach. The following is a description of an exercise that uses the actions of "push" and "pull" as a foundation to approach different dramatic territories. The information is drawn from my own experiences of learning and teaching, and the description noted down by Simon Murray, a former pupil of Lecoq's, in his book titled simply *Lecoq*. The text can be considered a reliable source for an understanding of Lecoq's approach: Murray prepared the written description with Thomas Prattki, who became the pedagogical director of the school after Lecoq's death. The sequence as described would not take place in one session, but indicates how primary physical experience is first investigated to identify components of meaning, then consciously controlled to lead to dramatic expression.

Exercise: push and pull

The first step in the work demonstrates an attention to semantic detail. The dynamics of pushing and pulling are broken down into three pairings, or six distinct units: I push ... I pull; I am pushed ... I am pulled; I push myself ... I pull myself. It should be borne in mind that the verbs push and pull fall into Lakoff and Johnson's second category of neural modeling, "concepts of bodily movement," and that the same neural mechanisms used in perception and movement are also used in abstract reasoning, meaning that the exercises help students to make links between movement and thought and feeling.

The exercise leader invites the students to walk across the space individually, naturally, with no acting. The others in the class observe the movement of the walkers, and are asked to reflect on questions such as these:

Do they push the space, are they pushed by it?

Do they have to push themselves through the space, or are they pulled by something?

Do they push the space with the upper body, while some force appears to pull the pelvis back?

What images are generated by the different ways of walking? (Someone who pushes the space may appear powerful, someone who is pushed, reluctant, someone who is pulled, naïve.)

Do diverse ways of walking suggest different emotional states?

Is it possible to correlate different permutations of pushing and pulling with different emotions?[28]

This exercise alerts students to a number of factors – first, that posture and movement by themselves can suggest meaning; second, that their own personal walks have habitual patterns; and third, that push and pull actions can help to find physical characterizations in different styles. All of this rests on the fundamental recognition that movement communicates meaning, and begins the process of increasing students' sensitivity to this fact. By placing conscious attention on movement that has become unconscious through habituation, the exercise stimulates the neural connections between this movement and its conceptual expression. Having heightened students' awareness through observation, the components of the exercise can then be used to make conscious choices of physicality. Students can be invited to experiment with, for example, pushing the space with their chest, or pulling the space with one shoulder. One development that I have used is to invite two students to work in the space simultaneously, moving in relationship to one another while focusing on "push" and "pull" with different parts of the body. In more than 20 years of teaching this exercise, I have found that students repeatedly report a changed sense of self when working in this way. Comments on pushing with the chest report a sense of aggression, or confidence, or cockiness, for example. Evidently, different students will have different experiences depending on their personalities and their habitual postures. What is significant is that there is a changed sense of self through consciously chosen muscular activity (I will look at the physiological processes involved in a later chapter), and for players and observers alike, a recognition that the dynamics of non-verbal spatial interaction communicate meaning and suggest narrative.

In Lecoq's approach, the work on push and pull and other primary physical activities serves as a foundation for exploration in other dramatic "territories," and as an approach to text. As Murray points out:

> When students work with text it is important to register the relationship between words and actions, or physical behaviour. Is the body expressing the same emotion as the words, or do they counterpoint each other? In Commedia there is sometimes a complete congruence between a character's body and verbal language. However, in many of the other dramatic territories there is often a strong contradiction between body and language. A character might push with words, but the body is pulled back. A character may state he is not scared, while his body expresses the opposite.[29]

In the vocabulary of psychological realism, this understanding would refer to the communication of "subtext," something that is better defined as non-verbal meaning, as described in the previous chapter. Lecoq's approach offers the student a way of defining, naming, and working on the components of physical expression that make up nvc.

The use of nvc in defining acting style

For analysts of written drama and observers of performance, the concept of congruity and contradiction in nvc and speech also offers an empirical basis for considerations of character and style. Where there is consistent congruence between verbal and non-verbal features of communication, we would understand the character to be "simple" (all thoughts and feelings declared, as in farce, for example), whereas frequent contradictions in this area would suggest complexity (conflicts between declared information and thought and feeling, as in psychological realism). This can also be one of the components that identify different genres of drama and their attendant styles of performance. The example of Commedia that Murray mentions could be logically extended to farce and sitcom, for instance. In a comedy of manners, however, such as *The Importance of Being Earnest*, much of the humor arises from the contradiction of verbal and non-verbal content, as indicated in the analysis in the preceding chapter.

Murray describes how the preparatory work on "push" and "pull" extends through several phases of development at Lecoq's school. He describes an exercise that is used in the development of melodrama, where the psychophysical implications of "push" and "pull" are heightened by the increase of force necessary to accomplish the actions. In the first phase of the exercise, students work in pairs, one behind the other, with the person behind holding the pelvis of the one in front, who leans forward against the pull. This leads to an experience of "dynamic balance" – a physical expression of stasis that is nevertheless charged with energy. Once again, Lecoq's awareness of the metaphorical connection between physical activity and thought is apparent in linking the physical experience of balance with a dramatic status quo. The next development of the exercise is for both the students to exert more force – the one in front to push the pelvis forward in order to walk, the one behind to pull the other back to prevent the walk. This generally results in an off-balance situation as one or the other succeeds. The heightened physical experience of the breaking of the balance gives both participants a strong sensation of the dramatic impact of a disruption of balance. This experience embodies the process described by McNeill in his definition of the mental development of a GP, where the state of balance would be the background, and the breaking away the focus, or "newsworthy" event. Once again Lecoq's focus on the semantic detail of physical activity parallels cognitive dynamics.

Lecoq then draws upon this heightened psychophysical experience in a silent improvisation entitled "The Departure," in which a member of a family leaves home. The metaphorical values of push and pull are employed in the spatially and physically expressed dynamics among the family members, some of whom may want to "push" the departing member out, others of whom may want to "pull" her back. The balance of a status quo and the imbalance that results from a departure are now expressed in dramatic narrative.

The neutral mask

While the exercises described above are conducted without masks, they encourage an awareness of physical expression that is deepened by the work with the neutral mask (see Figure 3.1). This is a full-face

Figure 3.1 Sartori's Neutral Mask

mask with symmetrical features, devoid of expression, that serves several functions. Lecoq talks about the way it produces a state of calm in the wearer and, consequently, receptiveness to the environment. While this may sound somewhat mystical, the physiological process by which this can happen is identified by Paul Ekman's work on facial expression and emotion, which will be described more extensively in Chapter 6.

The effect of the neutral mask is startling. From my own experience of training in it and teaching others, I see the mask demonstrate in a profound way the immense expressive potential of the body. It immediately uncovers the degree of engagement that the wearer has with his or her environment, both literal and imagined. From the perspective of observers, the actor wearing the neutral mask is somehow exposed – the corporeality of expression being difficult to fake. In daily life we are accustomed to watching faces as the primary communicators of meaning and emotion. When the face of an actor is covered by the neutral mask, the communicative aspects of other parts of the body shine out; posture, gesture, tempo, and rhythm of movement. In the primary phase of the work, this transparency allows the instructor to identify postural and gestural habits that might need correcting, habits that limit the range of expression. One actor might, for example, have a tendency to tilt the head to one side, which tends to communicate appraisal or consideration to observers. As an unconscious habit, this would lead to inappropriate choices in performance. Clearly, habits cannot be changed overnight, but the use of the neutral mask assists actors in making the essential first step, which is to notice and identify the habit. Other actors in a workshop format, observing, realize the potential for communication that is inherent in corporeality, and hone their skills in "decoding" nvc signals. This in turn enhances their own abilities in "encoding" such signals.

The work on neutrality is intended to enable the actor to discover a physical starting point, "a blank page on which drama can be inscribed."[30] It provides "reference points" – until one discovers neutral tempo in oneself, then it is difficult to gauge fast or slow. If one cannot discover neutral posture, it is difficult to use the full expressive range of expansion and contraction, symmetry and asymmetry in postural attitudes. This focus on physical expression develops an ability in the actor to be specific and expressive in their non-verbal communication, no matter what style of performance they perform.

Beyond the diagnostic and corrective features of work with the neutral mask lies the work of discovering the body's response to different environments, and then embodying the rhythms of natural elements, objects, and animals. Lecoq uses an improvisation entitled the Fundamental Journey, in which the masked actor moves through imagined natural environments. The focus is on the embodied experience, but introduces students to what Lecoq calls the "poetic aspects of the theme: ... The crossing of the river can be compared to passing through adolescence to adult life, with all the movements finding their reflection in emotional feelings: the currents, the whirlpools, the waves rising and falling, washing back and forth from one bank to the other."[31] This again recalls the metaphorical links between movement and thought that Lakoff and Johnson describe. In this phase of the work, the actor thinks of him or herself being acted on by different rhythms of nature. The next phase is to embody those rhythms, starting by physically identifying with the rhythms of the elements, and discovering the different senses of the self that they provoke.

The neutral mask and identifications

This process engages the actor in what Lecoq calls "identifications" – identifying and moving in the rhythms of natural elements and different materials. In the work with elements, the students seek to embody the different rhythms of fire, air, water, and earth. Working with water, for example, entails discovering the difference in rhythm between a bubbling spring and the steady flow of a mature river, or the difference between waves gently lapping at a beach and the sea in a violent storm. Materials might include oil, rubber, cellophane wrapping – each of which has a distinctive pattern of movement that can be embodied. Lecoq uses a developmental approach where the technical work of controlling the body so that it mimics different rhythms is subsequently transposed into expressive drama. These activities extend the range of the actor by establishing neuronal patterning that is beyond the normal everyday range of behavior. This approach can be contrasted with Method acting where "truth" resides in the biographical experience of the actor, which is brought to the fictional character as the vehicle for its expression. In this style of acting, the neuronal patterns are those belonging to the biographical experience.[32] This approach risks devaluing, if not negating, the function of imagination in creating a role, whereas Lecoq's work stimulates the imagination through extending the actor's collection of sensorimotor experiences that can become source domains for conceptual thought. For example, Lecoq describes elastic materials as "nostalgic to return to their original shape, even though they may not succeed."[33] A detailed physical embodiment of such a process can give the actor the muscular memory source material for varied characterizations: "After having experienced, by means of these identifications, the greatest possible number of natural or animal dynamics, the actor (or author) is in a position to use these experiences, sometimes unconsciously, to feed the characters which he must act (or write) and to bring out some of their fundamental characteristics."[34] In the example of "elastic materials" mentioned above, the somatic experience links with themes of striving, nostalgia, and failure.

The neutral mask and sensorimotor source domains

The use of the neutral mask heightens the actor's awareness of, and ability to draw on, the sensorimotor source domains of abstract thought, something that Lecoq makes explicit: "The main results of this identification work are the traces that remain inscribed in each actor, circuits laid down in the body, through which dramatic emotions also circulate, finding their pathway to expression."[35] Through consciously chosen muscular activity, repeated over time, actors develop "muscle memory" of a variety of different rhythms of movement that are linked to concepts and emotions. Lecoq suggests that these are then available to the actor when she subsequently works on a text: "These experiences ... remain forever engraved in the body of the actor. They are reactivated in him at the moment of interpretation. It may be many years later, when an actor finds himself with a text to interpret. The text will set up resonances in his body, meeting rich deposits awaiting expressive formulation."[36]

At this point, it is useful to recall Lakoff and Johnson's statement that approximately 95 percent of the brain's activity is unavailable to conscious reflection, and McNeill's observation that the processes involved in generating gestures are largely unconscious. Lecoq's method assists actors in accessing and training some of those unconscious processes, by creating a reservoir of defined somatic experiences for the actor.

Lecoq also proposes that the neutral mask also has the effect of "essentializing" the dramatic quality of themes that arise in improvisation, creating a sense of archetypal drama. Lecoq's use of the word "essential" can be troubling to contemporary scholars, with its implication of "universal" experience that neglects differences of culture, race, gender, or orientation. However, one of the key aspects of a cognitive understanding of acting is that there are common biological experiences of perception, cognition, and expression that underlie, and interact with, multiple cultures. It is in this context that the word "essential" operates. Wearing the neutral mask, the thoughts that we are accustomed to expressing through speech and facial expression have to be communicated in expressive physical action. This both *reduces* the complexity and detail of what could be expressed by language, but also *expands* its meaning by allowing more room for an observer's interpretation through imaginative engagement. In some senses this is analogous to the way in which poetry offers up multiple meanings through linguistic metaphors, imagery, and symbols.

The following exercise demonstrates how the "essential" quality can arise. Lecoq originated it, but I learnt it from Philippe Gaulier, who taught at Lecoq's school from 1972–82. I have also been teaching it myself for many years, so it is possible that it has been altered in some way by the transmission from Philippe, and my own perspective.

Neutral mask – waving goodbye

Actors are invited to imagine a situation where they arrive at a dock and wave goodbye to a loved one who is departing on a boat. The improvisation is conducted in small groups (five or seven members in each is the most practicable), with each individual wearing a neutral mask. Beyond the information that I've just described, there is no specification of given circumstances. This leaves each player free to create his or her own individual imaginative connection with the situation. The primary focus of each individual is on the imagined loved one, rather than on creating interaction with other members of the group, although if this happens spontaneously it is not forbidden.

The students are encouraged simply to work on creating the situation through successive attempts, each followed by comments from observers. This results in a cumulative learning process that is derived from a combination of somatic experience as the students participate, and observation, as they watch other groups. When I teach this, I follow a sequence of attention that is central to Lecoq's process, identifying in turn features of mechanics, dynamics, the dramatic, and the poetic. Students are encouraged to integrate comments on each of these components with their own experience. Here are some examples of features of each component:

Mechanics: To create the illusion of waving at the same boat, all members of the group need to be focused forward, with the vertical plane of the mask on the horizon. This necessity overrides individual "psychological" choices, such as "I won't look because I can't bear to see her go." Similarly, there needs to be some coordination in the actions of waving to suggest the moment when the boat pulls away from the dock, the moment at which the wavers realize that they are no longer visible to the people on the boat. How can this coordination be achieved in an improvisation, without pre-planned choreography?

Dynamics: As students observe successive experiments with the exercise, they realize that rhythm plays an important part in creating dynamics. What is the pattern of arrival? If all the players arrive singly, at regular intervals, there is no variety, and the situation looks formulaic. If all the players arrive at once, again, there is no opportunity for variety. Similarly, the tempo of waving offers opportunity for dynamic shifts. What best creates the illusion of the departing boat – starting at a fast tempo and diminishing, or beginning slowly and accelerating to a climax that suggests the moment when the ship disappears beyond the horizon? How are the individuals arranged in the space? What does it suggest if two people stand closer to one another than to the rest? Or if one person stands apart from the group?

Dramatic: It becomes clear that, without the use of language, story can arrive through the manipulation of temporal dynamics (variances in rhythm and tempo), and spatial dynamics (variances in proximity and orientation). Players are encouraged to respond to their impulses, which arise both from a connection to the imagined situation *and* from a response to the physical environment created by their colleagues. The exercise encourages them to channel their impulses through an awareness of the principles of embodied action and ensemble improvisation. As the exercise is performed, observers notice the ways in which various aspects of the participants' behavior communicate meaning; the individual who arrives after the other members of the group and who turns abruptly to leave; the person who continues to wave after the rest of the group have departed, and so on.

Poetic: Evidently, the performance is neither naturalistic (the duration of the event must be shorter than it would be in real life), nor a realist portrayal of the situation (the wearing of the neutral masks). Nevertheless, it incorporates lived experience (waving) and a recognizable situation. The activity of waving is central both in performance and in observation, and through proprioception and empathy, prompts emotional identification with a theme of personal loss. As in much verbal poetry, this is achieved without portraying an explicitly detailed set of fictional circumstances. The experience therefore has the capacity to become a personalized metaphor for each individual that performs or observes it. In this sense the activity becomes "essential."

Encounters with language

Having developed a foundational awareness through investigating the movement of the body, Lecoq's training process progresses to encounters with text:

> Words are approached through verbs, bearers of action, and through nouns, which represent a designated object. We consider words living organisms and thus we search for the body of words. For this purpose we have to choose words which provide a real physical dynamic. Verbs lend themselves more readily to this: to take, to raise, to break, to saw, each contains an action which nourishes the verb itself.[37]

Again, the approach demonstrates a remarkable congruity with the principles identified by Lakoff and Johnson of metaphoric transference from sensorimotor experiences to conceptual thought. Also, by focusing first on singular units of linguistic meaning, Lecoq's process is sympathetic to the way in which the brain makes meaning of written language. As McNeill points out, written language is processed in a "bottom-up" fashion, with meaning constructed from the constituent parts. These synchronies between Lecoq's exercises and empirically identified processes of cognition mean that students are sensitized to the micro processes of communication in ways that make them more likely to become aware of the GP phenomenon. The consciousness of the relationship of movement to speech develops a greater facility and variety of non-verbal expression, as well as offering a foundation for performance in non-realist styles.

The next step in Lecoq's progression is through written poetry. He reads the students poems and invites them to work in groups of three or four. Lecoq chooses poems that address natural elements, and invites the students to improvise physically to discover a group movement in response to the poem. The poems are richer in imagery than everyday language, making the transition from image-based gesture to segmented language an easier one. Music is also used as a stimulus for movement before the students approach dramatic texts. Lecoq uses a neologism – "mimodynamic" – to describe a way of working that includes both imitation (mimesis) and also "physical movements which translate into bodily action the sensations aroused ... by colours, words, music."[38]

The approach to dramatic text encourages this translation of response into physicality: "In our way of working we enter a text through the body. We never sit around and discuss, but adopt the 'mimodynamic' method. In the same way as we did for music and poetry, we explore the different texts: working through movement, we ask the actors to get to grips physically with the text, its images, its words, its dynamics."[39] While it may appear that this approach lacks psychological subtlety, the physical groundwork that has been laid down by the time the students approach text leads to a refined and nuanced expressiveness. This means that they are highly responsive to, and expressive of, the impulses that lead to "utterances" in McNeill's analysis of thinking for speaking.

While Jacques Lecoq's work predates the findings of cognitive science that Kendon, McNeill, and Lakoff and Johnson describe, it displays synchrony with the principle that physicality is often an equal component of meaning with language. Through an approach that begins with physical activity, Lecoq's exercises offer a training that perfects an actor's ability to create both iconic and metaphoric gestures, and an awareness of the link between movement and conceptual thought. It also develops sufficient voluntary control of expression to effectively mimic involuntary expression. As I'll describe in later chapters, this frequently has the effect of creating affective states in the performer.

Conclusion

For some in mainstream theatre, there is an assumption that Lecoq's work, because it is physically based, leads graduates of his school to do "physical theatre," and dictates a style of performance. Simon McBurney of Complicite has countered this view by stating that "all theatre is physical,"[40] meaning that no matter what style of performance an actor is engaged in, a certain proportion of meaning is communicated through the body. Lecoq himself was fond of saying that he trains the actor for a theatre that hasn't been invented yet, and was insistent that his graduates discover their own style. It is true that he has influenced companies who are radically experimental in their style, such as Complicite and Théâtre du Soleil, but he has also trained actors such as Geoffrey Rush, who is well known for naturalistic film performances. Lecoq's approach prepares the actor for a variety of styles by focusing on fundamental cognitive and expressive activities. The creative mental orientation that this generates is illustrated by the fact that, at time of writing, Lecoq graduates have founded at least 35 independent theatre companies in the UK, Europe, the US, and Canada that create and perform their own material. Ariane Mnouchkine, speaking in a video documentary about Lecoq, said "His down to earth style ... showed me a certain truth which is not to imagine that everything takes place in the head ... the theatre is flesh. It's from the verb made flesh and Lecoq transmits that."[41]

Lecoq's focus on the meaning of the body incorporates an insistence on the observation of daily life and naturally occurring phenomena. There is, however, a marked difference in philosophy between Lecoq and proponents of a style of psychological realism that depends on autobiographical experience as source material:

> In my method of teaching, I have always given priority to the external world over inner experience ... It is more important to observe how beings and objects move, and how they find a reflection in us ... People discover themselves in relation to their grasp of the external world, and if the student has special qualities, these will show up in the reflection. I do not search for deep sources of creativity in psychological memories ... I prefer to see more distance between the actor's own ego and the character performed ... Neither belief nor identification is enough–one must be able genuinely to play.[42]

Lecoq's statement again displays coherence with the basic principle expressed by Lakoff and Johnson that our experience of movement in the physical world shapes our conceptual thought. It also raises questions about the degree of metaphorical distance (or level of identification) between actor and character. This is also a topic that can be investigated using the findings of cognitive science, and is the subject of the next chapter.

Key points

- Gesture and language form part of one system but operate in different ways.
- Around 90 percent of spoken utterances in daily life are accompanied by gesture; acting that does not incorporate gesture (both physical and vocal) will appear stiff and unexpressive.
- Speech forms and gestures are co-expressive of the same underlying thought unit.
- The Growth Point (GP) describes the moment where a new idea is added to existing contextual information.
- The GP is made visible in the onset of a new gesture.
- The GP concept can be applied to script analysis.

- Recurring features of gesture, such as shape, movement, space, orientation, and dynamics demonstrate how a speaker groups or separates meaning within a speech.
- Repetitive gestures show that an actor has not established variety at an ideational level.
- The work of Jacques Lecoq is remarkably coherent with current understanding of cognitive processes, both in overall conceptualization and in the particulars of specific exercises.
- Lecoq's exercises encourage gestural specificity, create an expanded range of expression, and sensitize actors to the metaphorical connections between physical activity and thought.

Chapter 4

How does the actor create a character?

The process of creating a character is at the heart of acting and theatre, and is at once both obvious and mysterious. Obvious, because the character is who we see and hear on stage, mysterious, because we generally cannot see or hear the relationship between actor and character. Indeed, in most Western styles of theatre, an audience considers the apparent melding of actor and character evidence of "good" acting.[1] The process by which the actor melds self and character is one that is frequently described by contemporary actors as having two possible starting points – "internal" or "external," and two possible pathways – "inside out" or "outside in." Although there are many variants of what precisely is meant by this, in broad terms these reflect ideas of "psychological" or "physical" starting points, and sometimes "sameness" (of self and character), or "difference" (between self and character). I've put these terms in quotation marks because these notions reflect the split between body and mind in Western thought that we now know is mistaken, and rest upon a *metaphorical concept of the individual* – that of the body as a container, with thought being something that occurs "inside," and expression something that happens "outside."

This perception springs from phenomenological experience and is part of the "recessive body" phenomenon described by Mark Johnson. Ultimately, what is happening when an actor prepares and performs a character is that patterns of neurons firing in the brain provoke physical action that can be perceived by an audience. The process by which this occurs is largely unavailable to conscious reflection; we define those aspects of it that we can become aware of in metaphorically shaped concepts. *Many of the proclaimed differences between approaches to acting are actually differences in the types of metaphors used to describe self and process.*

Several aspects of current cognitive studies facilitate a better understanding of what is actually happening when an actor embodies a character. Identifying these help us to make better choices about training and rehearsal, and recognize strands of agreement between different approaches. In this chapter, I'll first review some examples of the prevailing "inside/outside" dichotomy in acting discourse, and then describe some areas of cognitive research that relate to this issue. The first of these is a description of the connectionist view of the brain, which models mental activity as a series of neural networks. This model of the brain's operation offers us a way of understanding how abstract concepts are linked to motor activity, a fundamental feature of the bodymind concept. These concepts are metaphorically formed from physical experience in the world, and I focus on one that is particularly significant for this topic, the "mind as container" metaphor. From here, I describe Lakoff and Johnson's analysis of the metaphorical construction of the concepts of self and different selves. This leads on to an examination of the idea of the "essential self" in acting discourse, which is followed by a summary of neuroscientist Joseph LeDoux's concept of the Synaptic Self, in which consciousness depends on unconscious cognitive processes.

I describe some of the cognitive research that relates to imagination and its relationship to written language, which are, of course, significant features of an actor's approach to creating a character. This is also true of proprioception, a faculty that is partially described by the term "kinesthetic awareness" familiar to many actors. I also summarize Merlin Donald's description of the way in which mimesis is central to cognition and precedes language in human evolution. After a brief biography of Michael Chekhov and a description of his process, I turn to Fauconnier and Turner's theory of conceptual blending to offer a description of how the model of "mental spaces" can be used to understand the way in which we can combine different concepts while maintaining an awareness of their differences – something that explains how we can simultaneously be aware of actor and character while performing. This information is interwoven with more information about Chekhov and his exercises.

"Internal/external" in Western theatre

This consideration of actor and character seeks to discover foundational cognitive principles that underlie multiple acting and theatrical styles. The advantage of using cognitive science as a foundation for a theory of acting is that it is derived from empirical research into human behavior and is not entangled in the subjective terminology of competing theatrical schools of thought. While much current scholarship acknowledges the centrality of the body, it struggles to find useful terminology to approach the issue of actor and character. An example can be seen in theatre scholar Robert Gordon's analysis of trends in contemporary acting in *The Purpose of Playing*:

> All theatrical performance starts from the assumption that a performer is using her body to represent a virtual body ... For the actor, the central paradox of acting is always the way in which her real body is used to represent a virtual body. No matter what aesthetic forms are employed, or how abstract the conception of the performing body is, the actor's body must always be cultivated as an instrument capable of varied and subtle expressive forms. All theories of acting start from this point, but each proposes a different solution according to *what* each aims to represent, and *for what purpose* the representation is being made.[2]

While Gordon pinpoints the crucial phenomenon of theatre as an embodied art, his use of the term "virtual" highlights the difficulties of talking about the fictional characters of theatre, and is misleading. The fictional character has no body but that of the actor who portrays him or her. If actors imagine a character's body from reading a script it is more accurate to describe this as the "imagined" body without the associations that arise from the idea of virtuality. When audience members think of characters, they generally picture them as actors have embodied them. My intention is to examine the phenomenon of the actor's real body communicating a character's fictional being rather than the varied theories that lead to different styles, while recognizing, of course, that discourse about acting tends to get framed by references to different methodologies or theories. Certain metaphors recur; twentieth-century, Western concepts of acting translate Diderot's nineteenth-century paradox of "sensibility" and "technique" into the "inside/outside" conceptualization mentioned above, and, following the publication of *An Actor Prepares* in 1936, often defined the dichotomy with reference to Stanislavski, and later Strasberg, as representatives of the "internal" approach.

The English actor Michael Redgrave, writing about Stanislavski in 1946, observed that:

> There are in England today, roughly speaking, two styles of acting: the acting in which the effect springs from the cause, and that which begins with effect and which rarely, and only in part, seeks the cause. The latter style is still very much preponderant.

It is very seldom we see a production in which more than a few actors are faithful to the author, the director, and their artistic conscience. "Always he sought," said Nemirovich-Danchenko, "the essence of the play in the times and events described; and this he expected the actor to understand. This is what Stanislavsky called the core, and it is this core which must stir the actor, which must become part of him for the time being."[3]

In talking about cause and effect, it seems that Redgrave is talking about thought and expression. The juxtaposition of the quote from Nemirovich-Danchenko links "cause," "artistic conscience," "essence," and "core." The latter term implies that these are all "interior" qualities, and that consequently, for theatre to be art, the actor must move from cause to effect, from "inside" to "outside."

John Gielgud expresses a similar sentiment after working with a Russian director who had been close to Stanislavski:

Komis' [Komisarjevsky's] interest and help had encouraged me tremendously, and I began to feel that I could study a part from the inside, as he taught me, not seizing at once on the obvious showy effects and histrionics, but trying to absorb the atmosphere of the play and the background of the character, and then to build it outwards so that it came to life naturally, developing in proper relationship to the other actors, under the control of the producer.[4]

Again, the notion is that "showy effects and histrionics" are external and therefore superficial, and that "inside-out" is the preferable way to create a character, with internal thought leading to external expression.

Laurence Olivier also uses the "inside/outside" dichotomy, although he identifies himself as working in the opposite direction to Gielgud and Redgrave. In response to a question about how he had created his characterization of Richard III, he talks about how he started with two "extraneous externals;" a voice that was an imitation of old actors imitating Henry Irving, and a big nose:

I'm afraid I do work mostly from the outside in. I usually collect a lot of details, a lot of characteristics, and find a creature swimming about somewhere in the middle of them. Perhaps I should mention now what everybody's been talking about for years, and that's the Actors Studio and the Method. What I've just said is absolutely against their beliefs, absolute heresy. And it may be, as long as you achieve the result of, don't let's call it naturalism, don't even let's call it realism, let's call it truthfulness, that it doesn't matter which method you use. ... Some people start from the inside, some people start from the periphery. I would say, at a guess, that Alec Guinness is what we'd call a peripheral actor. I think I'm the same. The actor who starts from the inside is more likely to find himself in the parts he plays, than to find the parts in himself; perhaps not necessarily in himself, but to find the parts, go out to them and get them, and be somebody else.[5]

Several intriguing concepts emerge from Olivier's statement. He feels the need to apologize for his "external" approach, and then justify it by saying that it can lead to "truthfulness," and then makes a separation between character and self that suggests that the internal approach leads to autobiographical acting, and that there is a distinction between characters as autonomous beings, and characters as facets of one's own "self." The full significance of these distinctions will be clarified later by the work of Lakoff and Johnson; for now it is intriguing to note the amount of thought and feeling provoked by what is ultimately a metaphorical distinction between "internal" and "external."

Peter Brook also refers to the concept of "internal" and "external" in *The Empty Space*, and like Olivier, references Method acting as an example of an "internal" approach:

There have been times in theatre history when the actor's work has been based on certain accepted gestures and expressions: there have been frozen systems of attitudes that we reject today. It is perhaps less obvious that the opposite pole, the Method actor's freedom in choosing anything whatsoever from the gestures of everyday life, is equally restricted, for in basing his gestures on his observation or on his own spontaneity, the actor is not drawing on any deep creativity. He is reaching inside himself for an alphabet that is also fossilized, for the language not of invention but of his conditioning.[6]

The observation suggests that the desired feature – "invention" or creative choice – is no more likely to proceed from an "inside-out" process than from "external" codified gestures.

While these comments range in date from 1939 to 1968, it is evident that the "inside/outside" conceptualization persists in current discourse about acting. During a discussion about acting and cognitive science that took place at the Philoctetes Center in New York in 2007,[7] talk turned to the question of "mirroring" in the sense of imitation of gesture. Moderator Adam Ludwig, an experienced professional actor, responded to a comment about Delsarte by observing that "you can do this 'outside in' thing where you imitate just the form … but over years that form becomes hollow because the intention isn't learned also." Tony Award-winning actress Blair Brown, invited to talk about her own experience of "external approaches" commented that "I had worked with a lot of English directors who took much more that approach, which was – just in broad terms – Americans work 'inside out' and British – the Brits – work 'outside in', and I work both ways." Ludwig perceptively links a comment by neuroscientist Vittorio Gallese to an exercise of Michael Chekhov's; "You create an other you can relate to and imitate in your head. You close your eyes and imagine the character, then you begin to imitate it through gesture." In the context of the discussion, it is clear that Ludwig considers this an "external" approach because of the imitative element involved. The potential difficulties and contradictions that arise from using the "inside/outside" concept to describe acting become clear as one investigates the statement. Ludwig thinks of the activity as "external" because it involves physical imitation, but in the parameters of this concept, the initial act of imagination would have to be one that is "internal" in that it is done through thought alone. This analysis of his comments is not intended to be critical, simply to demonstrate the difficulties in using the shorthand of "internal/external" to describe the intangible phenomena involved in acting.

Current texts on acting, intended for use as practical instruction, also use the concepts of "inside/outside" to talk about an actor's relationship to character. Robert Benedetti's *The Actor at Work* was first published in 1968 and is now in its tenth edition:

> During the first half of the twentieth century, the British acting tradition stressed the importance of externals in the acting process, working "from the outside in." Our American tradition, on the other hand, stressed the importance of internals, working "from the inside out." For the past sixty years, however, a real effort has been made in both countries to combine these two approaches. … If your performance consists only of external movement and speech unconnected to an inner energy, it will seem hollow and lifeless; if it consists only of inner intensity, without skillful outer expression, it will seem vague and self-indulgent.[8]

Benedetti's statement differs from others in saying that both "external" and "internal" activities are necessary, rather than proposing an either/or relationship. Nevertheless, notions of what happens "outside" and "inside" the actor's body are used to define the quality of performance, and are set up as a dichotomy. Although the proposition sounds reasonable, the dualism that is established is complicated the moment one asks how an actor *communicates* "inner energy," or, indeed, how an audience member will perceive it. The answer has to be that it is through audible or observable communication, which would be considered "external" in the conceptual system used by Benedetti and the others quoted. Beyond these complications lies the factor that cognitive science now shows that conceptual thought and physical activity frequently share the same neuronal pathways in the brain. This means that the separation of thought and expression is both inaccurate and reductive.

Robert Gordon, whose work I mentioned at the beginning of this section, further confirms that the "internal/external" conceptualization of acting is widespread in Western theatre. He introduces his book by summarizing 11 common topics of debate among contemporary practitioners and critics in a series of questions. In one of these he asks: "Should the actor work from the 'outside in' (commonly associated with the traditional British acting practice of characterization through techniques of voice and movement) or from the 'inside out' (some what misleadingly assumed to be a Stanislavskian approach)?" When one considers this question in the light of the findings of cognitive science about cognition and expression, it becomes apparent that the premise on which this question is based is a false duality that misleads practitioners and theorists alike. The origin of the dichotomy is understandable – the body is visible, thought is not – but even before one delves into its metaphorical formation, the complications mentioned above demonstrate its lack of coherence under examination.

The "mind as container" metaphor

We now have information that offers more empirically-based insight into the actor's process. One of the features of cognitive science's understanding of the mind is the fact that a large proportion of the brain's activity occurs unconsciously and is consequently unavailable to introspection. The abstract concepts that we are conscious of are shaped metaphorically by our physical experience in the material world, as described in the Introduction and Chapter 1. In the analysis provided by cognitive linguistics, metaphor is not just a feature of language, but is fundamental to cognition through the transference of meaning from one domain to another. Mark Johnson explains how the metaphor of the body as a container arises:

> We are immediately aware of our bodies as three-dimensional containers into which we put certain things (food, water, air) and out of which other things emerge (wastes, air, blood, etc.). From the beginning, we experience constant physical containment in our surroundings (those things that envelop us). We move in and out of rooms, clothes, vehicles, and numerous kinds of bounded spaces.[9]

The kinesthetic experience of the body as a container is transferred to feelings and concepts of the mind, and therefore creates a notion of the mind as something with a boundary that separates interior from exterior, and that has contents.

One of the corollaries of this is that our experiencing consciousness, the foundation of our sense of self, is also shaped metaphorically in a variety of ways. Investigating the way this happens is essential for an empirically responsible description of the relationship between the self of the actor and that of the character. It is worth remembering at this point that the concept of the embodied mind that Lakoff and Johnson describe in *Philosophy in the Flesh* is fundamentally different to the Western notion of the mind that separates reason from the body:

> our conceptual systems and our capacity for thought are shaped by the nature of our brains, our bodies and our bodily interactions. There is no mind separate from the body, nor are there thoughts that have an existence separate from and independent of the body, nor are there thoughts that have an existence independent of bodies and brains. But our metaphors for mind conflict with what cognitive science has discovered. *We conceptualize the mind metaphorically in terms of a container image schema defining a space that is inside the body and separate from it.*[10]

This metaphorical conceptualization of the mind is what gives rise to the "inside/outside" conceptualization of work on a character. When mental activity is thought of as "inside" the body and separate from it, and expressive activity as "outside" the mind, it is inevitable that the two will be seen as separate. The metaphor of mind as container is the foundation of the perception that "[i]deas and concepts are internal, existing somewhere in the inner space of our minds, while what they refer to are things in the external, physical world. This metaphor is so deeply ingrained that it is hard to think about mind in any other way."[11]

When we consider the earlier quotes from theatre practitioners in this light, it is easy to see how notions of truth, imagination, and self are identified as "internal" because they are mental concepts. Gestures without intention are considered "hollow" because they lack "internal" substance, and Olivier's approach to characterizing Richard III by imagining a big nose and an imitated voice is identified as "external" because these are things of the body. Yet Lakoff and Johnson state that "There is no true separation of mind and body. These are not two independent entities that somehow come together and couple ... [r]ather, mind is part of the very structure and fabric of our interactions with the world."[12] For theatre practitioners to make a division between "internal" or "external" results in identifications of process that do not reflect how the bodymind actually works and therefore are of limited use to the actor, if not actively counter-productive. *Consequently, rather than trying to argue the relative merits of "psychological" or "physical" approaches to characterization, it makes sense to acknowledge that the two are intertwined, and to investigate how.*

The connectionist model of mind

The activities of the brain and their relationship to the bodymind are, of course, immensely complex. The advances that cognitive science has made in defining and understanding them have come from a combination of empirical experiments and hypothetical models, with some models being affirmed by experimental data. Connectionism is a model of the mind as a system of overlapping networks in the brain, a theory that became popular with cognitive scientists in the 1980s, and tends to be considered an alternative to the "mind as computer" model that prevailed prior to this. Connectionism creates models of mental activity based on the hypothesis that it is a result of the processes of interconnected networks of simple units. This modeling is used in a variety of different ways. For example, each unit in a network could represent a word, and the connections between the units would represent semantic similarity. The most common forms of connectionist models identify neurons as units, and synapses as connections. These models cannot come near to matching the scope of the brain's activity (it has an estimated 100 billion neurons, each with multiple synapses that can connect it to thousands of other neurons), but suggest the nature of the process that is involved. There is general agreement among connectionists that one type of neural network – the "recurrent" network, is a better model of what happens in the brain than a "feedforward" model. In the "recurrent" network, connections can form a "directed cycle," meaning that (in the case of a neural network) some synaptic connections will have more "weight" than others, and that with repetition over time, patterns of connection emerge and become confirmed (in the "feedforward" model no such directed cycles occur). The emergence and confirmation of connections between networks is the way in which associations between physical experience and conceptual thought arise.

Connectionist modeling is used to describe cognitive tasks such as visual and aural perception, or the processing of language, and is supported by empirical data gathered through the use of PET and fMRI scans, which can identify which parts of the brain are active during particular mental operations. Beyond these cognitive activities, however, certain researchers have proposed that neural network theory can also be applied to mental activity that involves abstract concepts. For example, neurobiologist Paul Churchland has proposed that moral behavior emerges from cognitive processes.[13] His central contention is that moral knowledge is a set of skills that can be described using the connectionist modeling described above. In the model, an abstract neuronal space of potential activation is configured by weighted synaptic connections to create prototypical moral categories such as "morally good action" or "morally bad action." Actual sensory input is assimilated to these categories with varying degrees of closeness as we make assessments of moral behavior. This analysis is supported by two clinical studies conducted by Hanna and Antonio Damasio in the 1990s. These studies showed that in two different subjects, moral behavior was different following trauma to a specific area of the brain.

George Lakoff describes how models of neuronal activity can be used to explain the way in which conceptual metaphors arise:

> In the neural theory, conceptual metaphor arises in childhood when experiences regularly occur together, activating different brain regions. Activation repeatedly spreads along neural pathways, progressively strengthening synapses in pathways between those brain regions until new circuitry is formed linking them. The new circuitry physically constitutes the metaphor, carrying out a neural mapping between frame circuitry in the regions and permitting new inferences. The conceptual metaphor MORE IS UP (as in "prices rose," "the temperature fell") is learned because brain regions for quantity and verticality are both activated whenever you pour liquid into a glass or build any pile. AFFECTION IS WARMTH (as in "She's a warm person," or "She's an ice queen") [is learned] because when you are held

affectionately as a child by your parents, you feel physical warmth. Hundreds of such *primary metaphors* are learned early in life. *Complex metaphors* are formed by neural bindings of these primary metaphors. And metaphorical language expresses both primary and complex metaphors.[14]

Experiences that repeatedly activate neural mapping between different brain areas create "directed" networks by establishing and reinforcing patterns of "weighted" synaptic connections. Through this process, we create cognitive connections between the different areas *before* we create linguistic ones. It will be useful to bear both these features in mind later, when considering the concept of mental spaces in relationship to self and character.

Metaphors of self

The process of creating weighted synaptic connections is in operation when we construct metaphors of self as a way of defining different aspects of personality. This metaphoric system of mental life, which we all use, is called the "subject–self metaphor system" by Lakoff and Johnson. In this system

> there is always a Subject that is the locus of reason and that metaphorically has an existence independent of the body. As we have seen, this contradicts the fundamental findings of cognitive science. And yet, the conception of such a Subject arises around the world uniformly on the basis of apparently universal and unchangeable experiences.[15]

Because the subject is that aspect of a person that is the experiencing consciousness it exists only in the present. "The Self is that part of a person that is not picked out by the Subject. This includes the body, social roles, past states, and actions in the world. There can be more than one Self. And each self is conceptualized metaphorically as either a person, a place or a location."[16] There are four types of everyday experience which form the source domains of the system:

1 manipulating objects, e.g. "I didn't fit in that job"
2 being located in space, e.g. "I'm always getting ahead of myself"
3 entering into social relations, e.g. "I felt like I'd just met my true self"; and

4 empathic projection – conceptually projecting yourself onto
someone else, e.g. "If I were you I wouldn't do that."

There is a fifth special case; each person is seen as having an
essence that is part of the subject. The subject may have many selves,
but only one of these selves is compatible with the essence, and this
is called the "real" or "true" self.

This conceptual understanding of subject and different selves
underlies most attempts to describe the relationship between actor
and character. This can be seen in Olivier's description of how an actor
can "find himself in the parts he plays, or find the parts in himself." The
first part of the statement implies an "essential self" of the actor –
this would be what Lakoff and Johnson identify as the subject – "the
locus of consciousness, subjective experience, reason, will and our
'essence' – everything that makes us who we uniquely are."[17] This is
projected onto the character. In the second part of the statement, the
notion is more related to the different selves that are linked to the
subject. Similarly, in the earlier quotes from Redgrave and Gielgud,
each describes the Stanislavskian way of working as one that enables
the actor to align the "essential self" with the fiction of the play. So
although Redgrave and Gielgud think of themselves as "inside-out"
actors, and Olivier sees himself as an "outside-in" actor, all three
conceive of the relationship between self and character in a way that
is unconsciously shaped by the subject–self metaphor system. The
identification of this system alerts us to the fact that the "essential
self" is a metaphorical construct.

The "essential self" in acting discourse

Much of twentieth-century discourse about acting, self, and character
draws on the work of nineteenth-century psychologist William
James, and his idea of multiple selves and the "essential self." While
today's cognitive scientists regard some aspects of James' work as
prescient, the concept of the "essential self," and the way in which it
has been taken up by acting teachers, is inaccurate. A prime example
of this phenomenon is Uta Hagen's widely-used book *Respect for
Acting*. Hagen explains how she relates the selves that are embodied
in different social situations to the "essential self" by stating that each
situation provides the actor with different "behaviorisms," and that
recognizing these helps the actor in the "continuing job of learning to
find out who you *really* are ... "[18] The sense is that there is a self that
one "really" is, and that the multiple selves, defined by behavior and

feeling, demonstrate different aspects of this self. This "essential self" is then used as "the source for the character."[19] Viewed in the light of Lakoff and Johnson's analysis, this would be the special case in which one of the metaphorically constructed selves contains the essence that is compatible with the subject. Hagen considers that source to be vital for the creation of a performance that will affect an audience:

> The Representational actor deliberately chooses to imitate or illustrate the character's behavior. The Presentational actor attempts to reveal human behavior through a use of himself, through an understanding of himself and consequently an understanding of the character he is portraying. The Representational actor finds a form based on an objective result for the character, which he then carefully watches as he executes it. The Presentational actor trusts that a form will result from identification with the character and the discovery of his character's actions, and works on stage for a moment-to-moment subjective experience … I believe that the illustration of a character's behavior at the cost of removing one's own psyche, no matter how brilliant the performance that results, creates an alienation between audience and actor … the vital empathy with human behavior, the emotional involvement between actor and audience will be lacking.[20]

Hagen's description suggests that the difference between the "Representational actor" and the "Presentational actor" is essentially one of "identification with the character," which results in "subjective experience." When viewed in the context of the subject–self system, the distinction between the approaches that Hagen describes is metaphorical rather than actual. Both activities that she describes involve a subject (an experiencing consciousness) and one or more selves in the form of people or objects ("forms"). The notion of an "essential self" is implied in "the use of himself" and "one's own psyche," and equates with Olivier's description of an actor "bringing himself to a role." So Hagen's progression of thought is that an actor can only move an audience by knowing his or her "essential self" and projecting it into the role.

Robert Benedetti proposes a similar view in *The Actor at Work*, another acting text that is popular in the US:

> You play a role every time you enter a social situation … It is this interaction with your world – this give and take of acting and reacting, this adjustment of your behavior to fit your

circumstances and those with whom you interact – that shapes and expresses your personality, your character, in everyday life ... William James's idea [is] that human personality contains various "me's" that one adopts in various situations but that are all versions of one's central identity, the "I."[21]

Benedetti's "versions of one's central identity" equate with Hagen's multiple social selves as aspects of "who you *really* are," with both depending on the metaphorical concept of the "essential self." However, Benedetti's view of how this understanding applies to performance has a different emphasis than Hagen's. Rather than insisting on authenticity through the investment of "who you really are" in the character, Benedetti talks about a character as " ... a new version of yourself, perhaps quite different from your everyday self ... "[22] Interestingly, Benedetti proposes an exercise in which the actor repeatedly performs an expressive physical action in order to discover an altered sense of self, which echoes the exercises of Michael Chekhov that I will describe later in this chapter. Benedetti also summarizes this section by saying that character grows out of action, which is congruent with the cognitive principles that I describe here. He does not, however, distinguish between narrative action and behavioral actions. The difference between Hagen's and Benedetti's conceptions of character and self perhaps reflects the change in understanding of Stanislavski's theory that has occurred in the period between the writing of the two books (Hagen's published in 1973, the ninth edition of Benedetti's book dates from 2005), and Benedetti's exposure to the physically-based practices of Grotowski. Both, however, refer to biographical experience as the source of the actor's repertoire of experience and behavior, which, in comparison to Lecoq's work for example, limits the actor's expressive range.

Lakoff and Johnson describe another category of metaphoric conceptualization that is key to the debate about self and character and underlies notions of whether the character is similar or different to the actor's "essential self." This is where the subject can project him or herself onto another person in one of two ways: advisory projection and empathic projection. In advisory projection, "I am projecting my values onto you so that I experience your life with my values."[23] In empathic projection, "I am experiencing your life, but with your values projected onto my subjective experience."[24] In the example quoted above, Hagen clearly favors advisory projection, and the two types of projection illuminate the distinction that Olivier makes between "finding oneself in the part" and "finding the part in oneself."

Lakoff and Johnson relate this metaphoric system to the capacity to imitate: "Imitating makes use of an ability to project, to conceptualize oneself as inhabiting the body of another. Empathy is the extension of this ability to the realm of emotions – not just to move as someone else moves, but to feel as someone else feels."[25] Empathy as a cognitive mechanism is immensely important to a consideration of acting, and I will talk about it in depth in the next chapter. For now, Lakoff and Johnson's statement serves to highlight the fact that the dichotomies of "internal/external" and "same/different" are based on metaphorical conceptualizations that are inaccurate representations of how the bodymind works.

The synaptic self

Current thinking on the self in the field of cognitive studies distinguishes between those aspects of the self that we are, or can become, aware of, and those aspects that exist outside of conscious awareness. Neuro-scientist Joseph LeDoux's position (in common with most working in this field) is that consciousness depends on unconscious cognitive processes. He defines those things that we are conscious of as *explicit* aspects of the self. This category would include the multiple situational selves mentioned by Hagen and Benedetti, along with one's conscious perception of one's body, known as the body image. The *implicit* category includes those aspects of self "that are not immediately available to consciousness, either because they are by their nature inaccessible, or because they are accessible but not being accessed at the moment."[26] This category includes most aspects of what are known as body schema – a system of motor functions operating below the level of consciousness.

The categories of *explicit* and *implicit* also apply to types of memory, and this is especially significant for the discussion of self and char-acter in acting. As LeDoux points out: "To the extent that our life's experiences contribute to who we are, implicit and explicit memory storage constitute key mechanisms through which the self is formed and maintained."[27] In referring to "life's experiences" he is talking about those aspects of self that are learned rather than the result of genetic heritage. It is those learned aspects that the actor is concerned with because they are, to varying extents, malleable, while genetic heritage is not.

Explicit memories are, naturally, those that we are conscious of and would include the everyday experiences in different situations that Hagen and Benedetti regard as the actor's repertoire of behavior.

In the approach that their writings characterize, it is this conscious awareness of self that is considered to include the "essential self" whose application to a role is necessary for authenticity. This approach does not take account of those aspects of self that are not available to consciousness, but these implicit memories are operating all the time. As LeDoux states: "The way that we characteristically walk and talk and even the way we think and feel reflect the workings of systems that function on the basis of past experience, but their operation takes place outside of awareness."[28] *The majority of factors that go to make up the self are not conscious.* The idea of the essential "I" simply does not agree with current convergent opinion in cognitive science about the nature of the self. To whatever extent we can know what our essential "I" is, it is unlikely that we can consciously make it be part of one of our situational selves. Consequently, *it is misguided to think that we can achieve authenticity in a role by investing the essential "I" in it.*

Imagination

This cognitive understanding of the notion of "self" serves as a foundation for a look at the pathways from self to character. Much discourse about the role of the imagination in contemporary acting derives from Stanislavski's concept of the "magic if." This involves the actor behaving "as if" they are themselves in the fictional situation of the character, and was originally described in *An Actor Prepares*. As Sharon Carnicke has pointed out, Elizabeth Hapgood's translation often distorted the meaning of the work, so I quote from the recent translation by Jean Benedetti: "The word 'if' is a spur, a stimulus to inner and outer creative dynamism. All you have to do is say 'What would I do, how would I handle it if the story of the madman turned out to be actually true?' and immediately you are dynamic and alive."[29] In light of the features of self that I've described, this process encourages the actor to respond from his or her own personality, to use what Lakoff and Johnson call "advisory projection." While this links the actor imaginatively to the fictional situation, *the actor's personality defines the character's response.* This has always seemed illogical to me. My personality is not the same as that of Falstaff or Leontes, and I would not respond to their fictional circumstances in the way that they do. This is true both at the level of narrative action and behavioral action. While it is understandable that Stanislavski sought to promote credible behavior in actors, if this particular idea is followed literally, it limits the activity of the imagination in preparing a role. This is one of the main reasons for Michael Chekhov's disagreement with Stanislavski's early ideas, and many subsequent teachers of Stanislavski's system have amended the concept to "what would I do if I were the character in the situation?" This involves imagining both the fictional circumstances *and* the fictional character.

Recent research has given us a more sophisticated understanding of imagination than was available to Stanislavski. Cognitive science demonstrates that the imagination is not a discrete or specialized function, as was often thought, but that it is a feature of cognition that is woven through much of our mental processes as metaphoric activity. In one way, theatre is the supreme expression of this because we experience the actor and the character simultaneously – a living, embodied metaphor. Beyond this, researchers point to the role that the imagination plays in interpersonal communication. This is described by what is known as theory of mind – our capacity to understand and sometimes predict the behavior of other people. We do this by attributing to them mental states that include beliefs, desires, and intentions, which requires a degree of imaginative activity.

The most recent explanation of how this occurs is known as simulation theory and incorporates the activity of mirror neurons, which are neurons in an observer's brain that fire in a similar pattern when an action is observed as when that action is actually executed.[30] This is a topic that I'll investigate in depth in the next chapter, as it links mimesis, empathy, and the imagination; for now a brief introduction is helpful for an understanding of the following material. Vittorio Gallese was one of the neurophysiologists who discovered mirror neurons, and describes their activity as follows (his use of "act" as noun and verb is in the everyday sense, not the theatrical sense):

> When I see a goal-directed motor act, not only the visual part of my brain is stimulated, but also a part of the motor brain. We discovered not only that the human brain behaves in a similar way – the motor strip is activated not only when we act, but when see other individuals acting – but [also that] the same mirroring mechanism is applied to other domains of social cognition, emotions and sensations.[31]

Gallese is careful to point out that mirror neurons fire only in response to a goal-directed motor act, so the connection to emotions and sensations in an observer arise via the parts of the observer's brain that perceive and control movement. Thus *the very capacity to engage in, and make meaning of, social interaction depends on our own experience of movement, the perception of movement, and its simulation as a cognitive activity*. This phenomenon is another feature of mental activity that is central to acting. It is in operation in daily life, and when actors interact with one another as characters, and it is also active in the individual actor as he or she reads and responds to a script with their imagination.

Even with the advances in understanding that have occurred in the last 30 years, the activity of imagination is still difficult to analyze. A simple definition is that it is the holding in mind of a representation that is not supplied by current perceptual information. An act of imagination works with representations of past perceptions and a knowledge of the material environment to recreate memories or imagine future events. Most humans have the ability to imagine things that they have, or have not, seen before, and to imagine doing things that they have, or have not, done before. It is worth remembering that cognitive science shows us that much of the way in which we make meaning occurs below the level of conscious awareness, and beneath representational structures such as language. Imagination can operate in response to a conscious choice, but is also at work in activities such as remembering or planning a route. As with other types of thought, *imagination is tied to bodily processes, but can also creatively transform the experiences of perception.*

While most of us would probably be comfortable with the idea that imagination occurs mentally, for many it may be difficult to conceive of the imagination as physical activity. Cognitive linguist George Lakoff joined Gallese to propose that "imagination, like perceiving and doing, is embodied, that is, structured by our constant encounter and interaction with the world via our bodies and brains."[32] They draw upon a number of research studies to argue (using the example of the concept of "grasping") that imagination actually uses the same neural networks as perception and action:

> Our ability to imagine grasping makes use of the same neural substrate as performing and perceiving grasping. According to our proposal, imagining is a form of simulation – a mental simulation of action or perception, *using many of the same neurons as actually acting or perceiving.*[33]

The concept of simulation means that the experiential distinctions between imagining, acting, and perceiving are much less clear-cut than previously thought, which disrupts the traditional Western view of conceptual thought as symbolic and abstract. This understanding of imagination is reinforced by work from neuroscientists Randy Buckner and Daniel Carroll. They refer to data that suggest that thinking about the future involves the ability to mentally project ourselves into alternative situations, and propose that a number of activities – all of which appear in humans at the same age (four years) and were previously thought of as distinct – actually reflect the workings of the same core brain network. These activities are: envisioning the future, remembering the past, conceiving the viewpoints of others (theory of mind), and some forms of navigation.[34]

Imagination and written language

Given that the majority of performances begin with an actor reading a script, the big question is, how does the imagination respond to written language? Another exciting feature of Gallese and Lakoff's work is the concept that language is related to many aspects of the brain's functioning:

> circuitry across brain regions links modalities, infusing each with properties of others. The sensory-motor system of the brain is thus "multimodal" rather than modular. Accordingly, language is inherently multimodal in this sense, that is, it uses many modalities linked together – sight, hearing, touch, motor actions, and so on. Language exploits the pre-existing multimodal character of the sensory-motor system.[35]

This means that, far from being a feature of "abstract" reason, language piggybacks on networks in the brain that are involved in perception and movement. Neuroscientist Lisa Aziz-Zadeh designed a brain imaging experiment[36] to test Gallese and Lakoff's thesis, and found that specific brain areas that are known to control movements of the hand and the mouth were activated both by watching videos of certain actions involving the hand and mouth, and also by reading sentences that described those actions. Marco Iacoboni, one of her colleagues in this experiment, described the implications:

> It is as if mirror neurons help us understand what we read by internally simulating the action we just read in the sentence. Lisa's experiment suggests that when we read a novel, *our mirror neurons simulate the actions described in the novel, as if we were doing those actions ourselves.*[37]

Iacoboni has also conducted his own experiments that show that a part of the brain known as Broca's area "is essential not only for language, but also for imitation."[38] Other studies also show that the brain's motor mechanisms are connected to mental imagery, and can aid visualization.[39] *This suggests that the vividness of an imaginative representation is greater if motor systems are in action.*

This account of how our brains respond to written fiction is fascinating, but leads to another question: How does an actor engage in simulation in response to a *script?* Scripts differ significantly from novels in that they include very little, if any, descriptive text. Remember Gallese's statement that mirror neurons fire in response to a goal-directed motor act; a script does not generally describe actions, but can only *imply* them through dialogue. Stanislavski displayed one of his most impressive leaps of intuition by recognizing the need to invest dialogue with specific actions. At first, he sought to do this by writing novelistic prompt books that described the characters' behavior in minute detail. After realizing that this allowed his actors little freedom, he developed the "task/action" process that is now so familiar to Western theatre practitioners, finally arriving at the Method of Physical Actions towards the end of his life. It is this phase of his work that correlates so well with current understandings of imagination. The cognitive information now available to us shows that the use of physical actions stimulates the imagination.

Proprioception and character

Proprioception plays a crucial role in our sense of self, and this feature makes it of particular interest in the relationship between physical activity and the actor's creation of character. Habitual gestures and postures contribute somatically to a feeling of one's "normal" or everyday self. When different gestures and postures are used, the feedback system creates a different sense of self (I will investigate this more in the next chapter). Consequently, *the investigation of a script in rehearsal without using movement and action significantly reduces the range of imaginative prompts to the actor.* This information further validates the exercises of Lecoq that I described in the last chapter, and explains why Stanislavski intuitively chose to move from the seated analysis of scripts early in his career to his Method of Physical Actions (described in more detail in the next chapter).

Exercise: Lecoq's seven levels of muscular tension

An emphatic demonstration of the power of proprioception can be gained by experimenting with different levels of muscular tension. Jacques Lecoq developed the following scale, and exercises based on it are still taught at his school. The following description is from his book *Le Théâtre du Geste*, re-published as *Theatre of Movement and Gesture*:

> Sub-relaxation: an expression of survival, like just before death; the image of sea birds that are tarred up on the beach; one speaks with difficulty, for oneself, incoherent, using swear words.

> Relaxation: a smiling expression of the body on holiday leaving the arms to swing freely and playing on gravity's pendulum, the body rebounds on itself. One speaks to others and seeks out groups of friends.

> The economic body: neutral, as if programmed for a minimum of effort for a maximum of return. Everything is said, politely but no more than that and without passion.

> The supported body: one carries the weight of one's own body. This is the first sensation of the space under pressure: discovery, interest, suspicion, one calls, one designates, a sort of state of alert. One seeks a partner. There is no relaxation. Themes are at the level of the realistic theatre, sensitive to situation.

> The first muscular tension is decisiveness. I go. It is action that starts it. Words are precise, clean. In the theatre this is the level of realistic acting, in action.

> The second muscular tension is the arrival of passion. Anger is the natural state. Put an angry person on stage, and he will be at the level of play-acting. The actor must also have this level but without getting angry, or shouting. It must be play. The theatre is close to mask and one cannot replay this level in life. It is already stylized theatre at this point.

> The third muscular tension is the maximum. The gesture plays to resistance, slowly and without a trajectory, as in Noh. One can only simulate the tension of this level, which is close to asphyxiation. Words are no longer spoken, but inter-cut with sounds that lengthen them.[40]

These states are described in note form below, with some minor differences in wording. The exercise can be done individually or in a group.

Experiment moving around with each of the following levels of muscular tension giving two minutes to each level and paying attention to your affective state and sense of self at each level. First of all, return to neutral in between each of the levels, making sure that your breathing is regular before moving on to the next level. The second time around, try moving directly from one level to the next, giving one minute to each level. Rest at the completion of this phase and make sure your breathing is regular. In the third and final phase, move up the scale from one to seven, and then back down again, taking a minute for each level.[41]

Table 4.1 Lecoq's seven levels of tension

The scale of the seven levels

Level I   Without contraction

MOVEMENT:	As if you had no spine, falling down, trying to get up, staggering.
FOCUS:	None.
VOICE:	Groan, grunt.

Level II   Relaxation with a smile

MOVEMENT:	Arms swinging, feet as if kicking a soccer ball with each step.
FOCUS:	Wandering.
VOICE:	Slang, minimal energy. "Hey."

Level III   Economy of movement

MOVEMENT:	Just enough energy to accomplish a task, no more, no less. Minimal swinging of arms when walking. Efficient, but not robotic.
FOCUS:	On the goal.
VOICE:	Efficient and complete. "Hello."

Level IV   The alert

MOVEMENT:	Suspended. Symmetrical. Arms suspended away from body. Grounded. Responding to the empty space as if it were another player. Awake. Hyper-aware.
FOCUS:	The space, the horizon, the emptiness.
VOICE:	Questioning. Listening to the echo. Calling out to the empty space. "Hello?"
STYLE:	Neutral mask.

Table 4.1 (continued)

The scale of the seven levels

Level V   Decision

MOVEMENT: Deliberate. Urgent.
FOCUS: Intensely on the task.
VOICE: Command. "Go!" "Stop!" "Move!"

Level VI   Colorful action

MOVEMENT: Asymmetrical. Unpredictable. Impulsive. Cartoon,
               Looney Tunes, Bugs Bunny. Intensity. Surprise.
               Quick changes of tempo and rhythm.
FOCUS: Intense, but rapidly changing from one point to
               another.
VOICE: Extreme.
STYLE: Commedia dell'arte, Italian comedy.

Level VII   Asphyxiation

MOVEMENT: Complete muscular tension.
FOCUS: Intensely fixated.
VOICE: Beyond speaking.
STYLE: Tragedy.

Having completed the third phase, take note of your experience. Did you feel more comfortable at one level than another? Did one seem habitual? Did your sense of self change in any of the levels? If so, which ones and how?

Mimesis

Mimesis also plays a role in the creation of character. Cognitive psychologist Merlin Donald, who has taken a particular interest in the evolution of the human brain, offers a description of the development of mimesis in human evolution. In his analysis, mimesis preceded the development of language as humans evolved: "Mimesis is an analogue or holistic style of thought that is more basic to our uniquely human way of thinking than language or logic. Indeed, on present evidence language and logic evolved much later, from a mimetic platform."[42] This statement is consonant with McNeill's differentiation between written language and gesture, and proposes that gestural and postural action is actually a "style of thought," further undermining the conceptual divide between physical and mental activity. Donald's description of mimesis also indicates its centrality to the acting process:

> The term mimesis describes a cluster of activities that were made possible by a single neuro-cognitive adaptation ... The four central mimetic abilities are mime, imitation, gesture, and the rehearsal of skill ... Mimesis seems to have evolved as a cognitive elaboration of embodiment in patterns of action. Its origins lie in a redistribution of frontal-cortical influence during the early stages of the evolution of species *Homo*, when the prefrontal and parts of the premotor cortex expanded enormously in relative size and connectivity. The cognitive significance of this lies in the fact that, in virtually all social mammals, the frontal regions are concerned with the control of action and behavior ... [43]

Obviously, the control of action and behavior is a central feature in the process of acting, and the fact that the evolution of mimesis is tied to the development of the prefrontal cortex also links mimesis to character, as this area of the brain is the one most strongly implicated in the creation and expression of personality. It is likely that the connection between physical action and conceptual thought occurs because there is neural circuitry from the premotor cortex to other, non-motor domains, which allows the networks that control movement to be used by conceptual domains such as emotion, sensing, and thinking.[44]

An understanding of these links between movement and conceptual thought helps make it clear how imaginative responses to fiction occur. As with most of the cognitive information that I describe, researchers are generally not concerned with the theatrical application of this knowledge. Theatre practitioners and researchers are therefore very fortunate to have a record of the discussion on mirror neurons and acting that I mentioned earlier in which Vittorio Gallese was a participant – it is rare that eminent neurophysiologists comment directly on matters of theatrical practice. Gallese made this observation during a phase of the discussion that focused on the creation of character:

> Your relationship with a character you're supposed to play is intrinsically relational, so you try to enter into the – metaphorically or even literally – into the body of someone else. In the body, in the gesturing, in the mind. So more than a mirroring mechanism, it's an *imagery* mechanism which partly impinges upon the same neuro-circuits which are involved in action observation.[45]

Gallese's conception of the character coincides remarkably well with the work of Michael Chekhov. Actor Adam Ludwig evidently notices this, for shortly after Gallese's comment, he describes the "imaginary body" Chekhov exercise in the comment that I quoted earlier in this chapter. Given the features of the discourse about character that I've mentioned above, it is significant that Gallese identifies the character as "someone else" rather than "self in character." It is also instructive that body and image feature strongly in his description, and how the container metaphor of self is applied to the identity of the imagined character, not the actor. I suspect that when he distinguishes between metaphorical and literal ways of entering the body of someone else, that "literal" means the assumption of physical characteristics, since there is an implicit understanding that the character is fictional.

Michael Chekhov

Michael Chekhov's conception of the relationship between actor and character bears a lot of congruence with the cognitive principles that I've outlined. Originally a student of Stanislavski, he acted and directed at the Moscow Art Theatre, but while Stanislavski's work and life have been extensively documented, Michael Chekhov is less well-known, although his ideas have contributed significantly to actor training in the latter part of the twentieth century, with a significant resurgence of interest evident since the 1980s.

Born in 1891, Michael Chekhov was the nephew of the playwright Anton Chekhov. At the age of 19 he began working as an actor with the Maly Theatre in St Petersburg, and was then invited to join the First Studio of the Moscow Art Theatre (MAT) by Stanislavski in 1912. In the following 15 years, Chekhov achieved fame for his innovative and unusual performances with both the first and the second MAT, but as the new communist regime tightened its grip on artistic activity, his aesthetic principles and his interest in the philosophy of Rudolf Steiner made him a target for the hard-line Marxists within his company. In 1928, his autobiography became an unexpected best-seller, and his increased fame led to denouncements by Moscow newspapers – portraying him as a mystic and a "sick artist" whose work was "alien and reactionary" – and the subsequent preparation of an arrest warrant. To escape imprisonment, he traveled first of all to Berlin, hoping to mount a German-language production of *Hamlet*.

Chekhov lived a nomadic existence for the next six years, working in Austria, France, Latvia, and Lithuania. In 1934, at the invitation of impresario Sol Hurok, he and other MAT émigrés formed a company called the Moscow Art Players, which toured the United States in 1934–5. They performed a repertoire of seven plays and an evening of adaptations of Chekhov stories and played on Broadway to full houses and highly favorable reviews. At this point Chekhov was invited by Stella Adler to join the Group Theatre, and also by actress Beatrice Straight to lead a theatre company and training studio at Dartington Hall in Devon, England. No doubt attracted by the school's links with the philosophy of Rudolf Steiner, and the financial security afforded by its backing by the wealthy Elmhirst family, Chekhov chose to go to England. From 1936 to 1939 he taught at the Michael Chekhov Theatre Studio in Dartington, but moved back to the US at the outbreak of the Second World War.

Based in Ridgefield, Connecticut, Chekhov started another studio and staged some performances with an ensemble that included a young Yul Brynner that were poorly received. However, his production of *Twelfth Night* was favorably reviewed on Broadway in 1941. His Ridgefield studio was forced to close in 1942, when the draft removed most of its male actors, and he moved to Los Angeles in 1943. He then began a film career as an actor that included an Oscar nomination for his role in Hitchcock's *Spellbound* in 1945, and resulted in a total of ten films. He continued to teach during this period, and actors who trained with him included Gary Cooper, Marilyn Monroe, Gregory Peck, Patricia Neal, Clint Eastwood, Leslie Caron, Anthony Quinn, Ingrid Bergman, Jack Palance, Mala Powers, Lloyd Bridges, and Yul Brynner. His book *To The Actor* was published in 1953, two years before his death from a heart attack.[46]

During his time at MAT, Chekhov rejected certain elements of Stanislavski's system, notably his approach to characterization:

> Stanislavski's viewpoint was that when an actor gets a part he has to imagine the character he will play is, figuratively speaking, seated within himself-absolutely and completely occupying the actor's inner self- ... In sum, the character dwelt within the actor, and the actor's voice and body expressed in a true-to-life manner what the character was supposed to think and feel and do ... yet in such a way that it was also true to the psychology or inner life of the actor himself.[47]

What Chekhov describes is an example of advisory projection, where the actor's values are projected on to the character, since the values of the character have to be "true" to those of the actor. That Chekhov took a different approach, and favored empathic projection, is clear from the following quote, where he invites the student of acting to ask three questions about the character that is being approached:

1   What is the difference between my way of thinking and the character's way of thinking?
2   What are the differences between the feelings and emotions of the character and myself?
3   What is the nature of my will and inclinations against those of the character?[48]

The focus is constantly on becoming aware of differences, rather than the similarities that Stanislavski's approach favors, and which Chekhov believed led to "weary repetitions" of the actor's autobiography. This approach evidently invites the subject (the student of acting) to experience the life of the character with the character's values projected onto the Subject's subjective experience.

Conceptual blending

The work of cognitive linguist Gilles Fauconnier and cognitive scientist Mark Turner offers an endorsement of Chekhov's approach. Their theory of conceptual blending describes the cognitive process that underlies innovation. Briefly, a cognitive blend is a mental construction, initially composed of at least three mental spaces, that occurs at the level of short-term or "working" memory. Each of these contain aspects of meaning that, when integrated with the others, creates a fourth mental space and new conceptual material. The process starts when two concepts, or domains of experience, are framed together in linguistic or imagistic ways, making the mind scan automatically for underlying similarities. This is the process that occurs when an actor thinks of "self" and "character" – in Chekhov's approach, these would be two different domains of experience, framed together by the fact that they will share the same body. Fauconnier and Turner suggest that if the two domains have traits in common (in the example of character, these could be personality traits), then the result of the scanning will be the recall from long-term memory of a third or "generic" space containing the outlines of these traits. This justifies Chekhov's statement that "the similarities take care of themselves." The presence of this generic space primes the mind to project or "map" connections, resulting in yet a fourth space, the blend itself. In Chekhov's process this would be the mental space in which the actor embodies the realized character. Chekhov's description of his process in *The Path of The Actor* has remarkable similarities with Fauconnier and Turner's analysis:

> If an actor prepares his role correctly, the whole process of preparation can be characterized as his gradual approach to the picture of his character as he sees it in his imagination, in his fantasy. The actor first builds up his character exclusively in his fantasy life, and then tries to imitate the character's inner and outer qualities.[49]

The mental space that represents the character is first experienced as an imagined "picture." The actor maintains a separate mental space that represents his or her self – this is indicated by the metaphor of "approach," and the intentional activities of "building" and "imitating." The blend occurs when the actor "imitates" the character. His approach of concentrating on the differences between actor and character is more aligned to the principles of conceptual blending than the idea that an actor can completely identify with a character, often associated with Method acting.

While Fauconnier and Turner are describing a mental process that operates in many areas of activity, they do make mention of what they call "drama connectors." In the quote below, they begin by describing the phenomenon of the blended actor and character from the audience's perspective, but nevertheless, the principles described are pertinent when addressing the process of the actor:

> Dramatic performances are deliberate blends of a living person with an identity. They give us a living person in one input and a different living person, an actor, in another. The person on stage is a blend of these two. The character portrayed may of course be entirely fictional, but there is still a space, a fictional one, in which that person is alive. In the blend, the person sounds and moves like the actor and is where the actor is, but the actor in her performance tries to accept projections from the character portrayed, and so modifies her language, appearance, dress, attitudes, and gestures.[50]

It is clear from the last sentence that Fauconnier and Turner, like Chekhov, conceive of the character as someone different from the actor. One of the very significant factors for the consideration of theatre as a whole is that audiences are simultaneously aware of actor and character without losing their engagement with the fictional circumstances:[51]

While we perceive a single scene, we are simultaneously aware of the actor moving and talking on a stage in front of an audience, and of the corresponding character moving and talking within the represented story world. Common to the two frames are some language and action patterns.[52]

While this simultaneous perception of "fictional" and "real" is something that Fauconnier and Turner describe from an audience's point of view, it seems reasonable to identify the same mental processes in an actor creating and performing a character. A core feature of Michael Chekhov's approach to characterization, which he called "dual consciousness," is congruent with this principle. This idea arose from an experience that he had while playing the character of Skid in a play called *Artists*[53] in Berlin, directed by Max Reinhardt:

> Skid was speaking, and it suddenly seemed to me that I really understood for the first time the meaning of his words, his unrequited love for Bonny and his drama. My exhaustion and calmness had turned me into a spectator of my own action ... I looked at Skid sitting down there on the floor and I was struck by it, as if I could "see" his feelings, his pain and agitation ... Now I was able to conduct Skid's acting. My consciousness had split into two – at one and the same time, I was in the auditorium and standing beside myself ... [54]

Although Chekhov describes this as a unique, even transcendental, experience, he links it to an ongoing phenomenon of his experience of acting: "Earlier it had been familiar to me in a somewhat less pronounced form,"[55] and identifies it as an experience of inspiration. Having studied the ideas of Rudolf Steiner, he identifies inspiration as being a function of "the higher ego," a part of consciousness that is creative, and distinguished from "the lower ego" which is identified with ambition, passion, and egotism: "A kind of division of consciousness occurs, with the higher ego acting as the source of inspiration and the lower ego as the bearer, the agent."[56]

While the terms "higher ego" and "lower ego" do not correlate with current understanding of the mind, the way that Chekhov describes his experience can be understood in the context of the subject–self system identified by Lakoff and Johnson. Chekhov "observing" himself would be the subject (experiencing consciousness), the "higher ego" would correlate with the "essential self," the "lower ego" with another self, Skid as yet another. The simultaneous awareness of these selves correlates with Fauconnier and Turner's description of blended "mental spaces." Chekhov saw dual consciousness as essential to an actor's control; the higher ego

> observes and directs the lower ego from outside, guiding it and empathizing with the imagined sufferings and joys of the character ... although the actor on stage suffers, weeps, rejoices and laughs, at the same time he remains unaffected by these feelings on a personal level. Poor actors pride themselves on the fact that they sometimes succeed in having such "feelings" on stage to the extent that they forget themselves completely! Such actors break the furniture, dislocate their fellow actors' arms and suffocate their lovers while on stage.[57]

This was the root of Chekhov's antipathy to "affective memory" – another significant difference between his practice and that of Stanislavski's at that stage of his development. Chekhov played Skid in 1928, and while his communication with his former teacher is not known, Stanislavski acknowledged the existence of "dual consciousness" by the time *An Actor Prepares* was published in 1936, while maintaining his belief in the usefulness of "affective memory." Before examining Chekhov's approach to emotion, it is instructive to look at a key exercise in the creation of character, described in *To the Actor*. This is the "imaginary body" exercise, partially described by Adam Ludwig in the Philoctetes Center discussion that I described earlier.

Exercise: the imaginary body

Chekhov invites the actor first of all to pose the questions of difference mentioned above, and by answering them, identify those characteristics of the character that are different from the actor. In the hypothetical example that he gives, the character is "lazy, awkward and slow":

> As soon as you have outlined these features and qualities of your role – that is, compared with your own – try to imagine what kind of body such a lazy awkward and slow person would have. Perhaps you will find that he might possess a full, plump, short body with drooping shoulders, thick neck, long arms hanging listlessly, and a big heavy head ... You are going to imagine that in the same space you occupy with your own, real body there exists another body – the imaginary body of your character, which you have just created in your mind.
>
> You clothe yourself, as it were, with this body; you put it on like a garment.[58]

The process described in this exercise is remarkably congruent with both Fauconnier and Turner's analysis, and Gallese's comment about character. The differentiation, and then melding, of self and character through imagery offers a useful conscious and physical corollary of Fauconnier and Turner's mental spaces, which would be present unconsciously in the creation of character. The "wearing" of the imagined body offers an imaginative corollary of the "blended" space of actor and character.

Chekhov also displays an intuitive understanding of mimesis as a type of thought, as defined by Merlin Donald:

> When really taken on and exercised, the imaginary body stirs the actor's will and feelings; it harmonizes them with the char-acteristic speech and movements, it transforms the actor into another person! Merely discussing the character, analyzing it mentally, cannot produce this desired effect, because your reason-ing mind, however skilful it may be, is apt to leave you cold and passive, whereas the imaginary body has the power to appeal directly to your will and feelings.[59]

Chekhov displays an inclination that is opposite to the Cartesian separation of reason from body. I read his use of the phrase "reasoning mind" to suggest that reason is only a part of mental activity, not synonymous with it, while the rest of the statement makes clear that the body can stimulate experiences in response to the imagination.

A further example of this can be seen in a statement that Chekhov made while teaching actors in the MAT First Studio, making clear the link between his idea of character and the creation of emotion on stage:

> Do not try to feel your own personal feelings. It is the character who has to feel, not the actor, and the actor must only sacrifice himself to the character ... In imitating and depicting what my fantasy gives me, I don't have to try to appear inside the char-acter, because then the actor ceases to be an artist and becomes a madman.[60]

Once again, the notion is that character is distinct from actor, and the statement adds the element of emotion to what we have been investigating so far. At first, it may be difficult to understand how it can be the character that feels – after all, it is the actor's body that experi-ences and expresses the affective state. However, the statement fits into the idea of the character as a situational self that arises in response to the imagined fictional circumstances, and the actor as the experiencing subject. As the actor's body expresses the physical behavior of the situational self, emotions can be stimulated through the proprioceptive system, described earlier in this chapter. I'll investigate this phenomenon in detail in Chapter 6, but for now the basic principle is that muscular activity affects the autonomic nervous system, and thence our experience of emotion. Chekhov displays an awareness of this phenomenon in the exercise that is described below.

Exercise: gesture and affective state

Lift your arm. Lower it. What have you done? You have fulfilled a simple physical action. You have made a gesture. And you have made it without any difficulty. Why? Because like every action, it is completely within your will. Now make the same gesture, but this time color it with a certain quality. Let this quality be caution. ... Your movement made cautiously, is no longer a mere physical action, it has acquired a certain psychological nuance. What is this nuance? It is a *Sensation* of caution which now fills and permeates your arm. It is a psychophysical sensation. Similarly, if you moved your entire body with the quality of caution, then your entire body would naturally be filled with this sensation. ... Now ask yourself if you forced your feelings. Did you order yourself to "feel caution"? No. You only made a movement with a certain quality, thus creating a sensation of caution through which you aroused your feelings.[61]

Again, physical activity is experienced with conceptual thought in a form of "moving as thinking." The activity stimulates the imagination through the neuronal links between motor activity and conceptual thought. Trying the exercise as I sit and type, I feel a distinct difference between my state of being simply thinking the word "caution" without movement, and my state of being as I move my arm cautiously. I also notice retrospectively that as I moved my arm, my eyelids narrowed and my eyes darted from side to side, without any conscious command. This is a behavior that I (and probably many others) associate with caution and which arose spontaneously.

Perhaps the most widely known, and simultaneously least understood, of Chekhov's exercises is the Psychological Gesture (PG). A common feature of the misunderstanding is that the PG is shown to the audience and that this leads to stylized or contrived behavior in the actor. Chekhov intended this exercise to be a preparation for performance as an image that was held in the imagination, but not shown to the audience; " ... the PG itself must never be shown to the audience, no more than an architect would be expected to show the public the scaffolding of his building instead of the completed masterwork."[62] The root of the PG is in the actor defining what the character's strongest wish is. This strongly resembles Stanislavski's idea of the "super-objective"; while Chekhov asserted many differences between his approach and that of Stanislavski, he emphatically endorsed "units" and "objectives" as tools of script analysis. The distinctiveness of the PG is that it expresses the character's strongest wish in a physical and imagistic way. The process begins with making a gesture with hand and arm that expresses the wish. With successive repetitions the gesture is developed to include the whole body, so that the final expression is both postural and gestural. This is done repeatedly through a rehearsal period, with adjustments and refinements as the actor's understanding of the character develops. A muscular memory of the image of the wish is developed that subliminally affects the performance of the character, but can also be consciously recalled during performance to inform the character's physicality and affective state. Subsidiary PGs can be created to reflect the strongest wish of the character in each scene – akin to Stanislavski's scene, or "beat" objectives.

As with Chekhov's other exercises, the imagination is stimulated through physical activity: "So we may say that the *strength* of the movement stirs our will power in general; the *kind* of movement awakens in us a definite corresponding *desire*, and the *quality* of the same movement conjures up our feelings."[63] These specific correlations are not as direct as Chekhov proposes, nor so distinct from one another, but the overall way in which the PG can stimulate thought and feeling is explained by the proprioceptive provocation of Feelings, the metaphorical relation between physical actions and conceptual thought, and the blending of mental spaces that represent self and character.

The metaphor of the self as a container is a central feature of the "internal/external" dichotomy. While Chekhov was not immune to this, he seemed (as described in Chapter 2) to have an imaginative conception of the container as both permeable and malleable:

> The body of the actor must absorb psychological qualities, must be filled and permeated with them so that they will convert it gradually into a sensitive membrane, a kind of receiver and conveyor of the subtlest images, feelings, emotions and will impulses.[64]

Many of his exercises demonstrate this concept, including those of molding, floating, flying, and radiating described earlier. He also incorporated physical work that expresses primary actions, such as grasp, push/pull, and throw in much the same way that Lecoq did. These features of his approach constantly link physical with mental activity in ways that fit with the role of mimesis in art described by Merlin Donald, and usefully integrate the differences between the cognitive processes of written and spoken language described by David McNeill.

Conclusion

In this chapter I have outlined some of the research in the field of cognitive studies that informs an understanding of what is happening as an actor conceives of, and embodies a character. This research shows that the prevalent conceptual dichotomy of "internal" (psychological) versus "external" (physical) approaches to characterization is mistaken, because it is based on an idea of mind separate from body. The findings that I've described show that mental and physical activities are both ways of thinking (or "minding"), are frequently linked, and that our conceptual thought is based on physical experience. Because of the way that we represent different aspects of our personalities to ourselves (the subject–self system), we have a metaphorical system of multiple selves that forms the framework for discourse about the relationship between actor and character. Much of this discourse has associated successful acting with the investment of the "essential self" in the character. Chekhov's approach, however, identifies a character as one of many "selves" whose actions are controlled by his experiencing consciousness, an approach that is congruent with the model of conceptually blended mental spaces proposed by Fauconnier and Turner. That his approach was successful in practice is indicated by the high praise that he received as an actor and teacher in both Russia and the US.

Chekhov was prescient in the way that he structured *To The Actor*; of the key figures in early twentieth-century theatre to write about their approaches (Stanislavski, Brecht, Copeau, Craig, Artaud, Vakhtangov, Meyerhold) he was the first to include practical exercises for the actor to follow, rather than describing them in narrative form or as general principles. His analysis of the lure of naturalism in acting identifies a stylistic trend that has only become more marked as theatre as an art form is increasingly subsumed by the entertainment industry:

> Moreover, under the hypnotic power of modern materialism, actors are even inclined to neglect the boundary which must

separate everyday life from that of the stage. They strive instead to bring life-as-it-is onto the stage, and by doing so become ordinary photographers rather than artists. They are perilously prone to forget that the real task of the creative artist is not merely to copy the outer appearance of life but to interpret life in all its facets and profoundness, to show what is behind the phenomena of life, to let the spectator look beyond life's surfaces and meanings.[65]

The book's opening sentence is also prophetic: "It is a known fact that the human body and psychology influence each other and are in constant interplay."[66] The statement has a certain bravado; when he was writing, the concept was neither well-known nor widely believed. Empirically derived proof of the statement is only now finding its way into discussions of acting, and Chekhov deserves credit for intuitively creating an approach that is in accord with the current understanding of the bodymind.

Key points

- Current discourse about character relies heavily on the mistaken "internal/external" dichotomy.
- This dichotomy rests upon a metaphorical concept of the individual as a container, with thought inside and expression outside.
- Many of the proclaimed differences between approaches to acting are actually differences in the *types of metaphors* used to describe self and process.
- Connectionism models the mind as a system of overlapping networks in the brain.
- These overlapping networks create neural circuitry that forms metaphoric concepts.
- Cognitive science offers an understanding of metaphoric concepts of the self, and undercuts the idea of the "essential self."
- Consciousness depends on unconscious cognitive processes.
- It is misguided to think that we can achieve authenticity in a role by investing the essential "I" in it.
- The capacity to engage in, and make meaning of, social interaction depends on our own experience of movement, the perception of movement, and its simulation as a cognitive activity.

- Imagination is tied to bodily processes, but can also creatively transform the experiences of perception.
- Imagining is a mental simulation of action or perception, using many of the same neurons as actually acting or perceiving.
- The vividness of an imaginative representation is greater if motor systems are in action.
- Proprioception is the neural feedback system that gives us information about bodily position and well-being, and contributes to the sense of self.
- Altered postures and gestures work proprioceptively to create a different sense of self.
- Mimesis is a holistic style of thought that preceded language in the evolution of the brain.
- Michael Chekhov distinguished his approach from Stanislavski in several key areas, by focusing on differences between actor and character, rather than similarities, by identifying the concept of "dual consciousness," by rejecting "affective memory" as indulgent, and by using physical means to prompt the imagination and emotion.

Chapter 5

How does the actor identify with the character?

This chapter focuses on the relationship of self to character. As with most aspects of acting, it is somewhat artificial to separate this out from other features of the process, but doing so helps us to gain clarity about the process as a whole. As the previous chapter showed, the concept of approaching a role from "the outside in" or "the inside out" is a false dichotomy when viewed from a cognitive perspective. Similarly, the idea of bringing one's "true" or "essential" self to a role is a metaphorical construct that reflects the transposition of values rather than a difference at a cognitive level. Nevertheless, it is commonly used to describe how authenticity in a role is achieved. So what is actually happening at the cognitive level? Whether you think of "self in the role" or "role in the self" the same process is engaged – the conceptual blending of mental spaces that connote concepts of self and character.

In this chapter, I'm going to talk about how the process of melding operates in the preparation of a role for performance as the actor combines his or her experience with that of the character. In theatre parlance, this tends to get called "identification with the role," and sometimes "investing," although this term is also used to mean "to make emotionally significant." Current debate about this topic is shaped by the concepts of "persona acting" and "transformational acting," which I examine before investigating the work of American actress Anna Deavere Smith in a case study. Smith's writings on her own process offer an intriguing insight into the creation of character through imitation. I then define the difference between narrative action and behavioral actions, and describe how this distinction can create greater clarity about how we define character. This is followed by descriptions of the proprioceptive sense of self and body schema and body image – cognitive mechanisms that participate in the sense of self.

The recent discovery of mirror neurons provides an account of the way that the neural circuitry of motor activity is involved in Empathy, Emotion, and responses to fiction. This information also relates to the way that the brain processes words and images. I also refer to the work of experimental psychologist Jonathan Schooler who has identified a phenomenon that he calls "verbal overshadowing" in which verbal descriptions of visual stimuli compromise visual memory, and apply this to a consideration of script analysis. I then trace Stanislavski's progression from linguistic analysis of a script to the "active analysis" that he used in the later stage of his life, proposing that the cognitive research that I've described validates the effectiveness of his Method of Physical Actions. This is followed by Case Studies of Vasili Toporkov, who acted in the last production that Stanislavski directed, and of contemporary actor Daniel Day-Lewis. The conclusion offers a cognitive definition of character in acting that underlies a variety of different approaches, normally considered to be distinct from one another.

Persona acting and transformational acting

The common understanding of the degree to which an actor identifies with a character involves yet another duality – that of "persona" acting versus "transformational" acting (also known as "personality" acting and "character" acting). Once again, this is a slippery subject to discuss – much of the discourse about it is expressed from a subjective point of view, in terms that mean one thing to one person and another to someone else. My understanding of the distinction is that the "persona" actor maintains a more or less constant personality from one role to the next, while the "transformational" actor embodies varying personalities according to role. I avoid the use of the term "character actor" to describe the latter, because that term is also used in "typing" to distinguish actors who play secondary roles from those who play leads.

> After *Blood Simple*, everybody thought I was from Texas. After *Mississippi Burning*, everybody thought I was from Mississippi and uneducated. After *Fargo*, everybody's going to think I'm from Minnesota, pregnant, and have blonde hair. I don't think you can ever completely transform yourself on film, but if you do your job well, you can make people believe that you're the character you're trying to be.
>
> Frances McDormand[1]

A number of issues are tied in with the "persona/transformational" dichotomy. While the difference is often understood in terms of finding one's "essential self" in a role, a more empirically reliable way to define the difference is to look at the range of actions that an actor uses to portray the character. Their actions link them to the fictional circumstances and demonstrate the personality of the character. The persona actor uses behavioral communicators that stay within a range that identifies his or her personality, which remains more or less constant from one role to the next. The transformational actor displays a variety of behavioral communicators according to the demands of character. In the case of the persona actor we see the more or less constant personality responding to the fictional circumstances with reasonably predictable results – we don't expect characters played by Tom Cruise or Harrison Ford to meekly surrender to adversity, for instance. We see a greater variety of behavior in actors such as Philip Seymour Hoffman and Daniel Day-Lewis in different roles, but in neither category can we state from observation that the actors are, or are not, identifying their concepts of their "essential selves" with the roles that they play. Consequently, the distinction that is based on behavioral action is more empirically useful. It identifies the phenomenon in the context of a range of behavioral communicators, rather than as a dichotomy.

Narrative action and behavioral actions

It is also useful to distinguish between narrative action, and behavioral actions that communicate meaning. Since Aristotle defined action as springing from character and thought, it has become a commonplace to say that character is expressed by action. However, what is often unconsidered is that action (in the sense of narrative development) is itself communicated by gestural *actions*, and that these have meaning that communicate personality: the hero is presented with an opportunity to kill the villain but he chooses not to – this choice is at the level of narrative action. At another level, the actor can choose whether this is done out of cowardice, indecision, altruism, or a malevolent desire to exact a more cruel punishment in the future, and *this* choice is communicated by the expressive behavioral actions of the actor/ character in delivering the language of the text. At this level, the actions communicate the values of the character, and hence, his or her personality. It is at this level that we talk of the "interpretation" of an existing role.[2]

It is useful to recall Lecoq's work on extending the range of an actor's behavior. The larger an actor's repertoire of behavioral actions is, the greater the range of personality he or she can play. It is also instructive to recall the neuronal links between motor activities and conceptual thought, and that there is a reflexive relationship between muscular activity and the experience of emotion. A variety of actions will also generate the experience of a variety of conceptual thoughts and feelings in the actor. This arises through the physiological process of proprioception, by which information about where the body is and what it is doing is relayed back to the brain. Recent research, which I will describe later in this chapter, shows that proprioception is strongly involved in a sense of self. So not only is character expressed by action, but also *actions create character by altering an actor's sense of self.*

Case study: Anna Deavere Smith

An example of this phenomenon can be found in Anna Deavere Smith's accounts of her work in creating *Fires in the Mirror: Crown Heights, Brooklyn, and Other Identities.* This was a solo show created by Smith from interviews that she conducted with residents of a neighborhood in Brooklyn, New York that had experienced rioting and conflict between Hasidic Jews and Afro-Caribbean Americans. Smith created her material by precisely imitating portions of the recorded interviews, providing an example of total imitation that is rare in contemporary theatre. First performed in 1992, the show was extremely successful, winning a Drama Desk Award and an Obie, as well as a Pulitzer Prize nomination. Much of the critical response to the play focused on socio-political issues, and the implicit commentary on identity afforded by Smith's impersonation of people of a variety of races and ethnic backgrounds. My focus, however, is on her process of embodying characters; the relevance of the piece for this discussion lies in Smith's coherent and explicit commentary on how the gestural actions of speech affected her. Smith's awareness of the difference between persona acting (which she describes as "self-oriented technique") and transformational acting is evident:

> A character from a play does not have a visible identity until the actor creates a body for that character. The self-oriented technique involves rendering characters who looked and acted like the actors. What are the subtleties in real-life behavior that could be used in the creation of

characters? There are linguistic as well as physical details that make a person unique.[3]

She also addresses the issue of the "essential self" as she describes attempting to teach students to imitate interviewees, and encountering resistance:

> They believed that they couldn't be someone else until they knew themselves. My argument was, and still is, that it doesn't have to be either/or, and that neither comes first. The discovery of human behavior can happen in motion. It can be a process of moving from the self to the other and the other to the self ... I knew that by using another person's language, it was possible to portray what was invisible about that individual.[4]

Smith's description has a lot in common with the principles that I've outlined of a reflexive relationship between self and character. Her comment on language, when seen in context, is about the gestural activity in speech patterns as well as the verbal content.

Smith's interest in the potential of speech to evoke somato-sensory sensations stems from her first experience of speaking Shakespeare: "In the first class we had to take any 14 lines of Shakespeare and say them over and over again to see what happened ... I knew nothing; it was my first acting class ever and I had some kind of a transcendental experience."[5] Smith expands on the description of this experience in her book *Talk to Me*:

> Everything happened. Not only did I feel as though I had become Queen Margaret, but I had what in the seventies we would have called a "transcendental experience," fully unaided by chemical substances of any kind. I, in fact "saw" Queen Margaret – she was a small vision, standing in my apartment. She came from the same place that the tooth fairy came from when I was a child. She came from my imagination. She was concocted somehow from the words. Words, it seemed to me, from then on were truly magical, not only by their meaning but by the way we say them, how we manipulate them.[6]

Similarly to Chekhov's experience when performing Skid, Smith finds her everyday perception altered through performance, and also has an experience of dual consciousness – sensing herself as Queen Margaret while also seeing a vision of the character. While the experience may sound mystical, my guess is that the breathing pattern necessitated by the multiple repetitions of the line, coupled with the rhythm of speech dictated by the verse linked with the linguistic content to stimulate the imagination. Neither in the book nor the interview does Smith attempt to explain *how* she thought this happened, although the experience forms a cornerstone of her practice thereafter. She takes a pragmatic, functional view of the phenomenon, as is revealed later in the interview when she describes working on Leonard Jeffries as a character for *Fires in The Mirror*:

> the point is simply to repeat it until I feel it and what I begin to feel is his song and that helps me to remember more about his body ... My body begins to do the things that he probably must do inside while he's speaking. I begin to feel that I'm becoming more like him.[7]

Smith is saying, that for her, direct physiological re-experiencing of the character occurs because of the repeated imitation of his speech patterns and vocal gestures; his "yawning, ... [his] way of lifting his soft palate."[8] By doing this, she feels she is able to "become the 'them' they present to the world."[9] Her experience supports the idea that behavioral communicators play a part in defining personality, and also calls to mind psychologist Paul Ekman's observation that the consciously chosen use of the vocal characteristics of an emotion can generate the experience of that emotion (I describe Ekman's work more fully in the next chapter).

Smith also talks about how her approach differs from the common understanding of Stanislavskian-based "psychological realism:"

> Psychological realism – this is a real over-simplification of Stanislavsky – saying: Here's Leonard Jeffries. You have to play Leonard Jeffries now. Let's look at Leonard. Let's look at his circumstances. Let's look at your circumstances. How are you two alike? How can you draw from your own experience? Contrary to that, I say, this is what

Leonard Jeffries said. Don't even write it down. Put on your headphones, repeat what he said. That's all. That's it.[10]

Smith's perspective, clearly, is tied to her own creative process of recording interviews, and doesn't concern itself with the more common challenge that faces the actor when approaching an existing script. Nevertheless, her experience and her stance tie in to the issues that are apparent in David McNeill's analysis of the difference between written and spoken language. It is significant that she says "Don't even write it down." In her personal process, she is experiencing the sensual impact of spoken language without going through the distancing of written analysis that she characterizes as Stanislavskian. At a phenomenal level, Smith is very aware of the difference between spoken and written language: "This project is at its heart about the act of speech, the physical action of dialogue, and was not intended for the printed word."[11] This awareness of a distinction between the two is surely involved in her choice to repeat several times during an interview that: "My grandfather said if you say a word often enough, it becomes you."[12]

Further comments by Smith echo Michael Chekhov's belief in identifying a difference between self and character:

What has to exist in order to try to allow the other to be is separation between the actor's self and the other ... I can learn to know who somebody is, not from what they tell me, but from *how* they tell me. This will make an impression on my body and eventually on my psyche. Not that I would understand it but I would feel it.[13]

Once again, Smith is drawing a distinction between language and speech, and stressing how the physical activity of speech integrates the character's personality and that of the actor. Her contrasting of "understand" and "feel" in the last sentence of the quote suggests that the difference is between an approach that prioritizes conscious mental analysis and one that works with somatosensory experience.

While Smith adamantly espouses imitation as the process by which she embodies a character, this has not prevented her from gaining work in popular naturalistic television dramas such as *The West Wing*, and *The Practice*, where, presumably, she has to work from a script. In a 2007 interview, entitled

"How do you get into character?" Smith does not reveal any change in the methods already described, but reaffirms her need, both as a playwright and as an actress to "feel" another person before her "imagination comes into play."[14]

The proprioceptive sense of self

The way in which Smith's process of imitation imaginatively generates a sense of character can be better understood by examining the role of proprioception in the sense of self. Philosopher Shaun Gallagher and psychologist Andrew Meltzoff investigate this aspect of proprioception in a paper that argues that it is more innate than previously thought. They state that all accounts of proprioception agree that "the organized and meaningful perception of self and others depends on a proprioceptive system of a developed body schema organized to allow for an intermodal translation between external and internal senses."[15] This description again challenges the "inside/outside" dichotomy of acting discourse, because the body schema depends on both internal (proprioceptive input) and external (visual and tactile) senses in combination.

Body image and body schema

Gallagher and Meltzoff take care to point out the difference between body image and body schema. The body image is the mental representation of the varying levels of *conscious* awareness of the body, and includes perceptual and conceptual understanding, along with emotional attitude. The body schema is:

> a system of motor functions that operates below the level of self-referential intentionality, although it can enter into and support intentional activity. It involves a set of tacit performances, preconscious subpersonal processes that play a dynamic role in governing posture and movement. In most instances, movement and the maintenance of posture are accomplished by the close to automatic performances of a body schema, and for this reason the normal adult subject neither needs nor has a constant body percept. To the extent that one does become aware of one's own body in terms of monitoring or directing perceptual attention to limb position, movement, or posture, then such an awareness helps to constitute the perceptual aspect of a body image.[16]

The definition of the body schema helps us further understand the distinction between persona acting and transformational acting.

As I mentioned earlier, I define persona acting as a style in which the actor projects a more or less consistent personality from role to role. In transformational acting, the actor uses a greater range of behavior to embody varying personalities according to role. It seems likely that the persona actor is working more closely with the unconscious body schema than the body image, which is more conscious, because he or she is not consciously attempting to alter physical behavior to express a character. In transformational acting, the actor is working consciously to control aspects of physicality, and this takes place in the realm of body image: "The body image, consisting of a complex set of mental representations of the body, involves a form of explicit and self-referential intentionality."[17] This activity can be linked to the "conscious competence" model of learning described in Chapter 2. Stages 2 (conscious incompetence) and 3 (conscious competence) describe conscious attempts to master a skill (expressing the imagined or perceived behavior of the character). When the actor reaches Stage 4 (unconscious competence), the skill has been assimilated to the extent that it has become part of the body schema. Of course, both aspects of proprioception are involved in all activities, so it is a question of emphasis and degree rather than exclusivity.

Whether an actor uses a persona or transformational approach, intentionality is at the core of the acting process. Studies of body image often distinguish three elements of intentionality:

(a) the subject's *perceptual* experience of his/her own body;
(b) the subject's *conceptual* understanding (including mythic and/or scientific knowledge) of the body in general; and
(c) the subject's *emotional* attitude toward his/her own body.[18]

When the actor consciously directs attention to postural or gestural actions, all three elements are involved, but at varying levels of conscious awareness. For example, when Smith sought to imitate Jeffries as described above, (a) is involved as she adjusts the movement of her soft palate to imitate "his way of lifting his soft palate." Smith's conceptual understanding of her body, (b), evidently includes the notion (among many others) that her body is different from the character's body and that, although female, she can successfully embody a male character. While her writing gives no explicit indication about her emotional attitude, (c), it is likely that she has a degree of comfort with her body, given her success in making it follow her conscious promptings, and her willingness to experience public scrutiny in performance.

There are distinctions between the process of the actor and the experience of daily life; (b) and (c) are not always at the level of conscious awareness in daily life, but are likely to be consciously considered by the actor at some stage of training. One of the goals of this book is to make theatre people more aware of what their conceptual understanding of the body is, and to include more scientific knowledge in that understanding. The conceptual understanding of the body will influence what one believes it to be capable of. Clearly, activities such as Lecoq's neutral mask work, by extending the range of behavioral expression, alter one's concept of what one's body can do. Even something as basic as the integrated posture can have an effect.

I received a vivid illustration of this during a movement course that I taught recently. In the early part of the course, I encouraged the students to heighten their awareness of non-verbal communication (nvc) by observing behavior as they moved around campus. One impassioned report came from a female student focused on the behavior of football players[19] whose demeanor on campus walkways forced other students to step off the sidewalks to avoid collisions. A few weeks later, after intensive work on the integrated posture, the same student, enthused by the sense of confidence that she had gained from her altered physicality, proposed to her classmates that they walk across the quad in a group, maintaining the integrated posture. They set off, still wearing their movement clothing and barefoot, and returned ten minutes later, whooping with laughter. Apparently two football players had stood aside to allow the group to pass.

Of course, increased self-confidence is not the only quality to be gained from work with posture, gesture, and movement. Embodying a variety of organic rhythms in the neutral mask, for example, will provide the actor with proprioceptive input that is significantly greater, and more differentiated, than the range that is encountered in daily life. Given that proprioception is linked to conceptual thought and emotional attitudes, it follows that *using postures and gestures that are different from those that we employ in everyday life is likely to create an altered sense of self.*

Exercise: transformation through imitation

Until the twentieth century, there were few formal training schools for acting. Actors learned through apprenticeship and imitation. This process is still in practice in styles such as Japanese Noh theatre, where precise choreography of gesture and movement is passed on from generation to generation, and in Commedia dell'arte, in which particular postures, gestures, and walks define both masked and unmasked characters. Following the advent of Method acting in the mid-twentieth century, the practice of imitation fell into disrepute as leading to psychologically "inauthentic" performances in realistic styles. However, Anna Deavere Smith's experience, and the cognitive evidence that supports it, shows that imitation is a useful tool in extending an actor's range in the creation of characters.

Step 1 Record a two-minute video of someone talking whose physical and vocal mannerisms are significantly different from your own. This is best taken from daily life, rather than a film or TV show.

Step 2 Refer back to Table 2.2 in Chapter 2 (p. 29) that describes the components of vocalics. Play back your recording multiple times, listening to the audio only. Listen for one vocalic component for three playbacks, (e.g. pitch, cadence, volume) speaking along with the recording and seeking to duplicate the original speaker's mannerisms.

Step 3 After you have imitated each of the vocal components in the chart separately, play the recording three times and integrate all the components simultaneously as you speak along with it.

Step 4 Refer back to Table 2.2 in Chapter 2 (p. 29) that describes the components of non-verbal communication (nvc). Play the video recording with the sound down multiple times. Observe one component of nvc for three playbacks (e.g. postural shifts, gestures, eye movements, facial expressions), imitating the movement as precisely as possible. Make sure to duplicate the physical circumstances (i.e. sitting, standing, or walking).

Step 5 Play the recording three times with the sound down, and imitate all of the nvc components simultaneously.

Step 6 Play the recording multiple times with both sound and image, imitating all the verbal and non-verbal components simultaneously. You will find that you have already learnt much of the speech and behavior. Continue until it is all memorized.

Step 7 Without playing the recording, communicate the content five times without interval between each iteration. Pause. How do you feel? What is your sense of yourself? Do you feel different aspects of will, confidence, emotion?

The emphasis that both Chekhov and Smith place on physical action in the creation of a character is validated by another study that shows that the proprioceptive system is more active in response to movement, and that this feature is linked to one's awareness of self through the agency of one's actions.[20] While Smith's actions come from observation of the interviewed subject, Chekhov's arise from the imagination, stimulated by a play text.

Both Chekhov and Smith acknowledge the difference between self and character, and in some senses are both imitating the character's gestures – Smith is using the perceptual stimuli gained from sight and hearing, while Chekhov responds to what is "seen" in the imagination. Both Smith and Chekhov explicitly differentiate their approaches from that of Stanislavski. Smith opposes an approach that focuses on similarities between character and self, and is also resistant to analysis in general. Chekhov challenged Stanislavski's conception of the relationship between self and character. Smith's experiences provide a vivid example of the physiological effect of imitation, but her approach of imitating interviewees has limited application to scripted drama. In this context, the narrative action is already determined, so the actor's choice is operating at the level of behavioral actions. Chekhov's approach demonstrates how actors can access these through the use of the imagination, but how is it that these can influence the actor's Feelings?

Empathy

The current understanding of the nature of empathy helps us to understand this imaginative response to written material. The everyday use of the word implies an emotional response of compassion or sympathy. Recent research, however, uses the term to describe a cognitive mechanism that is involved in unconsciously "mirroring" others' actions and emotions. This idea arises from both theoretical hypotheses and experimental approaches. Philosopher Robert Gordon was the first to propose that we simulate the mental states of others in order to understand their behavior, or to predict their decision-making. This proposition, known as simulation theory (ST), holds that if our brains are able to use their own processes to represent those of others, then it is not necessary to hold a mental store of knowledge about other people's behavior, a position known as "theory" theory (TT). Gordon's proposal would mean that one imaginatively places oneself in another's situation in order to understand them. However, in contrast to the activity typified by Stanislavski's "as if" question, Gordon's position allows for a continuum of adjustments that adapt to the other's situations. The default position would be one in which no adjustments are necessary, occurring at an unconscious level. Adjustments to take account of difference can be unconscious or conscious, and could include character traits, thus moving beyond the Advisory Projection of Stanislavski's approach.

Mirror neurons

As a theoretical model, ST has been strengthened by the discovery of mirror neurons (MNs). These are neurons that fire in the premotor cortex when one executes a goal-directed action, and also when one observes a similar action executed by someone else. MNs were originally discovered in macaque monkeys by a team of scientists including Vittorio Gallese who, with Alvin Goldman, built on this discovery to identify a mental mechanism in primates by which an observer mimics, resonates with, or re-creates the mental life of others based on direct observation of their movements. In a paper published in 2004, Gallese and others lay out the evidence that mirror neurons are also active in humans, both for action and emotions. They choose to call this process of internal replication "simulation," linking it with Gordon's theory but modifying the concept:

> the fundamental mechanism that allows us a direct experiential grasp of the mind of others is not conceptual reasoning but direct simulation of the observed events through the mirror mechanism. The novelty of our approach consists in providing for the first time a neurophysiological account of the experiential dimension of both action and emotion understanding.[21]

Obviously, we are able to reason about the actions and emotions of others at a conscious level when we choose to, but Gallese argues that mirror neuron system responses occur without any reflective mediation, without passing through the phase of conscious cognition. Thus, to a certain degree, we are actually experiencing the actions and emotions of others as we watch them.

Some everyday examples will help to illustrate the phenomenon in the case of actions: I notice that when I play tug-of-war with my dog, I clench my jaws and teeth tight, even though I'm holding whatever we're tugging with my hand. I notice that when watching a game of rugby on TV, I brace myself for impact as a player is about to be tackled. I also notice that I move my body to the side (a swerve) as a player attempts to evade a tackle. (This was brought sharply to my attention when running on a treadmill as I watched a game.) These responses are probably more marked in me as a former rugby player than if I had not played rugby; I have executed these patterns of movement repeatedly of my own volition in the past. An fMRI study of dancers from the styles of ballet and capoeira showed that they displayed more neuronal activity when watching dance in their own style than the other, and that both groups of dancers exhibited more neuronal activity than a control group of non-dancers.[22] *This suggests that the establishing of neuronal patterns through training and repetition plays a significant part in the activity of mirror systems, in that they are more likely to fire in response to observed action that is already patterned in the observer.*

Empathy and fiction

Clearly this discovery has significant implications for acting theory, but a significant step needs to be made between these effects in daily life, where individuals respond to other individuals, and the way actors might be employing these mechanisms in response to reading about, imagining, or improvising a fictional character. Might the same mechanism be involved in imaginative responses to a piece of writing? Gallese reports that it does:

> There is a part of your brain which is active when you do something, when you see someone else doing something, or when you are imagining either yourself doing something, or someone else doing something. The overlap is not perfect, so in other words, not all the same regions in your brain which are activated when you imagine doing something are activated when you imagine the same thing being done by someone else.[23]

Imaginative responses to fiction, then, *are to some extent the actual experience of what fictional characters do.* The degree of intensity will vary, presumably, from individual to individual, and probably from experience to experience within the same individual. Actors can increase their level of imaginative response to fiction by establishing a wide variety of neuronal patterning, as in the Lecoq exercises described in Chapter 3. This is further supported by a study that shows that the amount of neuronal activity involved in mirror systems is increased when one physically duplicates the activity that is observed.[24] This also confirms the value of Chekhov's work of imagining the character and duplicating the physical activity that one sees.

Another significant feature of the imagination's response to fiction is that it uses a very similar pathway in the brain to perceptual responses to external stimuli:

> There is no distinct anatomical region of the brain used for representing the merely imaginary; nor is there a distinct set of nerve fibers carrying information exclusively about the merely imaginary; nor does there seem to be a special affective, or, for that matter, motor region designated for receiving input about the merely imaginary.[25]

This information further destabilizes the "internal/external" dichotomy that exists in approaches to character. It also provokes an intriguing question: If imaginary stimuli use the same pathways as perceptual stimuli, why do we not carry out actions as a result of fiction? And what is it that inhibits physical action as a result of mirroring mechanisms? As my bruising encounter with the treadmill shows, the inhibition of motor activity in response to observed action is not complete. Schroeder and Matheson offer a possible answer to the first question: "actions are influenced more by belief than by mere representation in general, while feelings tend to be much more powerfully influenced by representation without regard to belief, regardless of whether the imagination is involved or not."[26] If this is true, our belief that what we are reading or improvising is a fiction will inhibit our actions, but not our feelings. On the other side of the footlights, this goes a significant way towards explaining why an audience can be moved by something an actor does, while knowing that it is a fiction.

These interlocking pieces of theory and experimental evidence show that an actor can successfully create a vivid embodiment of a character by using the imagination to stimulate an image of the character as a separate self, using physical actions to duplicate the imagined actions of the character, and by allowing Feelings to arise from these activities without questioning whether they are "authentic" expressions of the "essential self." For actors, then, it makes sense to train physically in the mechanics of behavioral expression to establish neuronal patterning that will facilitate these responses. For example, if one is a mild-mannered person, the neural patterns associated with the facial expression of anger might not be very well established. Daily practices of the configurations of the facial expressions associated with primary emotions would provide a wider range of neuronal patterns that will respond more effectively to imaginary stimuli. This gives the actor a wider range of experience to play from than if he or she is restricted to autobiographical experience.

Words and images

Much of the research that I've referred to deals with the differences between language and image, and how actors navigate from the printed words of a script to the embodied images of dramatic action. A further piece of information related to this topic leads the discussion back to Stanislavski. Psychologists Jonathan Schooler and Tonya Engstler-Schooler have conducted experiments at the University of Pittsburgh that show that verbal descriptions of visual stimuli impair one's ability to subsequently recognize what had been seen.[27] They have called this phenomenon "verbal overshadowing," because the verbalization of a visual memory overshadows, but does not eradicate, the original visual memory. Some experiments worked with memories of faces, but the principle also applies to other perceptual stimuli such as taste and hearing. The connection with Stanislavski arises because of his use of "table analysis" – a process where actors sit with the director at a table and verbally analyze the script, identifying motivations, objectives, and actions. Schooler's findings suggest that this process would inhibit unconscious imaginative responses to the fictional world of the script, since it replaces the perceptual stimuli that might arise in the imagination with word-based, largely conscious thinking. The process of table analysis will also influence subsequent rehearsal, since actors will mentally refer back to the verbal analysis of the script, rather than images or sensations it provokes. In the terminology that Schooler uses, this would be "recoding interference."

This hypothesis of what happens in verbal analysis of a script agrees with both McNeill's analysis of the difference between speech and gesture, and Merlin Donald's proposition that mimesis is an earlier evolutionary development than language. Mimesis is gestural, and gestures are processed as visual image in the brain. Images that arise through imaginative activity are more like perceptual stimuli than language. An approach that encourages the imaginative development of visual stimuli in response to a script will more readily provoke gestures and feelings in an actor than an approach that supplants imagery with verbal description. That is not to say that fine performances cannot arise from a process that includes table analysis;[28] it is a question of emphasis and sequencing. If the emphasis in a rehearsal is solely on conceptual ideas, the actor will have a significant jump to make when he or she gets to the gestural phase – embodying the character in action.

If, however, the investigation of the script's meaning includes gestural activity alongside conceptual analysis, the meld is more akin to what the actor does in performance, where meaning is communicated both by words and gestures.

Stanislavski seems to have come to an intuitive realization of these principles over the course of his life. As he developed his ideas, he turned from table analysis to "active analysis," a process that became the cornerstone of his later work, which he called the Method of Physical Actions. This phase of Stanislavski's work is much less well-known than his earlier approach; given the influence that his ideas have on actor training in the US, it is important that his later work, and the principles that explain its effectiveness, become better known.

The Method of Physical Actions

An understanding of Stanislavski's work is complicated by three factors; the development and change of his ideas over his lifetime; the history of translation and publication of his work; and the partial application of his principles by Lee Strasberg that became known and popularized as the Method. During the period that Chekhov was working with Stanislavski (1912–28), key features of his work included emotion memory, "inner" psychological drives, and, as Chekhov noted, the idea that character and actor should be the same. The approach that Stanislavski arrived at late in his life, and which is recorded in Vasili Toporkov's *Stanislavski in Rehearsal*, shows significant differences, which I will address later.

Stanislavski made several attempts to record his system, but only settled on the diary format in the late 1920s, beginning work in 1928 after a heart attack that prevented him from continuing to perform. What was intended to be one book, *An Actor's Work on Himself*, was eventually published in Russian in two parts in 1938 and 1953. The English publication of the first part as *An Actor Prepares* was in 1936, and of the second part as *Building a Character* in 1950. The first part of his book dealt with "internal" aspects, while the second focuses on physical and technical features of performance, although it remains unfinished because of Stanislavski's death in 1938. In the opinion of Jean Benedetti, who has translated the entire work and related fragments, the intended result is "a unified, coherent psycho-physical technique."[29] Benedetti acknowledges the way in which the splitting of the work has resulted in misunderstanding, and reports that Stanislavski feared that by printing just the first part, his system would be considered purely psychological, and a form of "ultranaturalism." Additionally, as we know from Sharon Carnicke's analysis in *Stanislavsky in Focus*, numerous distortions arose from confusions in the oral transmission of the system, and from Elizabeth Hapgood's translation.

Carnicke also addresses the way in which Stanislavski's system became distorted by Lee Strasberg as "the Method," describing how the founders of the Actors' Studio (Elia Kazan, Robert Lewis, and Stella Adler) favored the later version of the system, as described by Stella Adler following her sojourn in Paris with Stanislavski in 1934:

> When Adler spoke to the Group Theatre that summer about then unfamiliar aspects of the System, she split the group into camps and challenged Strasberg's sole authority. She specifically opposed his take on affective memory with new information on how the play's given circumstances shape character, the power of the actor's imagination and what would come to be known as the Method of Physical Actions.[30]

Strasberg reacted angrily to her description, and asserted the value of "his" method, and by 1951 had gained complete control of the Studio. Benedetti describes the difference between Stanislavski's system and the Method as follows:

> In the "system" the primary emphasis is on action, interaction and the dramatic situation, which result in feeling with Emotion Memory as a secondary, ancillary technique. In the Method, Emotion Memory is placed at the very centre; the actor consciously evokes personal feelings that correspond to the character, a technique which Stanislavski expressly rejected ... Strasberg's main concern was to enable the actor to unblock his emotions.[31]

This analysis is generally concordant with other accounts of Strasberg's emphasis, but Benedetti glosses over the question of how Stanislavski's ideas changed over time, and consequently may overemphasize the intended coherence of his system. As is clear from Chekhov's comments, in the 1920s Stanislavski believed in the character and the actor being the same. This advisory projection is confirmed by the passage about the "magic if" that I've quoted from the Benedetti-translated *An Actor's Work*. Another quote from a piece of Stanislavski's writing that preceded this work makes clear his belief that authenticity lies "inside" the actor: "Scenic action is the movement from the soul to the body, from the center to the periphery, from the internal to the external, from the thing an actor feels to its physical form."[32] So it is not only the splitting up of the original volume that led to the belief that Stanislavski's work focused only on the self of the actor, but also the change and development of his ideas over time.

Evidently, Strasberg resisted the changes in thinking that were reported by Adler. Despite the internal politics within the Studio, Strasberg's Method became associated with Kazan's success as a director, and the success of Studio-trained actors such as Brando – who, ironically, had been Adler's student. The fact that *An Actor Prepares* was the only available written information about Stanislavski's system until 1950 further assisted in the conflation of Stanislavski's system and the Method as an acting process that prized subjectivity and self-expression.

In addition to the historical accidents that led to this conflation, the growth in popularity of this concept of acting also reflected wider socio-cultural factors. Theatre historian Bruce McConachie investigates the way in which the concept of containment manifests itself as a social metaphor in a variety of ways during the Cold War period from 1947 to 1962. Of particular interest to this discussion is the way in which the container metaphor of self operates in the appeal of Method acting to the Cold War generation: "the model of self embedded in Method performance conformed to the contained, psychologized self of cold war culture." This self is seen as "an authentic inner essence trapped inside a repressive outer shell."[33] In this conceptualization, the boundary of the body creates a rigid distinction between the internal and the external; the interior authenticity can only partly be seen through the activities of the body, and any notion of a reflexive relationship between thought, feeling, and gestural activity is absent.

The way in which Stanislavski developed his work over his lifetime makes his ideas about character and process significantly different from Strasberg's Method. Stanislavski's Method of Physical Actions, described by Adler to the teachers of the Actors' Studio, and rejected by Strasberg, relates character to situation, emphasizes the actor's imagination, and discovers meaning in physical activity. This conceptualization is significantly different to the container metaphor of the body described above. Instead, the body integrates the fictional environment, the actor, and the character to communicate meaning to the audience. In the last production Stanislavski worked on, Molière's *Tartuffe*, he replaced "analysis of feelings" with "active analysis," after complaining that "after long discussions 'at the table' and individual visualizations, 'the actor comes on stage with a stuffed head and an empty heart, and can act nothing.'"[34] This experience could be seen as an example of verbal overshadowing, where verbal reasoning replaces the imaginative stimuli that follow perceptual pathways. To engage the actors in the fictional environment of the play, and to stimulate a shared imaginative response to the play, Stanislavski put the actors on their feet from the beginning of rehearsal, improvising the situations of different scenes, paraphrasing the dialogue, and discovering the spatial elements of Orgon's house, creating what Carnicke calls "collective fantasy."[35]

Case study: Vasili Toporkov

Vasili Toporkov's book *Stanislavski in Rehearsal* provides individual examples of how rehearsals were conducted at this stage of Stanislavski's life. Toporkov describes his own journey from joining the Moscow Art Theatre in 1927 to the production of *Tartuffe* on which Stanislavski was working when he died in 1938. Toporkov is frank about the challenges that he encountered in understanding Stanislavski's way of working, providing fascinating details about the rehearsal process, and his account is sensitively translated by Jean Benedetti. Toporkov recounts his first rehearsal in a play called *The Embezzlers*, in which he plays a cashier. Stanislavski watches his first attempt at a scene, and then questions him about the cashier's office. Toporkov has not given any thought to this, and Stanislavski proceeds to give a lengthy description of the imagined office that begins: "Here we have the cashier, Vanechka, a mild, modest young man. His office is his home. It is his holy of holies. It is the best thing in his life. Everything about it reveals the nature of his concerns ... "[36] The description continues to include details such as the cleanliness of the office, the well-oiled hinges of the safe, the cashier's pencil, how banknotes are arranged in the safe, and so on. It is intriguing to note how Stanislavski's elaborate word picture moves from physical details to the way in which they reflect aspects of the character's personality: "Vanechka can always tell how much is in there at any given moment. He loves the process of paying in and paying out. Issuing and checking money in the department is a holy ritual, a work of art for him."[37] The sense is that he uses perceptual stimuli to stimulate Toporkov's imagination, and then relates the physical environment to the values and traits of the character, by encouraging the actor to engage imaginatively with his fictional environment.

The process becomes more explicit when, in rehearsing another scene from *The Embezzlers*, Stanislavski instructs actors to focus on the physical circumstances of the fictional scene, repeatedly refusing actions that were illogical or contrived:

> Go on working, don't force anything, cautiously make your starting point the most simple, living, organic actions. Don't think about the character. *The character will emerge as a result of your performing truthful actions in the given circumstances.* You have just seen, in this example, how you can build a pathway by going from one small truth to another, testing yourself out, releasing your imagination and so achieve a vivid, expressive character.[38]

The injunction not to think about the character shows Stanislavski's intent to place the attention of the conscious mind on the fictional circumstances, and physical actions within those circumstances. The imagination is stimulated through perceptual information, and the character results from an unconscious combining of these elements. In Toporkov's report, Stanislavski frequently distinguishes between behavior, and "playacting," with behavior favored. Toporkov writes of his own response:

> At that time I still had not grasped the full significance of this type of work. I didn't know the meaning of Stanislavski's secret, that by truthfully performing physical actions and following the logic and sequence you can achieve the most complex feelings and experiences, those qualities which we had tried unsuccessfully to achieve in the first period of our work.[39]

This process creates an environmental fictional situation, provoking the development of character as a situational self through physical responses to the imagined circumstances.

While Stanislavski did not relinquish the concept of "internal" and "external" to describe the actor's relationship to character, the metaphors he uses towards the end of his life suggest an interlinked whole. He saw the three basic drives behind creativity – "mind," "will," and "feeling" – as being "inextricably linked to each other in a tightly bound 'knot' or 'bundle.'" This bundle is not experiencing a struggle between its internal essence and its external container, but rather is "'blended and interdependent!' like a 'harmonious' musical chord."[40] In Stanislavski's later practice, one can see a holism that is absent in a great deal of current acting training, and which achieves the development of character in a way that is sympathetic to what we now understand about the processes of imagination and empathic responses to fiction. There is no insistence on authenticity through the transposition of the essential "I" to the character, but a development of a "self" who behaves in a way that is credible within a set of fictional circumstances – a situational self. This process fits with the current convergence of opinion about self in daily life, summarized in this comment by psychologist Jerome Bruner:

> There is no such thing as an intuitively obvious and essential self to know, one that just sits there ready to be portrayed in words. Rather, we constantly construct and reconstruct our selves to meet the needs of the situations we encounter, and we do so with the guidance of our memories of the past and our hopes and fears for the future.[41]

In the rehearsal process that Toporkov describes, the character emerges from a similar process, and feelings arise without conscious bidding through a combination of physical actions and empathetic responses to a fiction that is embodied from early on in a rehearsal, and thus more likely to stimulate the imagination. This process is fundamentally the same as that described by both Michael Chekhov and Anna Deavere Smith. Although both these practitioners considered their work to be distinct from Stanislavski's approach, they are, in fact, engaged in the same cognitive processes that were emphasized in his Method of Physical Actions.

Case study: Daniel Day-Lewis

A more recent example of this process lies in the work of actor Daniel Day-Lewis, who is frequently cited as a "Method" actor, but whose approach derives from Stanislavski-based training at Bristol Old Vic theatre school. A certain mystique has built up around Day-Lewis for his practice of immersing himself in the physical circumstances of the roles that he plays, which frequently involves a degree of suffering.

Identifying with the role

My Left Foot (1989)

Playing the role of Christy Brown, an artist who suffered from cerebral palsy and was only able to control his left foot, Day-Lewis was wheeled around the film set in a wheelchair and spoon-fed by crewmembers. He taught himself to paint using a knife held between his toes, and damaged two ribs from remaining hunched in the chair for weeks of filming.

The Last of the Mohicans (1992)

Day-Lewis played Hawkeye, an adopted Mohican warrior fighting in the French and Indian War of the mid-eighteenth century. In preparation, he spent six months learning how to live off the land, camping, fishing, killing, and skinning animals. He carried a Kentucky rifle at all times during filming, and learnt how to load and fire it while running.

In the Name of the Father (1993)

For the role of Gerry Conlon, who was wrongly convicted of bombing a pub in Guildford, UK, in 1974, and jailed for 15 years, Day-Lewis lived on prison food, losing 30 pounds, and spent two days and nights in the jail cell on set, while crew duplicated the interrogation techniques that triggered the false confession.

The Crucible (1996)

In this filmed version of Arthur Miller's play about the 1692 Salem witch trials, Day-Lewis stayed in the film set's replica Massachusetts village, planting fields and building his own house with seventeenth-century tools, and living without electricity or running water.

The Boxer (1997)

Day-Lewis played a boxer just released from prison. For nearly three years, he trained in a gym twice a day, suffering a broken nose and a herniated disk in the process.

Gangs of New York (2002)

To portray the character of "Bill the Butcher," Day-Lewis apprenticed as a butcher, and hired circus performers to teach him how to throw knives. Having contracted pneumonia during the shooting of the film, he initially refused to have medical treatment as it was not true to the period.

There Will Be Blood (2007)

To build the character of oil-prospector Daniel Plainview, Day-Lewis started with the voice. Director Paul Thomas Anderson reportedly sent him recordings from the late nineteenth century to 1927, and a copy of the 1948 film *Treasure of the Sierra Madre*.

While some commentators consider Day-Lewis' practice excessive, there is a rationale behind it that is related to the stimulation of the imagination. He is reported, for instance, to have lived separately from his wife and children on the set of *The Ballad of Jack and Rose*: "I did ... but it was a token, symbolic separation which nevertheless to the imagination can have a powerful effect. I still saw my family every evening and spent the weekend with them but it would otherwise have been just too complicated for me to play the extremely conflicted life of Jack while in the presence of someone I was married to."[42] Another apparently extreme decision was involved in the filming of *In the Name of the Father*, in which Day-Lewis plays the real-life character of Gerry Conlon, a man convicted for a bombing that he did not commit. While on set, Day-Lewis spent two days and nights without food and water in a prison cell, a choice that he explained by saying

> You have to learn ... You need to understand what it is like to be interrogated by three two-man teams over a period of two days. If an innocent man signs a confession, which pisses away his life, it is part of your responsibility to touch on why a human being would do that.[43]

It is significant that in this and other choices, Day-Lewis *focuses on physical experiences to stimulate his imagination*. In the making of *The Last of The Mohicans*, his preparation included fitness training, and the outdoor activities that an eighteenth-century hunter-gatherer would need in order to survive. Some controversy arose over the fact that he kept his rifle with him at all times, even during breaks in filming, a behavior that some considered obsessive. Day-Lewis explains this, and other instances of maintaining character-specific activities, as being a response to the specific demands that film-making makes on the imagination:

> If you go to inordinate lengths to explore and discover and bring a world to life, it makes better sense to stay in that world rather than jump in and out of it, which I find exhausting and difficult. That way there isn't the sense of rupture every time the camera stops; every time you become aware of the cables and the anoraks and hear the sound of the walkie-talkies.[44]

Day-Lewis' choice to sustain a consistent set of behavioral actions for the duration of filming makes sense when we recall the way in which proprioception creates a different sense of self in response to behavioral actions: "I suppose it's like when painters talk about when they begin to make marks on a canvas and then 24 hours later they're still working and there's no sense of the ticking clock and no sense of the self. The self takes care of itself through the work, through the impulse."[45]

This choice also has a bearing on Day-Lewis' decision to work solely in films; he has not appeared on stage since 1989, when he walked off stage mid-performance in a production of *Hamlet* at England's National Theatre. At the time he attributed this to the shock of seeing the ghost of his own father as the ghost of Old Hamlet, an event that recalls Michael Chekhov's vision of Skid, and Anna Deavere Smith's vision of Queen Margaret. Since then, however, he has elaborated on the way in which he finds theatre rehearsals problematic in creating imaginative identification with the character:

> Theatre invites a nuts and bolts process to rehearsing in which all the actors are transparent to each other. For me, even if the truth I am looking for might be a specious one, I still need to believe in a kernel of truth. And I find it hard to do in a rehearsal situation where everyone is saying, "Are you going to do it like that?" It is distracting and deadly in the end to any discovery you might make.[46]

Actors who are asking "Are you going to do it like that?" are clearly not engaging in the "collective fantasy" that characterized Stanislavski's Method of Physical Actions, or supporting the creation of a physical and social environment that expresses the fictional circumstances.

A final quote from Day-Lewis demonstrates the value he places on the physical stimulation of the imagination: "When you don't know from experience, or you can't explore through the imagination, you better do some sort of practical work that is at least going to stimulate the imagination, because finally the whole thing is just an act of imagination."[47]

Conclusion

When viewed from the perspective of cognitive science, the examples of Chekhov, Smith, Toporkov, and Day-Lewis in different periods, styles, and media have a commonality that make descriptive categories such as "Method" or "physical" become redundant in talking about acting. This commonality is best described by saying that *an actor identifies with a character by developing a range of behavior that expresses his or her understanding of the character's intent, that is credible in the fictional circumstances, and that forms a temporary situational self through the imagination, with Feelings that arise through a proprioceptive combination of physical actions and empathetic stimuli in the fiction.*

Key points

- The duality of "persona" acting versus "transformational" acting is better understood in the context of a range of behavioral actions.
- Dramatic action is an expression of character, however, a distinction between narrative action and behavioral actions refines the concept of interpretation of a role.
- Through proprioception, consciously chosen behavioral actions can create character by altering an actor's sense of self.
- This phenomenon is exemplified by Anna Deavere Smith's creation of character through imitation.
- Proprioception incorporates both body image and body schema.
- Body image is the mental representation of varying levels of *conscious* awareness of the body, and includes perceptual and conceptual understanding, along with emotional attitude.
- Body schema are a system of motor functions that operate below the level of conscious intent; when conscious

awareness is used to monitor or direct movement or bodily position, this awareness becomes part of the body image.

- Using postures and gestures that are different from those that we employ in everyday life is likely to create an altered sense of self.
- The proprioceptive system is more active in response to movement, and this is linked to one's awareness of self through the agency of one's actions.
- Empathy as a cognitive term describes a mechanism that is involved in unconsciously "mirroring" others' actions and emotions.
- Simulation theory proposes that we simulate the mental states of others in order to understand their behavior.
- The establishing of neuronal patterns through training and repetition plays a significant part in the activity of mirror systems.
- Imaginative responses to fiction are to some extent the actual experience of what fictional characters do.
- A vivid embodiment of a character can be created by using the imagination to stimulate an image of the character as a separate self, using physical actions to duplicate the imagined actions of the character, and by allowing Feelings to arise from these activities.
- The phenomenon of verbal overshadowing arises when the verbalization of a visual memory overshadows, but does not eradicate, the original visual memory.
- Verbal overshadowing suggests that linguistic script analysis alone will not be as effective as analysis that incorporates movement and gesture.
- Stanislavski's journey from table analysis to the Method of Physical Actions demonstrates an intuitive recognition of the limitations of linguistic analysis.
- A cognitive description of identification between actor and character reveals a commonality that underlies different periods and styles.

Chapter 6

How does the actor embody emotion in fictional circumstances?

As with the other areas that I have covered, there have been significant advances in the understanding of emotion in the last 30 years. This has arisen through a shift of emphasis in scientific research from a psychological to a biological approach that has been facilitated by the ability to study the human brain in operation with technologies such as functional magnetic resonance imaging (fMRI), magnetoencephalography (MEG), and positron emission tomography (PET). Neuroscientists conceptualize brain functions as patterns of nerve cell activity; in fMRI, MEG, and PET studies, these patterns can be identified and traced. This process originated from work on the visual system, where objects in the environment have an effect on retinal receptive cells, with patterns of activation in the brain corresponding to external stimuli. The evidence from such studies, coupled with experimental research on animals, has allowed neuroscientists to offer empirically-based descriptions of emotional processes.

However, concepts of emotion in actor training are still largely derived from variations of Stanislavski's approach, which was inspired by his reading of the work of nineteenth-century psychologist Théodule Ribot. In this chapter, I'll look at Stanislavski's development of emotion memory, and the way his ideas about generating emotion changed over the course of his career. I'll then consider the implications this has for Lee Strasberg's insistence on emotion memory as the actor's central tool, and describe the current cognitive understanding of memory. This is followed by a summary of analyses of emotion by neuroscientists Antonio Damasio and Joseph LeDoux, and a description of psychologist Paul Ekman's discovery of the reflexive relationship between facial expression and specific emotions, along with his identification of the nine pathways to emotion. Further cognitive research demonstrates the way in which physical activity intensifies the imaginative stimulus of emotion, and is applied to an examination of Stanislavski's Method of Physical Actions. This is followed by a description of the different phases of Jerzy Grotowski's work, and how they can be understood in cognitive terms. The final part of the chapter looks at how cognitive information can be integrated into the studio, describing Susana Bloch's Alba emoting, and a sequence of exercises that I've developed that uses the voluntary control of eye movements to stimulate affective change in performers in improvisations and open scenes.

Stanislavski and emotion memory

Sharon Carnicke points out in *Stanislavsky in Focus* that Stanislavski's approach bore little relationship to Ribot's findings. The feature of Ribot's work that Stanislavski focused on was his research into the memory of emotions. Ribot distinguished between "concrete" and "abstract" memories. "Concrete" memories would be felt in the body in the same way as the original emotion, while an "abstract" recollection would be "intellectual." Although Ribot concluded that "[t]he emotional memory is nil in the majority of people,"[1] Stanislavski decided that actors could develop their ability to recall "affective memory" by becoming more attuned to the feelings of the senses: "Once you can grow pale or blush at the memory of something you have experienced, once you are frightened to think about something unhappy that you lived through long ago, you have a memory for *chuvstva* (feelings, senses) or a memory for emotion."[2]

Stanislavski seeks to explain the application of "affective memory" in *An Actor's Work*.[3] Ironically, his choice of example demonstrates the effectiveness of imagination more than that of memory. In an exercise designed to stimulate the "as if" phenomenon, Stanislavski's fictional alter-ego, Tortsov, asks his students to behave as if a violent madman were at the door. The actors improvise a scene where they blockade the door with furniture, hunt for potential weapons, and hide themselves. Tortsov is satisfied with the reality of their behavior. Some time later, he asks them to repeat the improvised scene, only to be disappointed with the lack of "internal" truth. As the narrator recounts: "Tortsov and Rakhmanov told us that while our earlier efforts had been direct, sincere, fresh and true, what we had done today was wrong, insincere and contrived … "[4] The distinction between the two outcomes is described by Tortsov as follows:

If, the first time, your actions were prompted by your feelings, your intuition, your everyday experience, today you followed a well-beaten track blindly, almost mechanically. You repeated the first, successful version, and didn't create a genuine, new life belonging solely to today.[5]

In response to questioning, Tortsov explains that this arose because the group "displayed an excellent memory for externals. But as for memory of feelings, that was not evident today." He goes on to explain that he has replaced Ribot's term "affective memory" with "emotion memory," and that recalling emotions is crucial to giving the scene life. Evidently, at this stage of Stanislavski's work, there is a pronounced emphasis on the idea of difference between "inside" and "outside;" the behavior in the second version of the event displays an "excellent memory for externals" but wasn't "genuine" because of the lack of "memory of feelings."

Stanislavski's belief that emotion in fictional circumstances needs to be accessed through memory is confirmed by a further quote from Carnicke's book:

"Actors can experience only their own emotions" Stanislavski explains. "They can understand, empathize, put themselves in their characters' shoes, and begin to act as the characters do. This creative action calls forth experiences analogous with the role ... You never lose yourself on stage. You always act in your own person as artist. There's no walking away from yourself."[6]

In a literal sense, it is true that an actor can only experience their own emotions; however the cognitive research on Empathy described in the previous chapter shows that one's own Emotion and Feelings can arise through the mirror neuron mechanism when observing another's Emotion, or when imaginatively responding to fiction. Similarly, Stanislavski's statement that "creative action" can only call forth "analogous experiences" from the actor's own life does not sit well with contemporary cognitive theory. As the previous chapter demonstrated, when we *imagine* an action, our brains operate in much the same way they do when we actually perceive or execute the action. Similarly, when we imagine actions that stimulate Emotion, the brain is using the same neural pathways that operate in the direct perception of those stimuli. Consequently, it is not necessary to pass through the step of discovering an analogous experience from one's own life to credibly enact an event. The true issue is how vivid the actor's imagination is.

This analysis explains the difference of approach between Stanislavski and Michael Chekhov that is apparent in the story described in Chapter 1, where Chekhov was expelled from the MAT studio for having an "overheated imagination." Stanislavski objected to Chekhov's process in enacting his father's funeral, because it was *imagined* rather than a lived experience. Over time, Stanislavski came to recognize that emotion cannot be controlled as easily as the body can, but that control of the body can bring forth emotion. As a result, his insistence on emotion memory as the resource for Feelings in the early and middle parts of his career gave way in the latter part of his life to his work with physical actions.

Lee Strasberg and emotion memory

Nevertheless, the use of emotion memory exercises in actor training in the US became widespread through the influence of Lee Strasberg, who took up this concept from Richard Boleslavsky and, as described in the last chapter, placed emotion memory at the center of the Method. This decision correlates with the emphasis on the biographical experience of the actor as the primary resource in creating a role. In Strasberg's conception of acting, the actor can only create "truth" in performance through the recall of lived experience:

> Affective memory is the basic material for reliving on the stage, and therefore for the creation of a real experience on the stage. What the actor repeats in performance after performance is not just the words and movements he practiced in rehearsal, but the memory of emotion. He reaches his emotion through the memory of thought and sensation.[7]

This formulation of what an actor does to successfully embody a character is notable for its lack of acknowledgement of imagination or craft, or of an awareness of the way physical activity can stimulate emotion. Strasberg's commentary on the subject of emotion is frequently contradictory. For example, in an interview published in 1964, Strasberg first of all states that affective memory "is the basic element of the actor's reality,"[8] but then that the "basic idea of affective memory is not emotional recall but that the actor's emotion on the stage should never be really real. It always should be only remembered emotion."[9] Clearly, Strasberg has some idea of differences between "reality" and the "really real," and between "emotional recall" and "remembered emotion," but what they are remains unclear.

Even those who advocate for the effectiveness of the process fail to provide any meaningful criteria about the distinction between "real" emotion and "remembered" emotion. Wendy Smith explains one related exercise as follows:

> The actor [does not] try to recall the feeling directly, but rather to re-experience the sensory impressions surrounding it ... Then the actor went over the exact sequence of events, concentrating on re-creating as precisely as possible the physical reality of the moment. When done properly with a strong situation, the exercise almost invariably brought the emotion flooding back to the present. The actor could then play the scene with the appropriate feeling.[10]

If, as Smith states, the exercise can bring the emotion "flooding back to the present," how can one distinguish this from a "real" emotion?

Further inconsistencies arise in David Krasner's attempt to defend the practice against the critiques of writers such as Robert Brustein, Richard Hornby, and Colin Counsell. Krasner states that

> the feelings evoked during an episode of affective memory may surprise the actor (you may laugh when you thought you would cry), and that is significant—the performer has created a true, original and spontaneous sense or feeling in response to scenic events.[11]

Again, the avoidance of acknowledging the role of imagination in the process leads to a conceptual inconsistency – the "spontaneous response" is to the memory, not to the fictional circumstances of the "scenic events." Since the exercise is intended to generate emotions appropriate to the fictional circumstances, unexpected responses would appear to be counterproductive to the intended result, although Method practitioners would prize them for their apparent spontaneity.

A cognitive understanding of memory

Strasberg's insistence on biographical experience as the source of "truth" in the actor requires a belief that it is memory alone that provokes the experience of emotion in that actor. His contradictory explanations of the process of affective memory are based on concepts of self, consciousness, and emotion that Lakoff and Johnson call "Folk Theories" – ideas of how we function that originate from the limited conscious awareness that we have of processes that are largely unconscious. The current understanding of the brain derived from neuroscience and experimental psychology points in a very different direction from the notions put forward by Strasberg. Patrick Colm Hogan, drawing on the work of experimental psychologist Daniel Schacter points out that memories

> are not like little videotapes stored in our heads. [...] our minds reconstruct remembered events in relation to current concerns, experiences, and so on. Thus my recollection of a past event may change significantly, depending on the situation in which I am asked about it ... The reconstruction of memories is affected by current emotional states as well ... Thus I remember a past event differently if I am now sad than if I am angry, fearful, or whatever.[12]

This suggests that Strasberg's activity of encouraging sense memory in order to stimulate emotional memory is *as much an imaginative exercise as it is one of recall.* As such, it is affected by the current circumstances in which the activity is undertaken. Hogan also explains that

> it seems that our memory storage is in fact very fragmentary and discontinuous. We have partial and isolated memories of past events ... [i]n fact "retrieving" a memory is a highly elaborate and constructive process. We access fragments from the relevant time period and link them together, often using broad schemas. In other words, we do not really remember the past, we reconstruct it – often in a way that reflects our present concerns as much as our past experience, sometimes in a way that does not reflect our past experience at all.[13]

This once again suggests that it is imagination as much as memory that is in operation in the emotion memory exercise. Smith's comment quoted above that it is more important for the actor to "re-experience the sensory impressions surrounding [the memory]" recalls the information in Chapters 4 and 5 about the way in which somatosensory experience (perceived or imagined) stimulates Feelings. This analysis is not intended to deny that emotion memory is effective – it has been and continues to be a useful tool for many actors – it is, however, intended to dismantle the notion that only autobiographical experience can produce "truth" in a performance.

Joseph LeDoux offers an interesting perspective on this issue in *Synaptic Self: How Our Brains Become Who We Are.* The book is an examination of the brain mechanisms that create personality and self, and LeDoux refers to a wide range of clinical research on the synaptic processes of features such as perception, memory, and emotion. In a section titled "Reliving the Emotional Past," LeDoux describes the way in which a part of the brain called the amygdala is involved in both the storage and retrieval of memories that have a strong emotional component. The information gives us a clearer understanding of what is happening when an actor tries to use "affective memory" to generate emotion. LeDoux points out that "Explicit memories established during emotional situations are often especially vivid and enduring ... "[14] which probably explains the initial attraction of "affective memory" for Stanislavski, Strasberg, and others. Experiments by psychologist Paul Ekman also describe the potential that the memory of an event has to generate emotion in the present. In his experiments, subjects responded emphatically in a physiological manner to the invitation to remember an emotion-inducing event:

> For example, to call forth sadness we asked people to remember a time in their life when someone to whom they were attached had died. We asked them to visualize a moment when they had felt the most intense sadness and then to try to experience again the emotion they had felt when the death first happened.[15]

Instruments measuring heart rate, respiration, blood pressure, perspiration, and skin temperature showed that "the changes that occur when emotions are remembered actually resemble the changes that occur when emotions begin by other means ... "[16] These physiological indicators show that memory does indeed stimulate emotion.

LeDoux also describes how this phenomenon arises at the neurological level when the emotion of fear is engaged:

> During emotional arousal, outputs of the central amygdala trigger the release of hormones from the adrenal gland that return to the brain. ... By way of its connections with the hippocampus and other regions of the explicit memory system, the amygdala then modulates (strengthens) the consolidation of explicit memories being formed during emotional arousal.[17]

So far, this description would seem to support the idea that memories of emotional events would be useful resources for the actor. However, LeDoux concurs with Schacter in saying that "memories are more easily retrieved when the emotional state at the time of memory formation matches the state at the time of retrieval."[18] This poses a problem for the actor engaged in an affective memory exercise, since the conditions of a workshop or rehearsal are unlikely in themselves to provoke an emotional state that matches that of the memory – and if they did, the affective memory exercise would be redundant.

LeDoux points out that "[t]he unreliability of remembered emotion ... may be related to the fact that the emotional state at the time of retrieval will by necessity be somewhat different from the state at the time of the original experience."[19] In common with LeDoux's analysis, Ekman points out that "[w]e may replay the emotions we felt in the original scene, or we may now feel a different emotion."[20]

A further complication in the use of emotional memory arises from the degree of emotional arousal that occurred in the formation of the memory: "[A]s long as the degree of emotional arousal is moderate during memory formation, memory is strengthened. But if the arousal is strong, especially if it is highly stressful, memory is often impaired."[21] So on two counts, current empirically based knowledge about the brain's activities qualifies the effectiveness of affective memory. As I will show later, *the use of memory is just one of several potential pathways for generating emotion.*

Strasberg's insistence on the centrality of emotion memory and on autobiographical experience also disregarded the changes in Stanislavski's thinking that were reported to him by Stella Adler and others. As Stanislavski moved towards developing the Method of Physical Actions, he grew increasingly impatient with actors who indulged in private emotions:

> What's false here? You're playing feelings, your own suffering, that's what's false. I need to see the event and how you react to the event, how you fight people – how you react, not suffer ... To take that line ... is to be passive and sentimental. See everything in terms of action![22]

Implicit in the exhortation is an endorsement of the idea of imaginative engagement with the fictional "event," something that Strasberg's emphasis on biographical "truth" disregards. Also implicit is the notion that the action that evolves from imaginative engagement can stimulate emotion, a concept that became the foundation of the Method of Physical Actions. As with other practitioners that I have mentioned, this phase of Stanislavski's work displays a certain prescience of the current understanding of the nature of emotion, imagination, and action, which of course, has advanced considerably since Stanislavski's time.

Antonio Damasio and the neuroscientific understanding of emotion

Antonio Damasio has been one of the most prominent researchers and articulators of a neuroscientific understanding of emotion, disseminated through numerous research papers and articles, and the best-selling books *Descartes' Error*, *The Feeling of What Happens*, and *Looking for Spinoza*. In *The Feeling of What Happens*, Damasio draws on his experience as a clinical neurologist to investigate the nature of consciousness and, in the process of doing so, considers the nature of emotions. This is important information for theatre practitioners who seek to better understand emotional processes that, in daily life, often seem to have no relationship to cause or conscious intent, and are not directly controlled by the will. Understanding how emotions occur is a useful foundation for developing an approach to stimulating emotion in performance.

Damasio's research shows that emotions are brain representations of body states. He suggests that while the senses of vision, hearing, touch, taste, and smell function by nerve activation patterns that correspond to the state of the external world, emotions are nerve activation patterns that correspond to the state of the internal world. These patterns have a biological basis and have evolved through evolution as bioregulatory devices that support survival:

> For neuroscience, emotions are more or less the complex reactions the body has to certain stimuli. When we are afraid of something, our hearts begin to race, our mouths become dry, our skin turns pale and our muscles contract. This emotional reaction occurs automatically and unconsciously. Feelings occur after we become aware in our brain of such physical changes; only then do we experience the feeling of fear.[23]

The stimuli that activate these patterns can occur in the external environment, or within the body; "Representations of either the exterior or the interior can occur underneath conscious survey and still induce emotional responses. Emotions can be induced in a non-conscious manner and thus appear to the conscious self as seemingly unmotivated."[24] Thus, while we might be consciously aware of an event (external or internal) that stimulates an emotional response, it is also possible that we can have an emotion without being aware of the cause. Emotions use the "internal milieu" – the interstitial tissue, fluid, and lymph in which cells are bathed – and visceral, vestibular, and musculoskeletal systems, which affect "a fairly restricted ensemble of subcortical regions, beginning at the level of the brain stem and moving up to the higher brain ... [t]he collection of these changes constitutes the substrate for the neural patterns which eventually become feelings of emotion."[25] As we know from our own experience, different emotions can entail varying levels of conscious awareness about their causes, and Damasio offers a further level of specificity by identifying three categories of emotion:

> The primary or universal emotions: happiness, sadness, fear, anger, surprise, or disgust ... secondary or social emotions, such as embarrassment, jealousy, guilt, or pride; and what I call background emotions, such as well-being or malaise, calm or tension.[26]

Each of these categories of emotions have a biological core, but vary in the degree to which they are influenced by culture. For instance, "several secondary emotions begin to appear later in human development, probably only after a concept of self begins to mature – shame and guilt are examples of this later development; newborns have no shame and no guilt but two year-olds do."[27] Background emotions are what would commonly be called "moods" in daily life – emotions that recur frequently or are sustained over significant periods of time. Damasio, however, distinguishes between the two in his terminology; "a particular background emotion can be sustained over time to create a mood."[28]

Duration is another helpful indicator of differences between emotions: certain primary emotions (fear, anger, surprise, and disgust) have a rapid onset, a peak of intensity, and rapid diminishment. Other emotions, such as sadness and all of the background emotions, have a more "wave-like" pattern of gradual onset and gradual diminishment. Identifying the temporal pattern of emotions allows actors to relate them to the temporal components of Laban's efforts, "sudden" or "sustained," and thus to integrate them into a vocabulary of action. For example, the gestural action of "punch" (sudden, direct, and heavy) is easily associated with anger, and can be used as a metaphorical action applied to speech.

Another intriguing feature of the distinctions between primary and background emotions is the source of the immediate inducer of an emotion. In the primary emotions, this is usually an event that takes place in the physical environment, or a representation of such an event. In background emotions it is frequently the result of mental conflict. Being aware of this distinction can help actors with understanding the emotional life of their characters. For example, Hamlet can legitimately be said to be melancholic at the beginning of the play as he broods over the death of his father and the rapid remarriage of his mother (mental, sustained, process) but when he encounters the ghost of his father (environmental event provoking sudden responses) his emotional state evidently changes, and he is propelled into action.

All three categories of emotion are expressed physically. Primary and social emotions are mostly expressed through differentiated, explicit facial expressions, and although background emotions initially target the internal milieu and viscera, they also have effects on the musculoskeletal systems which are evident to observers: "We detect background emotions by subtle details of body posture, speed and contour of movements, minimal changes in the amounts and speed of eye movements, and in the degree of contraction of facial muscles."[29] It is important to remember that Damasio demonstrates that the conscious experience (Feeling) of emotion (using the word in its everyday sense) is actually dependent on physical symptoms. The implications for the actor are that consciously controlled physiological actions, such as altering the rate and tempo of breathing, changing muscular tension, adjusting body posture, controlling eye movements, and facial expressions not only communicate emotion to the audience (through the activation of mirror neurons) but can also generate an emotional experience for the performer. These findings challenge the conceptual foundation of one of the perennial dualities in acting theory – does the actor have to feel an emotion in order to express it, or does he or she simply reproduce the physical signs of the emotion? It is clear from Damasio's research that it is not an either/or situation. Since *physiological indicators are the stimulators of Feeling in many emotions, the conscious reproduction of those symptoms can provoke the affective experience of emotion.*

Joseph LeDoux

Joseph LeDoux confirms Damasio's findings. In *The Emotional Brain: The Mysterious Underpinnings of Emotional Life*, LeDoux offers a clear account of the relationship between perception and emotion, and describes his belief

> that emotion and cognition are best thought of as separate but interacting mental functions mediated by separate but interacting brain systems … The perceptual representation of an object and the evaluation of the significance of an object are separately processed by the brain.[30]

However, in the cases of some emotions, conscious evaluation is preceded by an automatic response:

> The emotional meaning of a stimulus can begin to be appraised by the brain before the perceptual systems have fully processed the stimulus. It is, indeed, possible for your brain to know that something is good or bad before it knows exactly what it is.[31]

This explains the phenomenon that most of us have experienced of physically responding to a potential threat before consciously realizing that the stimulus is not a threat – a snake in the grass that turns out to be a stick, an intruder in the house who turns out to be an unexpected family member. Generally the lag time between the physical response and the conscious appraisal is minimal, a matter of microseconds. Obviously, not all stimuli of emotional responses are as dramatic as this, and this phenomenon is more apparent in the evolutionarily earlier emotions (fear, anger, surprise, disgust). But these examples demonstrate an important principle:

> The linkage of appraisal mechanisms with response control systems means that when the appraisal mechanism detects a significant event, the programming and often the execution of a set of appropriate responses will occur. The net result is that bodily sensations often accompany appraisals and when they do they are a part of the conscious experience of emotions. Because cognitive processing is not linked up with responses in this obligatory way, intense bodily sensations are less likely to occur in association with mere thoughts.[32]

So Strasberg's insistence on emotional memory as the actor's sole pathway to emotion is further discounted; thinking of a past event is less likely to produce the sensations that are identified as Feelings when they are consciously perceived. Given that many of these sensations occur in physiological mechanisms that are subject to conscious control as well as involuntary impulse, such as breathing and the level of muscular tension, it would seem to make sense for the actor to use these as pathways to emotion. The viability of such an approach has reliable empirical backing in the work of experimental psychologist Paul Ekman.

Facial expression and emotion

Ekman has shown that consciously chosen muscular actions affect emotional state. While researching the configuration of facial muscles used in expressions of emotion, Ekman and his assistant discovered that they began to experience the conscious effect of the emotion as they controlled the arrangements of their facial muscles to denote primary emotions such as fear, anger, and surprise. Following this experience, Ekman devised a set of experiments to see if the phenomenon could be reliably reproduced. In a paper published in 1990,

Ekman, Wallace Friesen, and Robert Levenson reported the findings of experiments conducted to determine "whether voluntarily produced emotional facial configurations are associated with different patterns of autonomic activity."[33] Subjects were invited to create facial expressions through muscle-by-muscle instruction and then were invited to report on their feelings as well as having their autonomic activities monitored. These included heart rate, skin conductance, finger temperature, and muscle activity. The facial expressions were ones that had previously been identified by Ekman and Friesen in their Facial Action Coding System in the late 1970s. These muscular configurations each represented a universal emotional facial expression based on cross-cultural studies of both the recognition and expression of emotion. The configurations indicated emotions of anger, fear, hatred, surprise, happiness, and sadness, but when the subjects were invited to produce particular muscular configurations, they were not told what emotion was being targeted. The experiments showed that the subjects did indeed experience the emotion associated with the facial expression as a result of simply organizing the muscles of the face in a certain way. More recent studies support Ekman's findings; one showed that neural mechanisms involved in the generation of emotion were stimulated by the perception of emotion,[34] another that both observation and imitation of the facial expressions of emotion activate many of the same areas in the brain.[35]

Although it is now 20 years since this paper was published, there is little evidence to suggest that its findings are being employed on a consistent basis in actor training programs. Lecoq's training program, which consistently places focus and attention on the body, does not specifically address facial expression or emotion. Popular acting texts, such as Robert Cohen's *Acting One*, Uta Hagen's *Respect for Acting*, and Robert Benedetti's *The Actor at Work*, do not offer any exercises for the recognition or generation of facial expressions. Most practitioners agree that the emotions cannot be consciously controlled. Muscular activity can, however, and so it would seem to make sense to incorporate Ekman's findings into actor training programs. The simple task of consciously arranging one's facial muscles in certain configurations would not only develop facility with facial expressions, but also offer a route towards the generation of the experience of emotions. The process is more time-effective and specific than the affective memory exercise, and can be linked with other controllable features such as breathing patterns and levels of muscular tension – activities that will be addressed later in this chapter. In the same way that repeated practicing of scales gives a pianist increased dexterity through confirming neuronal patterning, practicing the controllable physiological features of specific emotions would increase the actor's ability to express emotion in response to fictional circumstances, either through conscious choice, or through an involuntary response to an imaginative stimulus.

Primary emotions

Ekman, in common with Damasio and other psychologists, initially identified six primary emotions: happiness, sadness, fear, anger, surprise, and disgust (he has since added contempt). Over a long career, his research has shown that these emotions are identifiable in a variety of different cultures, concurring with Damasio's view that they are biological in origin and not culturally determined. Ekman's Facial Action Coding System identifies the different muscular configurations that are associated with each of these primary emotions (see the exercise below). This specificity of description allows the actor to practice the generation of emotion through voluntary muscular activity in each configuration.

Exercise: facial expression and primary emotions

For each of the emotions, arrange your facial muscles in the facial expression described below. Hold them this way for a minute (except for surprise); how do you feel? Notice if there are involuntary changes in breathing patterns, posture, heart rate, and muscular tension. In between each one, return to a neutral expression and breathe normally for at least a minute or until the affective state has dissipated.

Happiness (see Figure 6.1): The corners of the mouth are raised, the lips parted (sometimes showing one or both rows of teeth); the outer, upper areas of the cheeks move outwards and upwards; the eyelids narrow; and there are "crow's-feet" wrinkles at the corners of the eyes.

Sadness (see Figure 6.2): The corners of the mouth are turned down, sometimes with lateral stretching of the lips; the chin is slightly pushed up; the eyelids narrow, with the lower lid pushed upwards; the eyebrows are pulled together and downwards towards the center of the forehead.

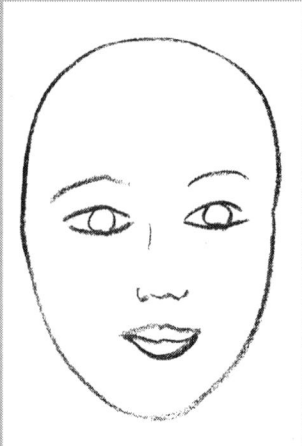

Figure 6.1 Facial muscles in configuration of Happiness

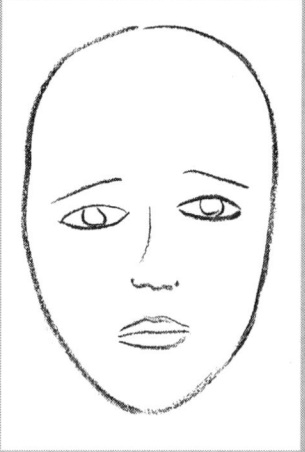

Figure 6.2 Facial muscles in configuration of Sadness

Fear (see Figure 6.3): The lips are parted and stretch laterally; the eyebrows are pulled together; the upper eyelids are raised; the lower eyelids tensed.

Anger (see Figure 6.4): The lips are pressed together and narrowed; the inner corners of the eyebrows go down towards the

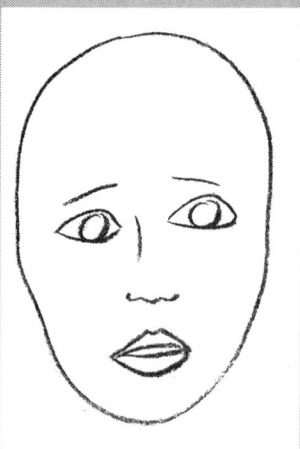

Figure 6.3 Facial muscles in configuration of Fear

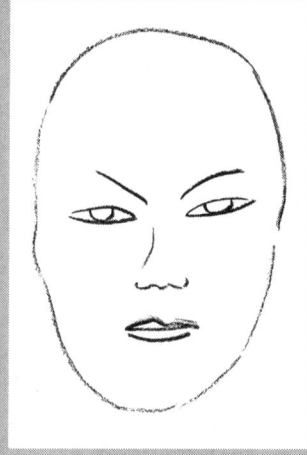

Figure 6.4 Facial muscles in configuration of Anger

nose; the eyes are open wide with the upper eyelids pushing against the lowered eyebrows; the chin is pushed forward. (In some cases the lips may be open, with teeth visible.)

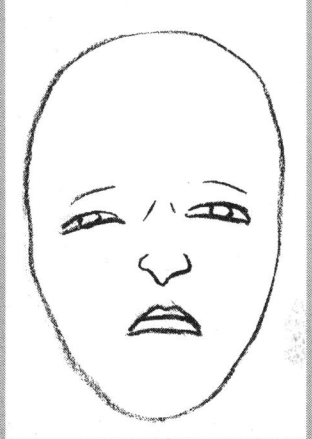

Figure 6.5 Facial muscles in configuration of Surprise

Figure 6.6 Facial muscles in configuration of Disgust

Surprise (see Figure 6.5): The mouth is open; jaw dropped; upper eyelids are raised as far as possible, eyebrows are raised. (This is best experienced in sudden, short, repeated iterations.)

Disgust (see Figure 6.6): The nostrils are raised, pulling the upper lip upwards to open the mouth slightly; the eyebrows are pulled down (sometimes creating a ripple shape); the lower eyelids are tensed; and the eye opening is narrowed.

In a number of experiments, Ekman has demonstrated that this activity produces the felt experience of emotion. For example, in working with the facial expression of enjoyment that communicates happiness, Ekman found a distinction in the brain activity that is provoked by related but different expressions. He proposes that spontaneous enjoyment is expressed by a smile activated by the *zygomatic major* muscle that extends from the cheekbones to the corner of the lips, and also by the contraction of the muscle that surrounds the eye, the *orbicularis oculi*. Part of this muscle is hard to contract voluntarily, and therefore its lack of contraction in an expression of enjoyment generally demonstrates that the subject is consciously attempting an expression of enjoyment, rather than involuntarily expressing enjoyment. These differences are visible in the patterns of brain activation provoked by the expressions. Smiling with both the eye muscle and the lips activated the left temporal and anterior regions, while smiling only with the lips did not.[36] One can test the phenomenal experience of the distinction by smiling with the lower part of the face only (raising the corners of the mouth), and then by smiling in a way that involves the upper part of the face (cheeks and eyes) as well as the mouth. The difference in affective experience of the two types of smile is often quite significant.

In addition to the primary emotions mentioned above, Ekman identifies a number of other distinct emotions, such as contempt, pride in achievement, embarrassment, and sensual pleasure. These correlate with Damasio's category of secondary or social emotions. Valuable information for the actor lies in a particular set of findings that suggest that many of these emotions can be thought of as groupings or "families" of emotions:

> [O]ur findings suggest that all of the positive emotions (amusement, sensory pleasure, pride, etc.) share a single expression, a particular type of smile ... An observer distinguishes which of these positive emotions is evident, not so much from the expression itself (although the timing and intensity of the expression may provide clues), as from the context, from knowledge of what emotion is likely in a given situation for a given person.[37]

Similarly, there is an "unhappiness" group of emotions – disappointment, sadness over loss, remorse, shame, and guilt – that share an expression, which Ekman describes as one in which "the corners of the eyebrows are raised, the cheeks slightly raised, and the lip corners are pulled downward."[38]

This level of empirically derived specificity about the facial expression of emotion gives the actor the ability to confidently research emotion and its expression in training, so that the activities of expressing emotion in performance can be fluid and responsive to the imagination. It makes sense for actors to develop facility in voluntarily creating the facial expressions of each of the six primary emotions. Given that many of the wider range of secondary emotions share, or are similar to, the facial expressions of the primary expressions, the ability to create the primary expressions would also extend to a communication of secondary emotions, especially when combined with the eye activities described in the "Five S's" exercise.

"Real" emotion

In addition to the potential for practical application that this information has for actors, cognitive science presents a significant challenge to the concept of "real" emotion that is used with such frequency by Strasberg and other practitioners. The research of Ekman and others shows that the brain activation patterns of emotions can be provoked in a number of ways, not just by memory. Most of us would consider a spontaneous response to a real-life event as the most "real" experience of emotion, but neuroscientific research shows that emotion that is stimulated by memory, imagination, or by the conscious control of physiological processes uses *the same neural pathways to create activation patterns*, but with less intense results. This suggests that, rather than attempt to define what is "real" or not "real" in the experience and expression of emotion, it is a more useful approach for actors to consider the origin and pathway of an emotion-inducing event. By doing this, and experimenting with different activities, they will be able to identify which pathway, or combination of pathways, works best for them in creating the expression of emotion.

That actors should focus on the expression of emotion, and not on the idea of creating "real" emotion is supported by a comment of Antonio Damasio. He confirms that "we cannot control emotions willfully"[39] and, as mentioned earlier, that we are often unconscious of what events or images have provoked an emotional state. Aspects of the emotional process that we can control include whether an emotion-inducing image remains the target of our thoughts once noticed, and also, to some extent, the expression of our emotions:

> We can also control, in part, the expression of some emotions – suppress our anger, mask our sadness – but most of us are not very good at it and that is one reason why we pay a lot to see good actors who are skilled at controlling the expression of their emotions ... [40]

What is especially significant here is that Damasio talks about actors controlling expression, rather than experiencing "real" emotion.

Nine pathways to emotion

Another feature of Paul Ekman's research identifies which aspects of emotional expression are controllable, and therefore of interest to the actor seeking to generate emotion in performance. Ekman identifies nine pathways that generate emotion.[41] The first, and most common, is through *automatic appraisal*, an unconscious scanning of the environment for events that are relevant to our survival. Our identification of what these events are is developed through a combination of biology, evolutionary natural selection, and individual experience. This process continues through life, with new stimuli that seem relevant to what we care about added to an unconscious database.

The next pathway is *reflective appraisal*. This "deals with ambiguous situations, situations to which the automatic appraising mechanisms are not already tuned."[42] At the point where the reflective appraisal results in the recognition of an emotion-inducing event, the automatic appraisal mechanism takes over to generate feelings. Ekman then identifies *remembering* an emotion-inducing event as a pathway to generating emotion, followed by *imagining* an emotional event, *talking* about past emotional experiences, and *empathy* – the provocation of one's own emotions by witnessing someone else's emotion. This occurs in real-life situations, but also in response to fictional representations, using the mechanisms described in the previous chapter.

The seventh pathway that Ekman identifies is *being told what to be emotional about*, and this tends to occur in early life in response to a caregiver or significant person. *Violation of social norms* is the eighth pathway – the emotions that we might feel in response to different violations will vary, of course, in type and intensity according to our individual opinions about the norm being violated. Ekman's final pathway derives from his experience of creating facial expressions – *voluntarily assuming the appearance of emotion*. While Ekman focuses on the facial expressions of the primary emotions, Damasio's work shows that breathing patterns, eye movement, and musculoskeletal activity are also involved in the expression of emotions.

Of these nine pathways, three would seem to be of especial practical use to the actor in the intentional generating of emotion – memory, imagination, and voluntarily assuming the physiological signs of emotion. The topic of memory has been addressed earlier in this chapter, and imagination in the previous chapter, although it is probably valuable to reiterate that when an emotion is stimulated by imagination, it follows the same neuronal pathways as one that is stimulated by an event in lived experience. As Shaun Nichols points out in his introduction to *The Architecture of the Imagination: New Essays on Pretence, Possibility and Fiction*: "research suggests that the affective response to imagining a scenario closely tracks the affective response that would occur if the subject came to believe that the scenario was real."[43] The neural scaffolding of this phenomenon is described by Vittorio Gallese:

The data reviewed here show that in the anterior insula, visual information concerning the emotions of others is directly mapped onto the same viscero-motor neural structures that determine the experience of that emotion in the observer. *This direct mapping can occur even when the emotion of others can only be imagined.*[44]

This phenomenon seems to be true for the six basic emotions, and recent research indicates that it is also true for social emotions. In a recent fMRI experiment, a group of Italian neuroscientists conducted a study to "investigate whether the same neural mechanism is activated both when experiencing and attending complex, cognitively-generated, emotions."[45] The emotion that they focused on was regret and their results showed that

observing the regretful outcomes of someone else's choices activates the same regions that are activated during a first-person experience of regret, i.e. the ventromedial prefrontal cortex, anterior cingulate cortex and hippocampus. These results extend the possible role of a mirror-like mechanism beyond basic emotions.[46]

Linking the two sets of findings suggests that a mirror-like mechanism for the activation of emotion through imagination is in operation for *both* primary and social emotions.

The ways in which actors are involved in imaginative responses to the fictional world of a drama are varied: a response to reading a script; an intentional act of the imagination such as Chekhov's visualization exercises; an imaginative engagement in an improvisation. In all these processes, however, the material about the cognitive aspects of emotion that I have surveyed here strongly suggests that *physical activity intensifies and particularizes the way in which the imagination can stimulate emotion.*

The Method of Physical Actions and emotion

As described in the previous chapter, Stanislavski's Method of Physical Actions sought to provide the actor with a physical pathway into the fictional world. Jean Benedetti, his biographer, describes the aim of the Method of Physical Actions as follows:

What Stanislavski wanted to provide was a method for actors to explore the play, the events as they unfold, in terms of what they would do in the various situations the author provided, using exercises and improvisations. It is active analysis on the rehearsal-room floor, as opposed to the reflective, formal analysis that takes place in the study; it first asks what happens, rather than what the dramaturgical structure is.[47]

Vasili Toporkov, reflecting on his work after Stanislavski's death, wrote:

> Stanislavski drew our attention to what is most tangible, most concrete in any human action: its physical aspect. In his directing and teaching, especially in his final years, he laid the greatest significance on this aspect of the life of a role when organizing the beginning of the work. Splitting off the physical aspect of human behavior from its other elements is, of course, artificial, but he used it as a teaching strategy. By diverting actors' attention away from feelings and the psychological, and directing them towards the fulfillment of "purely physical" actions, he helped them gain access to their feelings in an organic, natural manner as they performed them.[48]

As described in the previous chapter, Stanislavski worked with his actors through close and detailed stimulation of the imagination through constant insistence on features of the fictional environment and their physical behavior in response to it. The "organic" nature of the results that Toporkov describes seem to arise through the stimulation of emotion by a combination of imaginative engagement and physical behavior – the "symptoms" of Emotion that provoke Feeling.

Jerzy Grotowski

In many ways, Polish director and teacher Jerzy Grotowski can be seen as a successor to Stanislavski in his physically-based approach to training and directing. His work is widely characterized as "experimental," but the rigor of his approach, and its close connection to Stanislavski's Method of Physical Actions is less widely acknowledged. Grotowski's philosophy of "Poor Theatre" proposed that theatre should not attempt to compete with film in creating a visual spectacle, but should instead focus on the essence of the theatrical event, the creation of fiction that is jointly imagined by actor and audience. In order to do this, an actor should be capable of physical, vocal, and emotional action that far exceeds the expression of daily life.

Grotowski's work can be described in five phases.[49] The first starts in 1959, when he was invited by theatre critic and dramaturg Ludwik

Flaszen to become the director of the Theatre of the 13 Rows in Opole, Poland. Grotowski later called this phase the "Theatre of Productions," as it was the only period in which he created productions for public performance. The theatre was renamed the Theatre Laboratory, and research focused on classical texts by Romantic Polish authors such as Mickiewicz, Slowacki, and Wyspianski, whose works had a close to mythic role in Polish culture. Successful productions at Opole included Jean Cocteau's *Orpheus*, *Dziady* (*Forefathers' Eve*) by Mickiewicz, and Wyspianski's *Akropolis*. Many see the latter production as the first full realization of Grotowski's vision of the "Poor Theatre." The cast, playing concentration camp prisoners, acted out stories from Greek mythology and the Bible while they built a crematorium around the audience. This had particular resonance for the Opole audience, as the town was close to the Auschwitz concentration camp. This is also the production that stimulated international recognition of Grotowski's work, as scholars and theatre professionals promoted his work in their respective countries. In 1964, he moved his company to Wroclaw, where it was renamed the Institute for Research into Acting, partly to avoid the communist regime's heavy censorship of theatre performances. The success of *Akropolis* (1962) was followed by *The Constant Prince* (1965), and *Apocalypsis cum Figuris* (1968). Each of these productions was restaged several times and performed internationally, generating great interest in the idea of a "Poor Theatre." *Akropolis* was performed at the Edinburgh Festival in 1968, the same year that a book about Grotowski's approach (*Towards a Poor Theatre*) was first published. The following year, all three productions were presented to great acclaim in New York City.

In the first phase of his work, Grotowski stated that:

> In our opinion, the conditions essential to the art of acting are the following and should be made the object of a methodical investigation:
>
> A   To stimulate a process of self-revelation, going back as far as the subconscious, yet canalizing this stimulus in order to obtain the required reaction.
> B   To be able to articulate this process, discipline it and convert it into signs. In concrete terms, this means to construct a score whose notes are tiny elements of contact, reactions to the stimuli of the outside world: what we call "give and take."
> C   To eliminate from the creative process the resistance and obstacles caused by one's own organism, both physical and psychic (the two forming a whole).[50]

It is interesting to note that, while he is not entirely free of "inner/outer" terminology, Grotowski does not use it to describe the self of the actor, even though he addresses concepts such as the subconscious and communication. Instead, he identifies components of a process that connects the subconscious to the environment ("the outside world") through an organism that is a "whole."

The second phase of his work eliminated all but the two essential features of theatre, actor and audience, but in a way that sought to dissolve the boundary between them. In the work that became known as "Paratheatre," people were invited to participate in workshops and events. Actors did not work towards a performance, but became facilitators of activities that were designed to dissolve the everyday mask of the social selves. This was described as:

> the search for and try-out in practice of the conditions in which a man acting in unison with others could act sincerely and with his whole self, thus liberating the potential of his personality and realizing his creative needs; the searching for and practical exploration of what we would call the Paratheatrical fact.[51]

During the early 1970s, Paratheatre activities in Wroclaw attracted a growing number of people, culminating in the summer of 1974 with the "University of Research" in which more than 4,000 people participated, including Peter Brook, Jean-Louis Barrault, Joseph Chaikin, and Andre Gregory. Thematically, the process continued the idea that had been developed in the Theatre Laboratory of stripping away barriers of communication, but this time those of non-actors. Later in life, Grotowski acknowledged that he thought this avenue was of limited value, since in unstructured events such as these people simply reproduced cultural clichés.

In the late 1970s, Grotowski traveled widely, visiting India, Mexico, and Haiti among other countries, seeking ritual activities that could have an effect on a participant no matter what their culture or belief system. This research, known as the Theatre of Sources, linked anthropology and theatre, and led in to the next phase of his work, called "Objective Drama," which began in 1983. Grotowski had emigrated to the United States following the declaration of martial law in Poland, and was invited to institute a program at the University of California, Irvine. He led this work himself for three years, and thereafter the project continued until 1992, conducted primarily by people that Grotowski had trained. The continuation from the previous phase lay in the desire to employ ritual techniques in the training of performers:

> Objective Drama is concerned with those elements of ancient rituals of various world cultures which have a precise and therefore objective impact on participants, quite apart from solely theological or symbolic significance. Mr. Grotowski's intention is to isolate and study such elements of performative movements, dances, songs, incantations, structures of language, rhythms and uses of space. Those elements are sought by means of a distillation process from the complex through the simple and through the separation of elements one from the other.[52]

The term "Objective" seems to refer to a psychophysical effect, and the description overall to a desire to identify the constituent elements of performance. Although this identification is to be achieved through distillation and separation, the ultimate goal is holistic, a type of performance in which "poetry is not separated from the song, the song is not separated from the movement, the movement is not separated from the dance, the dance is not separated from the acting."[53]

The fifth phase, "Art as Vehicle," began in 1986, when Grotowski founded his Workcenter in Pontedera, Italy. Following his death in 1999, the work continues, led by Thomas Richards and Mario Biagini. The name of this phase seems to have been adopted from Peter Brook's assessment of what Grotowski's work means: "It seems to me that Grotowski is showing us something which existed in the past but has been forgotten over the centuries. That is that one of the vehicles which allows man to have access to another level of perception is to be found in the art of performance."[54] The training incorporates the "plastiques" and "corporels" of earlier phases with work on ritual practices, especially songs that can have a physiological effect on performer and listener through patterns of sonic vibrations. Grotowski's own description of the work is grounded in an awareness of the body and explicitly uses the physical frame of the body and its relation to the physical environment as a metaphor:

> When I speak of [...] Art as vehicle, I refer to verticality. [...] With verticality the point is not to renounce part of our nature – all should remain in its natural place: the body, the heart, the head, something that is "under our feet" and something that is "over the head." All like a vertical line, and this verticality should be

held taut between organicity and the awareness. Awareness
means the consciousness which is not linked to language (the
machine for thinking), but to Presence.[55]

Again, there are connections between Grotowski's thinking and the
cognitive research that I've described. When the experiencing consciousness attends to perception of the environment, it is not working
linguistically, but sensorily. This connects with Merlin Donald's
description of mimesis as an earlier cognitive development than language; proprioceptive and perceptual awareness of the environment
means that the experiencing consciousness is operating imagistically
and gesturally. Grotowski frequently stressed the necessity of the
actor being in relation to others and his or her environment, physical
or imagined:

> Again and again Grotowski turned our attention to the spaces
> around us, until finally we began to perceive that the world that
> we inhabit is not actually empty at all. It is filled with the imagery
> that we project into it, and therefore **everything an actor does is
> not so much an act of *doing* as it is a *response* to a real or an
> imaginary partner.**[56]

This sense of environmental relationship is a persistent theme in
Grotowski's practice. In working with actors in the Objective Drama
program, he insisted that technical movement sequences be invested
with precise associations to a person or object in the space, or to
mental images or memories. Lisa Wolford, who trained in this program, explains how this helps actors to avoid the workings of what
she calls the "discursive" mind:

> I have found that the temptation to follow the discursive voice
> becomes stronger when interacting with a memory or imaginary
> stimulus – there is always the possibility of allowing the conscious
> mind to manipulate the image/memory, playing it back as one
> would play a film, or elaborating it with the deliberation of an author
> writing a fictional scenario. The purpose of the work with memories
> and images was not to play them out in that way, as a type of
> internal projection, but rather to arrive to a state in which one
> does not anticipate or prescribe what details will emerge.[57]

The work with physical exercises (originally derived from yoga) was
designed not only to encourage actors to encounter their physical

limitations and challenge them, but also to develop the ability to allow spontaneity within structure. This prepares actors to develop a score of physical actions in a performance – the structure – and to find subtle nuances of meaning within that structure in response to impulses, other people, events. The idea of the physical score is often misunderstood to equate with "blocking," the pre-planned choreography of stage movement. Grotowski points out that there is a significant difference between "movement" and "action":

> If I am walking toward the door it is not an action but a movement. But if I am walking toward the door to contest "your stupid questions" to threaten you that I will break up the conference, there will be a cycle of little actions and not just a movement. The cycle of little actions will be related to my contact with you, my way of perceiving your reactions; when walking toward the door, I will still keep some "controlling look" toward you (or I will listen) to know if my threat is working. So it will not be walk as movement, but something much more complex around the fact of walking. The mistake of many directors and actors is to fix the movement instead of the whole cycle of little actions (actions, reactions, points of contact) which appears in the situation of the movement.[58]

One of the values of the information that I've presented about nvc and cognitive processes is that it gives us an understanding of, and a vocabulary for, these "little actions." This is certainly a different vocabulary than the one that Grotowski used, but there is a commonality of concept that physical action has meaning. For Grotowski this happens not through movement alone, but through the effect that movement has on the actor by making him or her more aware of subtle impulses and being simultaneously able to express them:

> If the actor reproduces an act that I have taught him, this is a sort of "dressage." The result is a banal action from a methodical point of view, and in my heart of hearts I find it sterile, for nothing has opened up before me. But if, in close collaboration, we reach the point where the actor, released from his daily resistances, profoundly reveals himself through a gesture, then I consider that, from a methodical point of view the work has been effective.[59]

The notion of revealing the self, of course, depends on the subject – self metaphor system described earlier, with the "daily resistances" being the self of the "social mask" that Grotowski sought to dissolve in his Paratheatre phase. However, the statement is interesting for the use of the word "gesture" as the means by which authenticity is revealed. Grotowski sees authenticity as something physical, rather than psychological. Despite the variety of the different phases of his work, this theme is apparent throughout, and originates with his experience of training as an actor in Stanislavski technique.

The lineage from Stanislavski's Method of Physical Actions to Grotowski's work with actors is indicated by the fact that Vasili Toporkov's book *Stanislavski in Rehearsal* was a required text in the Objective Drama program, where many of the people who now teach his techniques were trained. Long-time collaborator Thomas Richards, who is now the director of the Workcenter in Pontedera quotes Grotowski in his book *At Work with Grotowski on Physical Actions*:

> When I was a student in the school of dramatic arts, in the faculty for actors, I founded the entire basis of my theatrical knowledge on the principles of Stanislavski. As an actor, I was possessed by Stanislavski. I was a fanatic. I retained that it was the key that opens all the doors of creativity. I worked a lot to arrive to know all possible about that which he said or what was said about him.[60]

Richards goes on to describe his own experience in a workshop with Ryszard Cieslak, the actor who Grotowski felt best embodied his approach. In an exercise where Cieslak was working with a student to discover the way that he touched his (visualized) girlfriend's face, Richards observes Cieslak continually direct the student to focus on the physical details: "Don't act. What was the touch of her skin like? At what moment precisely do you touch your girlfriend's face? Is her face warm or cold? How does she react to your touch? How do you react to her reaction?"[61] The process echoes Toporkov's descriptions of Stanislavski's work, and Richards recognizes this as his "first insight into Stanislavski's 'method of physical actions.'" The focus on physical activity as a way to stimulate the imagination is validated by the cognitive perspective described in previous chapters, in which proprioception, memory, and imagination combine to connect the actor to fictional circumstances.

Richards also describes a moment in the workshop when Cieslak asked if anyone could cry like a child:

> A girl lay down on the floor and tried. He said "No, not like that," and taking her place on the floor, transformed himself into

a crying child before our eyes. Only now after many years, do I understand the key to Cieslak's success in the transformation. He found the exact physicality of the child, its alive physical process which supported his child-like scream. He did not look for the child's emotional state, rather with his body he remembered the child's physical actions.[62]

Richards' explanation of this phenomenon resonates with a statement of Grotowski's:

> It is thought that the memory is something independent from the rest of the body ... In truth, at least for actors – it's something different. The body does not *have* memory, it *is* memory. What you must do is unblock the *body-memory*."[63]

Once again, the intuitively derived statement concurs with current thinking about body schema, body image, and the proprioceptive sense of self.

This concentration on physical activity is also emphasized by Stephen Wangh, who, like Richards, studied with Grotowski, and now trains actors at the Experimental Theatre Wing of New York University (NYU). Wangh describes how, when he first encountered Grotowski at a workshop at NYU, he thought that "his approach was baffling, for he seemed to work differently with every actor in the group."[64] Wangh details the work that Grotowski did with a pair of actors on a scene from *Antony and Cleopatra*, indicating his amazement at the attention to physical detail:

> he led Tom through a long exploration of two sides of himself, *le petit* Tom and *le grand* Tom, an exploration that depended on Tom's control of his facial muscles! The requisite emotions, Grotowski explained, would arrive on their own if Tom would just pay attention to physical details. "Emotions come; they happen to us; they are not voluntary." ... Making a technical, physical choice, Grotowski insisted, could produce emotional truth.[65]

Grotowski displays an intuitive understanding of the way in which Feelings can arise from voluntary control of muscular activity. Familiarity with the findings of Damasio and Ekman explain how this occurs; to actors in the 1960s habituated to the Method, the process must have been startling. The statement recalls Toporkov's description of Stanislavski's insistence on precise physical action, and Grotowski's definition of the "cycle of little actions" quoted earlier. Like Chekhov, the metaphors that Grotowski uses in describing the actor's process, while not entirely free of the "internal/external" dichotomy, display a notion of the being of the actor as a permeable one: "Performer must develop not an organism-mass, an organism of muscles, athletic, but an organism-channel through which the energies circulate, the energies transform, the subtle is touched ... "[66]

Integrating cognitive research with studio technique

The final part of this chapter investigates ways in which little actions and subtle impulses – as Grotowski called them – can be approached using cognitive information. In the context of this discussion on emotion, much of the information in previous chapters has relevance because of the holistic nature of an actor's process. The postural and gestural elements of nvc are related to emotion through proprioception; the relationship of thought, speech, and gesture participate in how we define Feelings; the relationship of self to character is intimately bound up with body schema and body image, which in their turn engage in the experience of affective state. The performer who is familiar with this information has the knowledge to both stimulate Feelings and communicate Emotion to an onlooker. The following examples demonstrate two ways in which this information can be put into use in the studio.

Alba emoting

Susana Bloch is an experimental psychologist whose experiments on the effector patterns of emotions led her to propose a psychophysiological process to teach "acting behavior."[67] Her earliest experiments were conducted in the 1970s and therefore preceded the majority of cognitive research referenced here, but have a congruity with Ekman's findings on the reflexive relationship between facial expression and emotion, and with Damasio's explanation of the way in which the subjective experience (feeling) of emotion arises from physiological symptoms.

Bloch defines the effector pattern of an emotion as "a particular configuration of neurovegetative, hormonal and neuromuscular reactions"[68] from which she extracts those elements that can be consciously controlled; breathing, muscular tension and activity, and facial expression. She proposes that

> each basic emotion can be evoked by a particular configuration
> composed of: (1) a breathing pattern, characterized by amplitude

and frequency modulation; (2) a muscular activation characterized by a set of contracting and/or relaxing groups of muscles, defined in a particular posture; (3) a facial expression or mimicry characterized by the activation of different facial muscle patterns.[69]

The subjects of her experiments were a group of actors who had recently completed their training at the Theatre School of the Universidad de Chile and who, prior to the tests, were trained in techniques of controlling aspects of behavior such as tension in different muscle groups, respiratory rate, facial expression, and physical and vocal inhibition. Once this training was complete, subjects were asked to voluntarily adopt the breathing patterns, muscular configurations, and facial expressions of emotions without being told which emotion was being targeted. Electrocardiogram (ECG), pneumogram, and electromyogram (EMG) recordings were used to identify physiological changes and for comparison against control recordings of what Bloch calls "natural" emotions.

The scope of Bloch's work in these experiments was ambitious, and several aspects of her approach would probably be considered questionable by other experimental psychologists; for example, the control recordings of "naturally" occurring emotions were derived from subjects under hypnosis, and there is no description in her article of how the effector patterns were originally defined. There is no clear single hypothesis that is being tested, and the measurement of the degree of success of the training is unclear. There is mention of self-reporting from the subjects, and also of a test where a group of directors were asked to rate two performances of a scene, one prepared using a Stanislavskian approach, the other using a "melody" of effector patterns. Additionally, Bloch's definition of the six "basic" emotions is different from the current consensus; she substitutes "tenderness" and "eroticism" for surprise and disgust in the group described earlier. While these are undoubtedly useful for the actor, there is a lack of procedural rigor in making these substitutions without explanation or justification.

Given these, and other methodological issues, the standards of proof in these experiments do not come anywhere near the other cognitive data that I have described. Consequently, it seems best to consider Bloch's work as theatrical practice that is informed by a scientific perspective, rather than as empirically derived data. Viewed in this light, there is much that is of use to theatre practitioners, and Bloch's motivating impulse is certainly in accord with the central argument of this book:

What in our opinion is lacking in the curricula of most drama schools are instrumental techniques for learning how to express emotion. While the Gnostic-verbal (literary) and the body-expressive (physical) aspects of acting behavior are quite well covered pedagogically, the emotional expressive (psychophysio-logical) aspects are almost entirely left to the intuition, life experience or "emotional memory" of the student actor, with little or no technical support.[70]

The idea that technical training in communicative behavior is desirable is certainly something that I agree with, but as the information in the preceding chapters has indicated, the potential scope of such training is far greater than emotion alone.

Bloch designed a training system (now known as "Alba emoting") that instructs actors in the physiological expressions of emotion. Many of the aspects of this system resonate with the work of other practitioners that I have described. For example, the spatial expressions of different emotions are charted on "approach/avoidance" parameters, and postural expression in terms of muscular "tension/relaxation," both of which can be understood in the context of Laban efforts and Lecoq's work. Bloch contends that the configurations that she describes are more effective in triggering subjective emotional state than the use of Ekman's findings on facial expression. This assertion rests on the fact that these configurations incorporate breathing patterns and postural activity in addition to facial expression. Given the consensus of opinion among current research about the way that emotions create feelings, this would seem to be true, but the comparison with Ekman's work points up a major flaw in Bloch's approach that is apparent in the description of the configurations.

This flaw lies in Bloch's conflating of different levels of emotion into one pattern. For example, the configuration of behavior that she associates with happiness is described as follows:

Happiness–laughter. The breathing is characterized by a deep and abrupt inspiratory movement followed by a series of short saccadic expirations which may even invade the expiratory pause. The posture is relaxed; the distribution of the phasic muscular tonus is quite particular, with a tendency to diminish in the extensor muscles, especially in the antigravitational groups. As a consequence, during laughter, the subjects tend to sit or even fall. The mouth is open, and the contraction of the *musculus caninus* and *m.zygomaticus* results in the exposure of the upper teeth. The eyelids are relaxed, and the eyes are semi-closed.[71]

As we know from our own experience in daily life and in performance situations, the emotion of happiness can exist at lower levels of intensity than those that provoke laughter. By proposing the behavior of laughter as the expressive configuration of happiness, Bloch ignores the concept of progression and scale in behavior. It would obviously be inappropriate for an actor to laugh on every occasion that a character feels happiness – at some moments the facial expression alone would suffice.

Similar inconsistencies exist in the other configurations, and arise both from conflating different levels of intensity (for example, sadness does not always entail crying), and from combining primary and background emotions (fear and anxiety are generally considered to be distinct from one another). Bloch also makes a distinction between "real" emotion and that provoked by her configurations. As described earlier, this distinction does not have much significance in affective experience since the neurological pathways of emotion seem to be the same no matter what the origin of the inducing event is. The significant distinction that arises from different types of inducing event seems to be that of varying intensity levels.

Despite these inconsistencies, Bloch's work offers valuable pointers about the ways in which the conscious control of behavior to communicate emotion can be integrated into actor training. A particularly useful feature is the "step out" technique, in which subjects assume a neutral posture and facial expression and adjust their breathing to reduce the affective experience of the emotion that they have been working on. This offers actors who may feel apprehensive about experiencing emotion reassurance that the effects are temporary and within their control. It also facilitates rapid transitions from one emotion to another, something that is often required within performances, and which might be delayed if an actor were to await the organic diminishment of subjective feeling. Bloch observes that "by the systematic repetition (initiation and interruption) of the effector pattern, the subject may retain the expressive components of the emotion with very little of the subjective involvement."[72]

A description of the co-existence of Alba emoting with Method acting is offered by Pamela Chabora, an actor who has attained a "level 3" certification in Bloch's licensing system of the technique. Her article in *Method Acting Reconsidered* is largely descriptive – first of her work with Lee Strasberg and his assistants, and secondly of Bloch's approach. Chabora uses both emotion memory and Alba emoting in her work, but sees the two approaches as significantly different, and does not identify any links between them. Indeed, there is an implicit favorable comparison in some of her remarks:

> Alba Emoting provides an additional tool, a physiological and organic one, for creating genuine feeling onstage. Knowing how to express a specific emotion and which emotion it is brings actors one step closer to ideal self-use with an informed response to expressive use. Actors have a firmer grasp on the outcome of a role instead of having to depend on the director's guidance and/or the caprice of their feelings.[73]

The passage suggests that Strasberg's technique does not provide this level of specificity or control. Chabora also points out that sustaining emotion over extended periods is more easily achieved by using the Alba configurations:

> The role demanded that I portray high-pitched emotions for the entire day ... Had I relied solely on my Method training (ie., emotional memory and personalization), I probably would have collapsed halfway through the day. However, because I was able to utilize Alba Emoting patterns for fear, anger and sadness, I was able to sustain genuine emotional commitment for the duration of the performance and suffer no emotional hangover.[74]

Chabora also considers the Alba technique useful in her teaching, enabling her to offer accessible and achievable methods of inducing emotion to student actors.

Eye movements, thought, and feelings

The final practical activity that I will describe involves the movement of the eyes and their role in expressing thought and feelings. Eye movements are provoked both by perception of the environment, and by cognitive processes unrelated to the physical environment. As you may have experienced if you tried the "eye movements and imagination" exercise in Chapter 2, the conscious choice of the muscular activity can create affective states and provoke thought. The way in which this happens is described in part by the findings of an fMRI study conducted by a group of neurobiologists that were published in 1998.[75] These experiments investigated the relationship between eye movements and attention. This has long been a contentious topic, since eyes move in response to objects of attention in the physical environment, but it is also possible to pay attention to something that is at the periphery of one's visual field. This behavioral information suggests that different parts of the brain are used in the two activities, while other data suggested that the two activities are linked in the brain. The study conducted by Corbetta and his colleagues showed that visual attention and eye movement systems share the same areas of the brain and probably use similar neural mechanisms, indicating that common processes are involved in moving the eyes and shifting attention. This means that *voluntary control of eye movements can affect thought.*

This information links with the study that I mentioned in Chapter 2, in which psychologist Daniel Richardson and his colleagues refer to a number of experiments that demonstrate that we create a form of spatial indexing of information, whether that information is present in the physical environment or not: "Eye movement data thus reveal a powerful demonstration of how language about things not co-present is interfaced with perceptual-motor systems that treat the linguistic referents as if they were co-present."[76] Once again, this shows how neurological activity about imagined objects and events follows the same pathways as activity that occurs in response to perceived objects and events. For the actor, this information confirms the usefulness of the common practice when speaking monologues of "placing" imagined people and events in the physical environment. Several recent studies have also linked eye movement to emotion and used eye movement monitoring as a way of detecting emotional reactions.[77] Given that eye movements are linked to so many mental processes, including memories, expectations, and goals, the ability to make voluntary choices about them gives the actor an invaluable tool, both in defining expression and in proprioceptively generating thoughts and emotions.

Prior to learning about this information, I had recognized that many of my students made unconscious eye movements that contradicted what they wanted to communicate, and also that eye movements were significant communicators in interpersonal status interactions. Exercises that isolate these movements of the eyes give students a vocabulary for movements that are generally conducted unconsciously in daily life. Like other activities of the body such as breathing and muscular tension, they are also subject to conscious control. For the actor, awareness and control of the eye's movements are an invaluable part of the psychophysical process, since they are not only expressive features but also provide neurological feedback, assisting the intentional evocation of affective state. A progression of non-verbal exercises demonstrates how this phenomenon can be

extended into dramatic interplay. These exercises are ones that I have
developed and taught over the last 15 years in a variety of training
courses in England and America. In common with most of the other
exercises that I have mentioned, they were first developed without
knowledge of the cognitive research that I have described, and in
response to a practical training need. As I have learned more about
eye movements through studying the work of cognitive researchers,
I have adapted and refined the exercises. Their inclusion here will, I
hope, demonstrate how it is possible to integrate studio techniques
with scientific knowledge to provide effective training in the specifics
of psychophysical behavior.

Exercise: eye movements and ensemble improvisation

Step 1 Actors are introduced to these activities in a session in
which groups execute the different movements in response to
verbal guidance, while others observe, so that each person has
the experience of making the controlled movements, and also
seeing them in action. Each group conducts the sequence
described in Chapter 2. As a quick reminder, the activities are:

1 "Search." In this movement, the eyes move constantly, not
  resting on any one location any longer than another.
2 "Select." In this movement, the eyes come to a rest on one
  particular point.
3 "Shift." This involves moving the eyes directly from one
  selected point to another, without any intervening searching.
4 "Sustain." Here, the eyes sustain their focus on one point.
5 "Shut," in which the eyelids close briefly. The duration can
  range from a blink to a few seconds.

This stage identifies the terms, and allows the actors to correlate
the terms to the activities through experience and through
observation. For a group who is new to this work, it is useful
for the exercise leader to explain that these are all activities that
we carry out unconsciously in daily life, and that by becoming
aware of them, actors can gain greater control over their non-
verbal expression and give greater definition to their acting. For
this preliminary step, participants should concentrate on
moving the eyes only. They will notice that it is instinctive to
move the head to increase the range of vision. The exercise

leader should ask them to resist this impulse for the moment, so as to place attention on the eyes alone, explaining that subsequent stages of the exercise will incorporate the movement of the head. This part of the progression is designed to achieve clarity in definition of the activities and to focus the participants' attention on individual affective experience.

Discussion after the exercise can lead to the simple observation that movement of the eyes indicates mental activity as well as responding to external stimuli. For the onlooker, determining which of the two is in operation generally depends on correlating the eye movements to the physical environment. If there is no visible reason for the eye movements, the onlooker assumes that thought is prompting the movement, or that the individual being observed is deranged in some way. Thus a pattern of "search," "select," "shift," if not related to events in the subject's physical environment, can suggest the searching of thoughts, a decision, and then a change of mind. "Sustain" tends to suggest focused mental attention, and "shut" can suggest several things, depending on the duration of the closing of the eyelids. If this is slightly longer than a blink, it can suggest a pause for thought, or disagreement. Held a bit longer, it can suggest the thought "I can't believe my eyes," or intensify the expression of an emotion.

Step 2 In the second stage of the sequence of exercises, improvisations demonstrate the application of the eye movements in relationship to other people and space. In the first part of this stage, the exercise leader invites pairs of students to have an improvised "eye conversation" with one another, experimenting with turn-taking, proposition, and response. This is best conducted by all the pairs simultaneously, so that no one gets self-conscious by being observed. This can be done seated or standing, and the students are encouraged to allow expression of other physiological processes that are stimulated by the interaction – breath, gesture, posture – but not language. This step introduces the effects of social interaction, and alerts the students to the potential for communication through eye movement, the development of dramatic relationships, and the affective states that can arise. For example, A might "sustain" on B's eyes, while B "shifts" rapidly between A's gaze and his own hands. A clearly defined status relationship is quickly established, and the movements are likely to provoke thoughts of uncertainty or doubt in B, with feelings of guilt or embarrassment. After approximately five minutes of play, the exercise leader can invite reflective comments and discussion of the experience of this activity.

Step 3 This phase demonstrates how consciously chosen eye movements can stimulate the imagination to provide a fictional context for the activity. Players are invited to move in the space in response to the impulses generated by consciously chosen eye activities. As an example, the exercise leader can structure an initial guided improvisation as follows:

Two actors (A and B) enter the space "searching," allowing their physical activity to be prompted by the eye movements. A third actor (C) enters shortly after, "shifting" from A to B. A and B "select" C, and then "sustain" on him or her. C continues to "shift" from A to B. At this point, the exercise leader asks the actors to stop and recount what they have experienced. Frequently, all involved describe a narrative of looking for an item, and then suspecting C of having taken it. Observers usually report the same scenario. Those who "sustained" often reported that they thought that they were accusatory, with a low intensity level of anger, while the "shifter" frequently mentioned a sense of being accused and feeling intimidated, suggesting a low intensity level of fear. Simple physical choices have created an interpersonal narrative dynamic that provokes the imaginations of the players and observers alike, often with accompanying emotions.

This stage of the sequence of exercises is purposely conducted without language so as to heighten the students' awareness of the communicative potential of eye movements and nvc in general, and also to assist them in identifying their subjective affective states without distraction. The example described above is just one of many potential activities and scenarios. Improvisations can also be used to demonstrate aspects of interpersonal status, and to demonstrate the relationship between mental focus, visual focus, and dramatic focus.

Step 4 This stage moves on to incorporating language. As in the previous phase, players are invited to engage in improvisations that are prompted by consciously chosen eye activities, but to add speech as and when their imaginations prompt them. Participants often discover that language "takes over" once speech has been introduced, and that it's difficult to return their attention to originating action through eye movements. This isn't a failure; the goal of the exercise overall is to explore and discover these elements of communication and their relationships to one another.

Step 5 To make the transition from improvisation into working with scripts, pairs of actors memorize a short "open" scene (a scene without identifiable given circumstances in which dialogue can be interpreted in a variety of ways).

They then choose voluntary eye movements as they speak the lines of the script to one another. At this point, the choices should be improvisational, without any conscious rationale. As with the previous non-verbal improvisations, imagined contexts and motivations are generated by the eye movements, and in response to the actions of the scene partner. Frequently, a voluntary choice of eye movement will provoke other physiological symptoms, such as changes in posture, gesture, facial expression, and level of muscular tension, alongside affecting vocal rhythm, inflexions, and timbre. All of these stimulate the imagination through the proprioceptive system. Improvising the choices with dialogue multiple times can generate an interpretation of the open dialogue, which can later be complemented with conscious decisions about tasks and actions, and then rehearsed. By initially rooting the dramatic choices in non-linguistic actions, the potential inhibition of verbal overshadowing is decreased.

The developmental progression of these activities is intended to demonstrate the potential of consciously chosen eye movements to communicate meaning, provoke Feelings, and stimulate the imagination. This process can also be followed with work on scripted scenes, complementing the work of identifying tasks/problems and choosing actions. Clearly, the self-reported changes in affective state that I have described do not have the status of scientifically derived information about emotional process. However, given the empirically identified relationship between physiological symptoms of emotion and subjective Feeling, it is not unreasonable to suppose that consciously chosen eye movements, like consciously chosen facial expressions, can stimulate affective states through proprioception.

Conclusion

Practitioners from a variety of backgrounds have arrived at ways of using physicality to stimulate emotion. This underlines the biological foundation of the process that has now been identified. The cognitive research and the practices that I have described show that the emotion memory technique is only one of several pathways that can generate emotion. The actor can also use imagination, and the control of respiratory patterns, muscular tension, facial expressions, and eye movements to evoke specific affective states. These are no more or less "real" than Feelings that are stimulated through the recall of an emotional memory. The examples of the practical activities that I've described demonstrate how it is possible to integrate these activities into training, rehearsal, and performance in ways that stimulate and strengthen the actor's imaginative engagement with fictional circumstances. There is some indication that over time, habituation with the conscious control of the physiological symptoms can lead to their embodiment without the subjective affective experience for the actor. However, if the expressive components are well judged, they stand a good chance of evoking Emotion symptoms in audience members through mirror mechanisms, whether or not the actor experiences Feelings.

Key points

- Stanislavski's early use of "emotion memory" arose from readings of nineteenth-century psychologist Théodule Ribot.
- Stanislavski de-emphasized this practice towards the end of his career, in favor of physical action.
- The insistence on emotion memory by Lee Strasberg as the central feature of Method acting neglected the development and change in Stanislavski's practices.
- The idea that memory is the only path to emotion is contradicted by current scientific knowledge.
- Memory is as much an imaginative process as it is one of recall.
- Neuroscientist Antonio Damasio defines Emotions as physiological reactions to certain stimuli; Feelings arise when we become consciously aware of these physiological changes.
- Damasio identifies three different categories of emotion: primary, secondary (socially conditioned), and background emotions.
- There is a general consensus among psychologists that there are six primary emotions: happiness, sadness, fear, anger, surprise, and disgust (some psychologists have added contempt).
- Examples of secondary, or social, emotions include embarrassment, jealousy, guilt, and pride.

- Examples of background emotions include well-being or malaise, calm or tension, anxiety or confidence.
- Since physiological indicators are the stimulators of Feeling in many emotions, the voluntary creation of those symptoms can provoke the affective experience of emotion.
- Emotion that is stimulated by memory, imagination, or by the conscious control of physiological processes uses the same neural pathways as that stimulated by events in the physical environment to create activation patterns.
- Rather than attempting to define "real" emotion, it is more useful for actors to consider the origin and pathway of an emotion-inducing event.
- The nine pathways to emotion identified by Paul Ekman are: automatic appraisal; reflective appraisal; remembering an emotion-inducing event; imagining an emotional event; talking about past emotional experiences; empathy; being told what to be emotional about; violation of social norms; voluntarily assuming the appearance of emotion.
- Physical activity intensifies and particularizes the way in which the imagination can stimulate emotion.
- Stanislavski's Method of Physical Actions stimulates emotions by a combination of imaginative engagement and physical behavior.
- Jerzy Grotowski continued and developed the physical approach Stanislavski had created.
- The five phases of Grotowski's work are known as: Theatre of Productions; Paratheatre; Theatre of Sources; Objective Drama; Art as Vehicle.
- A central feature of Grotowski's approach is that the actor must always work in response to a real or imaginary partner.
- Grotowski makes an emphatic distinction between movement and intentional physical action.
- Grotowski asserted that emotion is generated through physical actions.
- Experimental psychologist Susana Bloch developed a process known as Alba emoting in the 1970s based on the effector patterns of different emotions.
- Some, but not all, of Bloch's assertions about emotion accord with current cognitive research.
- Bloch proposes that voluntary control of breathing, muscular tension and activity, and facial expression can generate emotion.

- Eye movements are provoked both by perception of the environment, and by cognitive processes unrelated to the physical environment.
- The voluntary control of eye movements can affect thought and participate in generating emotion.
- Neurological activity involved in eye movements show how language about imagined events interfaces with perceptual-motor systems that treat them as if they were physically present.
- The "Five S's" mnemonic gives actors a vocabulary of eye movement to use in training and performance.

Conclusion

The material that I have presented offers empirically derived descriptions of cognitive activities involved in key aspects of the actor's process: non-verbal communication; the relationship between thought, speech, and gesture; self and character; empathy; imagination; and emotion. In all of these areas, cognitive science shows that dualistic concepts of process are inaccurate. Approaches to acting that are based on those dualistic concepts reduce the potential of the actor rather than expanding it, and narrow the possible scope of expression and meaning in performance. An approach that acknowledges the holistic and interrelated nature of physical, mental, and emotional activities supports the actor in integrating all the cognitive and expressive features of the body.

In this conclusion, rather than summarizing the preceding material, I want to point out potential ways forward in using this information. The first section describes the work of three contemporary directors from a cognitive perspective, using concepts and terms from earlier chapters. The second section outlines some ways in which cognitive principles can inform actor training.

Cognitive principles in action

Much of the content of the book so far has focused on the individual practice of actors. This section focuses on three contemporary directors whose practice displays a resonance with cognitive principles. Katie Mitchell and Mike Alfreds have both read some literature on cognitive science, and integrated it with their existing methods, while Dan Jemmett's intuitive approach is based on his experiences, imagination, and trial and error. Examining their work from a cognitive perspective demonstrates several of the cognitive features described in previous chapters in practice: the relationship between physiology and emotion; the value of an understanding of the distinction between behavioral action, interpersonal actions, and narrative action; and the way in which the notion of conceptual blending is in operation in a non-realist style of performance.

Katie Mitchell

Katie Mitchell has directed for the Royal Shakespeare Company, the National Theatre, the Royal Court, the Young Vic, and the Donmar Warehouse, as well as numerous European theatres. She is considered one of the most adventurous contemporary directors in England both for her rehearsal process, and for her re-visioning of classic plays. Mitchell has incorporated the research of Antonio Damasio into her working practices and takes careful account of Damasio's analysis of the way in which Feelings arise after the mind becomes conscious of a stimulus to emotion. Describing experiments with actors after reading Damasio's *The Feeling of What Happens*, she says:

> We re-enacted situations involving one or more of the six primary emotions ... We studied what happened to the body in minute detail and quickly discovered that it was the half-second delay between the stimulus and becoming conscious of the change in the body that was either edited out of our perceptions altogether or the hardest to recall.[1]

Recognizing that audiences understand emotion by seeing physical changes in the actor, she identifies the risk that recalled emotion would not completely duplicate the physical reaction to the stimulus: "If we were to edit out vital frames in the film of an emotion as it is played by the body then it might not be legible to the audience."[2] Consequently she started encouraging actors to work in precise physical detail in recreating the physiology of different emotions.

Mitchell first put this discovery to work in her production of *Iphigenia at Aulis*, presented at the National Theatre in 2004. Early in the rehearsal session, having identified the dominant emotion of the play as fear, she asked the actors to re-enact a moment in their lives when they had been afraid. Other members of the group were asked to watch carefully how the bodies behaved and to avoid psychological analysis. One actor chose a situation in which he had to shoot a film scene with a lion, and re-enacted a practice session where he entered a cage with the lion in it. Mitchell's description of the physiological symptoms that he displayed is detailed and specific:

He entered, stood stock still for ten seconds, then kept wiping the palms of his hands on his thighs, taking tiny steps forwards and tiny steps back without moving towards the lion at all. He then turned his head repeatedly back and forth from camera to lion. His body temperature increased and he turned red. We could see his increased heartbeat as a vein on his neck pumped hard. His breathing was very shallow and we could see that his mouth was dry when he talked.[3]

The next step was to ask the actors where the physical symptoms that had been seen could be incorporated into the play, with many of the suggestions resulting in performance choices:

if you looked closely enough, you might have noticed the constant flutter of the background emotion of anxiety in the chorus, or Achilles's three-metre leap backwards when he is told he is going to get married, or Menelaus's panic attack when Iphigenia arrives.[4]

English theatre critics have not always been enthusiastic about Mitchell's productions, often disconcerted by her unconventional take on plays about which they have preconceived notions. This production, however, received very favorable reviews, with many critics commenting on its emotional potency:

What Mitchell never loses sight of is the emotional reality of the situation or the panicky imperatives of war.[5]

Mitchell's production retains the ending's ancient shock value and contrives to give it a chilling theatrical twist of her own.[6]

This is one of the finest productions the National has ever mounted: brilliantly imaginative, tense, powerful and essentially true to the ageing Euripides … this production brings poignancy and intensity to a family tragedy … [7]

Mitchell's willingness to experiment and apply novel approaches to her work clearly paid off, and the experience has had a major effect on her approach:

This discovery became a critical point of reference in my work with actors and radically altered how I directed emotions. I began to identify gestures and actions that were about romantic theatrical conventions and not true to life and began to weed them out of the actors' work. It was also sobering to find out that there is part of the brain which is dedicated to recognizing emotions in other people ... The physiology of emotions replaced psychology as my key point of reference for talking about – and working on – acting.[8]

Mike Alfreds

English director Mike Alfreds founded Shared Experience in the 1970s, and has since worked for the National Theatre, the Royal Shakespeare Company, and The Globe Theatre Company. He has staged more than 200 productions for numerous theatres internationally. In 1991 he took over the Cambridge Theatre Company, later renaming it Method and Madness and running it until 1999. He is highly respected within British theatre; Ian McKellen considers him one of the three best directors in England, and Mark Rylance has said: "To me he is a genius when it comes to acting and storytelling. I will spend my life trying to be true to what he perceives possible in the theatre."[9]

Alfreds, like most of us in Western culture, is inclined to use "inner/outer" terminology; "there are two fundamental approaches to acting: working from the inside-out in which the inner life (thoughts, feelings, objectives) influences the outer life (physical behavior); or vice versa, outside-in ... " However, his attitude towards the latter reveals his awareness of current cognitive thought (derived in part from reading the work of cognitive psychologist Steven Pinker). Rather than defining "outside-in" as technical or inauthentic, he acknowledges that "the state of the body can induce feelings and thoughts." Indeed, he states that having been "indoc-trinated" into a Method approach during his training in the States, he has come to believe that

> for certain situations, there is far greater efficacy in using the body to get in touch with inner experience. Any movement we make, the smallest gesture, evokes some feeling, autonomically connected with it. Often, by committing yourself totally to a physical action, you will make a more direct and natural contact with your need, thoughts and feelings than by trying to think or "feel" your way into them.[10]

Investigating Alfreds' work from a cognitive perspective demonstrates how a rehearsal process can be structured to be coherent with cognitive principles. His approach is designed to support total spontaneity within the fictional circumstances. He describes how moments of startling aliveness that happen in rehearsal become blunted by the time they get to performance:

> Those electric moments where an actor opens up and discovers something amazing or where two actors suddenly take off in a scene. That is usually contained and neatly reproduced and the impact is lost. The truthfulness, the immediacy and vivacity, the spontaneity, the daring and vulnerability, all the things that actors have, must be worked on to give them freedom.[11]

Alfreds differentiates the quality that he is seeking from the autobiographical notion of "truth" espoused by Method actors: "Their moments of truth were stunning, but were always about themselves, not their characters."[12] To avoid this, Alfreds has developed a way of working that develops immediacy and vivacity within the context of the fictional world of the play. Actress Pam Ferris describes his process resulting in performances that are "like an improvisation with carefully worked-out parameters, but within those limits, it's as free as any football match. I believe an audience knows when actors are 'in the moment' and Mike's work fosters that freedom more than any director I know."[13]

The methodology that Alfreds uses to achieve this spontaneity bears many resonances with cognitive principles. His rehearsal process varies, of course, from play to play, but he insists on the value of actors beginning with physical action in the social environment of the play. Each actor is asked to write four lists about the character that he or she plays:

i concrete facts about the character
ii what the character says about himself
iii what other people say about the character
iv what the character says about other people.[14]

Rather than asking the actors to make these inquiries in an isolated way, Alfreds invites the cast to read these lists to one another so that "everyone is exposed to the problems of the play as a whole, and not just that of their own character."[15] The emphasis is thus on engaging with the fictional world rather than relating autobiographical experience to an individual understanding of the character.

Within the context of this shared understanding, the process of interpretation begins simply; in reading what characters say in a script, Alfreds points out that "we have no idea whether what they say is true or false, we have no idea why or how they say what they say, we only know they say it."[16] He recognizes that "[d]ialogue is one of several means employed by characters to get what they want. (Others might be physical expression, gesture and attitude, demeanour, behaviour, 'business', activities, degree of energy, appearance ...)."[17] This statement indicates an intuitive understanding of the significant role that nvc plays in communication; confirming, modifying, or contradicting explicit verbal meaning. In order to discover the context of the verbal content, Alfreds states that "[w]e must take the dialogue at more or less face value, and decide what are the least indisputable actions it implies, that is, what the characters are *doing* when they speak."[18]

The first days of rehearsal are spent identifying these actions at a simple level; these include movement in the fictional environment such as "I enter with a book," as well as interpersonal actions such as "I beg you," or "I remind you." Once these have been identified, the actors run each act without speaking the lines, stating the actions verbally, and embodying them physically. Alfreds wants "the actors to meet the text in the most organic way possible, which means meeting the play holistically, not just with their intellects and their tongues, but also with their *bodies*, which contain their emotional and sensory life, their memories and their experience."[19] As David McNeill's analysis describes, utterances of speech and gesture arise from impulses that shape thought units. Alfreds' process allows the actors to begin to experience these utterances at an actional level. This concurs with cognitive information regarding the ways in which these features are rooted in physical experience, and how physical activity is more likely to stimulate the imagination than mental activity alone. Starting the rehearsal process in this way addresses the challenge posed by the difference between written and spoken language – lessening the potential for verbal overshadowing that arises in table analysis, and enabling physical activation of the spine of actions before speaking the dialogue. This process recalls Stanislavski's Method of Physical Actions, and follows cognitive principles, by establishing a fictional world that is initially defined by physical experience. Alfreds is insistent that the actors

> heighten the physicality of each action they play, so that while the playing is utterly *truthful*, it is not necessarily *naturalistic*. They should be seeking to play what is for them the absolute epitome of each action. If "*I enquire*," my whole body, energy and focus on my partner must be totally committed to and expressive

of the *act of enquiring*. The increased muscular commitment will help
actors to remember the structure of the scenes.[20]

He also utilizes Laban's "efforts" to help the actors define the characters
in a physical way long before any consideration of objectives. This
approach differs significantly from the traditional process of rehearsing
that derives from Stanislavski's early work where objectives are the
first thing to be identified in analysis. In contrast, Alfreds says of this
phase of his process: "At this point you have to assume you know
nothing about your character or the play. All you know is what the
characters do. You do not know why they do these things or how
you will do them."[21] Awareness of the characters' intentions grows
from this environmental and actional foundation. This progression
is also consonant with cognitive research, which shows that conscious
intent is generally assigned retrospectively to many of our actions.
A further consonance between Alfreds' work and ideas in this
book is the distinguishing of different types of action. By recognizing
that personal, behavioral actions are distinct from the dramatic
action of a play, he creates a situation in which actors become able to
make choices of personal actions that vary from night to night in
performance. The narrative action creates the parameters within
which behavioral improvisation can occur:

> They do an awful lot of work on the environment and space,
> their relationships, style and what the play's actually about,
> hopefully embodied in a very organic way through the very long and
> elaborate rehearsal process. Then, whatever they choose to play will
> be right, because it's true to that particular moment. They have to
> give up getting, say, a laugh on a specific line. You must be absolutely
> in the moment, playing whatever the moment demands.[22]

A review of Alfreds' production of *The Cherry Orchard* at the
National Theatre demonstrates the value of this approach. The
Observer newspaper's Michael Ratcliffe watched the production on
two consecutive nights, and describes how Ian McKellen as Lopakhin
played the climactic moment differently each time:

> The grieving triumph of the peasant Lopakhin at the purchase of
> Ranevskaya's estate was the more moving when … the victorious
> and the defeated fell weeping into one another's arms, but it
> made equal theatrical sense within Chekhov's character and
> McKellen's characterization for the boorish Lopakhin to whirl

the keys to the house around his head like a cowboy, kick over the daybed, and scatter the vase of scarlet flowers, together with Ranevskaya ... to the very edges of the white room.[23]

Ratcliffe's description predicts the title of Alfreds' book about directing, *Different Every Night*. The spontaneity that is generated through his process creates emotions that have the ability to empathically affect audiences. For Alfreds, this, not autobiography, is the distinguishing feature of truth in performance:

> ... truthful acting turns us hot and cold, makes us sweat, makes us blush, makes us gasp, makes our stomachs churn, makes us hold our breath, makes us laugh with joy, gives us a sudden intense sense of breathing sharp clean air, of being thrillingly alive and in touch with our humanity.[24]

Dan Jemmett

Director Dan Jemmett also values an audience's visceral response; "It's about being alive in the moment, when you feel your pulse quickening ... "[25] Jemmett began his theatrical career in England, performing a Punch and Judy show while also working with experimental theatre company Primitive Science. His work as a director, however, is best known in continental Europe. He has directed at some of Europe's most highly regarded theatres, including the Théâtre de Vidy-Lausanne, the Théâtre National de Chaillot, the Théâtre du Vieux-Colombier and the Bouffes du Nord in Paris, The Lyric Hammersmith and the Almeida Opera in London, the Deutsche Oper Am Rhein in Düsseldorf, Holland's Reisopera, and the Teatro Dell'Opera in Rome among many others. After being awarded the French critics' Revelation Théâtral prize in 2002, he was the first British director to be invited to work at the Comédie-Française, staging Molière's *Les Précieuses Ridicules* and De Filippo's *La Gran Magia*. His first film, *Curtains*, was selected for The Edinburgh Film Festival 2009, and more recently he directed Berlioz's opera *Beatrice and Benedict* for the Opéra Comique in Paris, followed by *Twelfth Night* at the Teatr Polski in Warsaw.

Equally comfortable with devising theatre as with working on scripts, he has conceived and directed four highly acclaimed shows in the USA, three presented by Quantum Theatre, and one by 404 Strand. *Dogface*, his adaptation of *The Changeling*, was performed in an abandoned steel mill, while *The Collected Works of Billy the Kid*, a dramatization of Michael Ondaatje's book of poems, was presented in a disused porn cinema. Both of these productions were subsequently invited to Madrid's prestigious Festival de Otoño. *The Museum of Desire* was another devised work, a presentation of stories by renowned art historian and writer John Berger that took place within a collection of old masters in Pittsburgh's Frick Museum. This was followed by an adaption of Marlowe's *Faust* called *faustUS* that was created and performed in a disused storefront in a run-down district of Pittsburgh.

As some of these examples demonstrate, environment is a significant feature in Jemmett's search for an experience that is vivid and visceral for actors and audience alike. For Jemmett, however, the concept of environment extends beyond the notion of physical location and relates the organization of time and space to dramaturgy. This links to his sometimes controversial adaptations of classic texts: "I've always questioned the validity of the writer's structure. Writers imagine the stage, but it's a very personal imagination, and they project very simplistic notions of space and time. Directors create the world of the live experience, beyond the illustration of the world of the play." This approach has its roots in his early work with Primitive Science on the texts of Heiner Muller: "In Muller's work the structure is not set – you can bang the text together like stones. If you work with a text with story, it's difficult to dislocate that."

For Jemmett, everything is open to question and creative exploration as he seeks an engagement that makes the audience imaginative participants in the live event. For example, in *faustUS*, I was one of five actors who collaborated in a long period of experimentation in which we played with every aspect of the event. Decisions were reached through improvisation and discussion, with a significant emphasis on embodying action (rather than discursive thought). This resulted in a production in which audience members surrounded a rectangular wooden structure that enclosed the action, and suggested the shelves of Faust's study, as well as a cage and a boxing ring. The form of the structure arrived intuitively through the process, but retrospectively, we realized that this was a visual metaphor for the way in which Faust's desire for knowledge paradoxically confines him, and creates the environment for the battle for his soul. We used portions of Marlowe's text, and each of us played, at times, Faust and Mephistopholes, with the transitions aided by Faust's habit of speaking to himself in the third person. The performance lasted Faustus' "one bare hour," with the audience inches away from the action within the shelf-cage. This proximity, and the eye contact that the spatial arrangement afforded, heightened the potential for empathetic physiological responses in the audience. Audience members and critics alike acknowledged the emotional intensity of the experience:

> "In the beginning I felt fear, absolute terror but was distant from it. I was curious about the terror. As the piece progressed I felt more trapped and claustrophobic."[26]
>
> "The production involves the audience in intimate ways ... It's impossible not to get involved."[27]
>
> "Sometimes, inside the horizontally barred cage, two actors would instantaneously switch roles, giving the visceral impression that soul-seller Faustus was confronting himself – or was, literally, beside himself."[28]
>
> "For some, it will be hard to watch. Faust is a man in torment, and his pain is raw. The actors often confront the audience directly with their plaints and pain."[29]
>
> "A very intimate performance that almost forces a Faustus-like condition upon the viewer, as I began to place myself right inside the 'box ... '"[30]

Even in conditions that necessitate a much greater physical distance between the dramatic action and audience members, such as a traditional proscenium theatre, Jemmett seeks ways to stimulate and integrate their visceral responses with the fiction of the play. For instance, in the 2011 Teatr Polski production of *Twelfth Night*, many of Feste's quips were replaced by contemporary jokes delivered to both the characters on stage and the audience, eliciting both laughter and groans. When Malvolio is imprisoned, Feste torments him with bad jokes, so the audience members have experienced what the fictional character goes through, and then find their emotions stretched between the pleasure of the laughter and the pain generated by Malvolio's pitiful begging for release. This strand of the play's action culminates, of course, in Malvolio's departure vowing "I'll be revenged on the whole pack of you."[31] The behavioral delivery of this line once again includes both the cast and the audience, unifying them as joint tormentors in Malvolio's eyes. When Orsino says "Pursue him and entreat him to a peace,"[32] none of the onstage characters depart, and he and Olivia look out at the audience, as if expecting one of them to obey the instruction. Through their inaction, audience members become participants in Malvolio's estrangement from the community.

Other features of this production of *Twelfth Night* connect with one of the reviewers' comments quoted earlier about Faust "confronting," or being "beside" himself. This highlights another aspect of Jemmett's style – the re-energizing of metaphors that have lost their visceral immediacy through linguistic repetition and removal from their physical origin. Conversations with him reveal that this is not a conscious choice on his part (he emphatically protects an intuitive way of working), but it re-appears in many productions. As we know from Lakoff and Johnson's analysis, much conceptual thought is shaped metaphorically by experience in the physical world, and Jemmett's work often reconnects language with physical expression. Readers familiar with *Twelfth Night* will be aware of Sir Toby's relationship with the weak-willed Sir Andrew Aguecheek, and would probably be comfortable with the use of the word "manipulation" to describe it. While the word was not current in Shakespeare's time, it has its etymological roots in the Latin for hand – *manus* – and handful – *manipulus*. In an earlier adaptation of *Twelfth Night* called *Shake* (2002), Jemmett represented the relationship between the two men by casting a ventriloquist's dummy as Sir Andrew, manipulated and voiced by Sir Toby. In the Teatr Polski version, the dynamic of control and dependence is portrayed by Sir Toby using his hands to wheel Sir Andrew around in an airplane seat. When, in Act V, Sir Andrew enters following his fight with Sebastian, he is free of the chair, but cannot walk, having been seated for so long, and thus has to drag himself on the ground. Once again, the choice stimulates a visceral response from the audience and increases emotional potency by emphasizing Sir Toby's exploitation of Sir Andrew.

Clearly, these examples are not realist in style, yet they provoke emotional responses through the stimulation of empathetic mirror systems in audience members. This phenomenon points to the way in which Fauconnier and Turner's notion of conceptual blending operates for audience members. As they watch a show, actor and character are two separate mental spaces – their similarities occupy a third space, with the blend being the actor/character in fictional circumstances – a fourth space. We are able to accept all of these concurrently, without losing awareness of the characteristics of the original mental spaces. Jemmett's choices frequently heighten awareness of these original mental spaces, drawing attention to the disparity between elements of the blend, rather than trying to create the illusion of a synthesized actor and character. When the actor generates physiological symptoms of emotion, the audience's mirror systems are stimulated to produce affective states in response, despite the intentional reminders of the fiction. This result is achieved because Jemmett, like Mitchell and Alfreds, insists on actors' technical physical precision, thus stimulating affective states in the audience.

A vivid example of this occurs in the Teatr Polski production of *Twelfth Night* where one actress, Lidia Sadowa, plays Viola and her twin brother Sebastian, who both believe that the other is dead. Until Act V, the characters are not on stage together, and are distinguished in costume only by one wearing a hat that the other does not. In the moment of recognition between the two in Act V, Sadowa directs her visual focus out to the auditorium and sustains it there as if seeing her twin, while speaking the dialogue of both characters. Simultaneously, she dons and doffs a hat to identify which character is speaking, an action that playfully acknowledges the audience's awareness of the conceit. In rehearsal, Jemmett had been attentive to the physiological signs of different emotions, symptoms that Sadowa accurately reproduced, and which resulted in empathetic audience responses in the performances that I observed. The explicit acknowledgement of theatrical artifice in this moment did not detract from the audience's engagement in the fiction.

This engagement is strongly linked to the stimulation of emotion. Jemmett seems to have come to the same recognition that Mitchell and Alfreds have about physical activity and its relation to emotion; "tempo is linked with emotion … the more abstract a moment is – the more open to interpretation – the more rhythm is important." He gives an example from a production of *Ubu enchaîné*, the first presentation of his company Comité des Fêtes:

> A moment in rehearsal might be just right, but then with five hundred people watching, it's wrong. He puts a hat down (like a street busker) at the beginning of the show. At the end he picks it up, looks inside – there's no money there – so he looks around at the audience. The actor wants to interpret this moment, but I ask him to make it shorter. I'm asking the actor to do something that's purely technical, not "felt" or "thought." The important thing is – what are the signs that are given off that serve the story or the universe of the event – the fabric of the theatrical event.

Jemmett is intent on increasing the potency of the event through the stimulation of the audience's imagination. Having worked in a variety of performance media, from puppetry to film, he asserts that "a painted piece of battered wood can do more than film [to stimulate the imagination]. Film is too literal a medium – it doesn't allow you to do the imagining. It does all the imagining for you." Intuitively, he has arrived at a way of working that uses embodied choices that, while not "realistic," succeed in engaging audience's imaginations and stimulating empathetic responses. Through this process he seeks to create a type of theatre event that is "something more than the play, or the writers or the actors ... it's a ritual, not in the service of religion, but of the human."

Cognitive principles and actor training

Most theatre practitioners probably recognize that few schools prepare actors for the types of rehearsal processes described above. A training course based on cognitive principles could be integrated with current script-based programs by incorporating a foundational phase prior to the approach to play texts. This phase could start with games and ensemble activities that alert the student to the communicative potential of nvc, and offer training exercises that would develop expertise in kinesic communication (facial expression, eye behavior, gesture, and posture), proxemics (the use of space, distance between individuals, and the idea of territory), and vocalics (the gestural features of vocalization). Exploration in these areas can be informed by Laban's categories of movement; weight, space, and time. Following this, exercises could be used to heighten awareness of the physical source domains of primary and complex metaphors, and the relationship between thought, speech, and gesture. By developing an awareness of, and facility with, the sensorimotor origins of certain words, actors can strengthen and define the links between thought and physical expression. Work with the neutral mask could be incorporated to increase the range of available source domains, and develop skill in physical expression and characterization.

As students begin to work with text, the following model of the dramatic act could complement the widely practiced process of identifying given circumstances, objectives, and actions:

- drama depicts change
- change is effected through action
- action is expressed through words and gesture
- words and gesture arise from impulse
- impulse is a neuronal process
- neuronal processes are generated in a physical, mental, and emotional environment
- a fictional environment stimulates neuronal processes that follow the same pathways as those that are stimulated by daily life.

Words *and* gestures integrate thought and action, make the invisible visible. Since words and gestures are the end result of impulses, reading a script is reverse-engineering, discovering the impulses that provoke action and, by doing so, creating the physical environment of the fiction. In improvised and devised pieces, the environment is often the starting point, creating a progression that more easily stimulates the actor's imagination than linguistically defined discursive thought. Each of the three directors described earlier seeks to prioritize the fictional environment in their practice, and by doing so stimulate impulses that are true both to the actor and the character. The process by which an actor generates these impulses is more likely to engage the imagination and emotions when it incorporates physical action. Stanislavski's Method of Physical Actions, and Michael Chekhov's character work offer coherent and accessible ways of doing this.

Within this phase of work, students can be introduced to concepts of performance that suggest integrative loops rather than oppositional dualities. For example, action can be seen to have distinct, but connected expression, ranging from primary through conceptual to narrative, all of which interact and affect each other. Primary actions are identified as those that have a defined physical experience. Work on these can start with the eight Laban efforts (*push*, *pull*, *stroke*, *dab*, *wring*, etc.), as they provide foundational examples of defined behavioral actions that have metaphorical expression and link to the earlier work on categories of movement in space. The work can then progress to other primary actions such as crumple, grasp, restrain, and knock. Conceptual actions are those that don't have a defined physical action – such as persuade, intimidate, or seduce – and that are communicated by primary actions. An actor can *punch* a line, for example, as a way of expressing the conceptual action of *intimidate*, or *stroke* it as a way of expressing the conceptual action of *persuade*. This level of specificity also allows the actor to make choices that surprise the audience by their incongruity, such as using *stroke* to *intimidate*. Narrative action describes events that change people, relationships, and situations, and can also be linked to physical experience. The status quo for example, is metaphorically in *balance*, which could be visually depicted on stage by compositional *balance*. The inciting incident *tilts* the *balance*. The *tilt* causes a narrative chain reaction of cause and effect, a concept that is based on the source-path-goal schema. The events of the narrative have a temporal pattern that can be thought of as *rhythm*.

Students would be encouraged to think of character in terms of situation and action, rather than in terms of identification with the "essential self." The process of characterization would be conceived of as forming a temporary situational self through the stimulation of the imagination, with feelings that arise through a combination of physical actions and empathetic stimuli in the fiction. This is achieved by discovering a range of expressive behavior that: (a) executes action in response to the mental, emotional, and physical environment of fictional circumstances; (b) is credible in the fictional circumstances; and (c) is congruent with the theatrical style. The accumulation of specific action choices defines the personality of the character. The discoveries of action choices can arise both from spontaneous responses to the imagination and from voluntary control of muscular activity, acknowledging the reflexive relationship between the two. This concept of character provides a coherent model that supports the activity of characterization in a range of styles. It is accurate for the actor who adopts the traditional posture and mannerisms of Pantalone in Commedia. It is also accurate for the actor who plays a character close to him or herself in age, experience, and personality in the style of psychological realism. The model is also applicable to both scripted and devised material.

A similarly holistic understanding of emotion would inform this cognitive approach to actor training. Students would learn about the current neuroscientific understanding of emotion as groups of physiological symptoms that, when consciously registered, produce Feelings. Information about the three categories of emotions (primary, social, and background) would help to define both behavioral and narrative action as well as character. Information about the nine pathways to emotion would inform exercises that develop facility with the three most controllable of those pathways: memory, imagination, and consciously chosen muscular activity. The latter would include work on eye movements, facial expression, muscular tension, postural attitudes, and respiratory patterns. Empathetic links between the actor's imagination and the character could be established through the use of the physiological configurations of relevant primary, social, and background emotions in the context of the fictional environment.

I hope that these brief examples illustrate how actor training can be approached in a way that is consistent with the relevant findings of cognitive science. The information that I have described undercuts some of the basic dualities that have informed acting theory in the twentieth century, and offers a new approach to training and practice that can nevertheless integrate some existing practices. A significant part of the goal of this book is to adjust actors' conceptual understanding of their bodies. This is a significant issue – one's conceptual understanding of the body defines what one believes it to be capable of, and this has implications for theatrical style. The ubiquity of the style of psychological realism in Western theatre leads to a literalism that encourages actors to "type" themselves in order to gain work, which is necessarily restricting. I hope that, as more practitioners become aware of the ways in which meaning can be communicated through embodied metaphor, a greater diversity of styles can flourish.

When I began researching the material that I've described, I feared that cognitive science would remove the magic from theatre. Now, I think that it will enable theatre practitioners to be better magicians. One way of describing magic is to say that we experience a result without being aware of the mechanisms that produced it. The actor's job is to understand and employ the mechanisms that create embodied life on stage. Given that at least 90 percent of the mental operations that are involved in embodied life are unconscious, cognitive science gives actors valuable information about processes that are not available to conscious reflection. This adds to the ability and range of the actor, and enhances his or her ability to embody fiction. Transformation of the actor occurs when this is accomplished to the extent that it affects unconscious neural patterns of empathy, of imagination, of emotion. When audience members, through empathetic processes, experience the actor's emotional state it feels as though they are experiencing real life because of a mirror mechanism firing in one part of the brain. At the same time they know with another part of the brain that they are witnessing a fiction. This is a lived paradox, a sensually experienced paradox, a paradox that feels magical.

Notes

1 Why should theatre people be interested in cognitive studies?

1 Diderot 1830: 60.
2 Hill 1746.
3 D. Gorodetski, "Iz vospominani ob AP. Chekhov" in *Chekhov I teatr*, pp. 208–9, quoted in Allen 2000: 4.
4 Allen 2000: 213.
5 Stanislavski 1967: 329.
6 ibid: 175.
7 ibid: 171.
8 Stanislavski 2008: 17.
9 Cole and Krich Chinoy 1970: 371.
10 ibid: 373.
11 ibid: 399.
12 Chekhov 1991: xiii.
13 Richards 1995: 6.
14 Grotowski, quoted in Drain 1995: 277.
15 ibid: 279–80.
16 Brook, quoted in Grotowski 1978: 11.
17 Lecoq 2001: 5.
18 ibid: 21.
19 ibid: 9.
20 A significant exception is Wolford and Schechner (2001) *The Grotowski Sourcebook*.
21 McConachie and Hart 2006: x.
22 Johnson 2008: 2.
23 ibid: 4.
24 Johnson 2008: 7.

2 How does the actor communicate meaning non-verbally?

1 Kendon 2004: 69.
2 Bateson 1968: 614–15, quoted in Kendon 2004: 71.
3 Argyle et al 1978: 16.
4 Bogart and Landau 2005: 215.
5 ibid: 216.
6 Argyle et al 1970; Birdwhistell 1970; Mehrabian 1968; Philpott 1983.

7 Carnicke 2000: 32.
8 Briñol et al 2009.
9 Strack et al 1988.
10 Leathers 1997.
11 Richardson et al (undated): 2.
12 Phelim McDermott of Improbable Theatre first introduced me to this mnemonic.
13 Beattie 2004: 15.
14 It is difficult to pinpoint the originator of this model. It became current in various forms of business management training during the 1970s, and is described in print in W.C. Howell and E.A. Fleishman (eds), *Human Performance and Productivity. Vol 2: Information Processing and Decision Making.* Hillsdale, NJ: Erlbaum 1982.
15 For many Eastern traditions of performance, this isn't an issue. In Noh theatre, for example, training focuses on the technique of executing detailed traditional choreography to tell a story.
16 Lakoff and Johnson 1999: 45.
17 Kendon 2004: 161.
18 ibid: 126.
19 David McNeill is the foremost among authors in this area, and I discuss his work in Chapter 3.
20 *The Importance of Being Earnest*, Act II.
21 *The Importance of Being Earnest*. Dir: Anthony Asquith. Perf: Michael Redgrave, Michael Denison, Margaret Rutherford, Edith Evans, Dorothy Tutin, Joan Greenwood. Paramount Pictures, 1952.
22 *The Importance of Being Earnest*. Dir: Oliver Parker. Perf: Judi Dench, Rupert Everett, Colin Firth, Frances O'Connor, Reese Witherspoon. Miramax Films, 2002.
23 Lakoff and Johnson 1999: 19.
24 ibid: 77.
25 ibid: 140.
26 ibid: 140.
27 ibid: 45.
28 Chekhov 1991: 43.
29 ibid: 41.
30 Lakoff and Johnson 1999: 47.
31 ibid: 52.
32 ibid: 48.
33 Chekhov 1963: 10.
34 ibid: 11.
35 ibid: 11.
36 ibid: 12–13.
37 Examples are *Laban for Actors and Dancers* by Jean Newlove, and Barbara Adrian's *Actor Training the Laban Way*.

3 What is the relationship between thought, physical action, and language?

1 McNeill 1992: 2.
2 McNeill 2000: 139.
3 ibid: 19.

4 ibid: 19.
5 ibid: 19.
6 McNeill 1992: 27.
7 ibid: 41.
8 This element, of course, is not the only feature that alters meaning from production to production; features such as location, environment, staging, scenography, lighting, and sound design also play their parts.
9 http://mcneilllab.uchicago.edu/writings/growth_points.html, accessed 29 May 2009.
10 ibid.
11 ibid.
12 Sher 2003: 20.
13 ibid: 22.
14 ibid: 20.
15 ibid: 21.
16 http://mcneilllab.uchicago.edu/writings/growth_points.html, accessed 29 May 2009.
17 Sher 2003: 21.
18 Lecoq 2001: 5.
19 ibid: 9.
20 Information about Lecoq's biography is drawn from the school website, www.ecole-jacqueslecoq.com/jacques_lecoq-biographie-uk.php?bg=01, accessed 5 September 2009, and *The Moving Body* (Lecoq 2001).
21 Lecoq 2001: 15.
22 ibid: 21.
23 Lakoff and Johnson 1999: 38.
24 ibid: 38.
25 ibid: 39.
26 Lecoq 2001: 35.
27 ibid: 21.
28 Murray 2003: 135.
29 ibid: 135.
30 Lecoq 2001: 36.
31 ibid: 42.
32 Daniel Day-Lewis' comments in Chapter 5 cast an interesting light on this.
33 Lecoq 2001: 45.
34 ibid: 45.
35 ibid: 45.
36 ibid: 45.
37 Lecoq 2001: 49.
38 ibid: 166.
39 ibid: 137.
40 Conversation with the author, 18 February 1990, London.
41 *Les deux voyages de Jacques Lecoq.* Roy and Carasso 1999.
42 Lecoq 2001: 19.

4 How does the actor create a character?

1 This is definitely not the case in many Eastern forms of performance. In Japanese Noh theatre, for example, audiences and critics savor performers' use of technique.

2 Gordon 2006: 2 (italics in original).
3 In Cole and Krich Chinoy 1970: 407.
4 ibid: 339.
5 ibid: 410–11.
6 Brook 1977: 125.
7 Brown and Ludwig's comments are transcribed from the video of the discussion available on YouTube: www.youtube.com/watch?v=loB-Lg0X1 qo&feature=PlayList&p=E42C219FA01A9888&index=0, accessed 21 December 2009.
8 Benedetti, R. 2005: 73.
9 Johnson 1987: 21.
10 Lakoff and Johnson 1999: 265–6, my italics.
11 ibid: 266.
12 ibid: 266.
13 Churchland 2000.
14 www.americanscientist.org/bookshelf/pub/the-functionalists-dilemma, accessed 5 January 2010.
15 Lakoff and Johnson 1999: 268.
16 ibid: 269.
17 ibid: 268.
18 Hagen 1973: 26.
19 ibid: 27.
20 ibid: 12. The terms "Representational" and "Presentational" are the subject of some confusion in themselves, with some practitioners and theorists using them in exactly the opposite way to Hagen. The more usual way of understanding them today is that Representational acting ignores the presence of the audience, while Presentational acting acknowledges audience members, plays to them, and responds to them.
21 Benedetti, R. 2005: 79.
22 ibid: 79.
23 Lakoff and Johnson 1999: 281.
24 ibid: 281.
25 ibid: 281.
26 LeDoux 2003: 27–8.
27 ibid: 28.
28 ibid: 28.
29 Benedetti, J. 2007: 51.
30 Mirror neurons have been directly observed in monkeys, and fMRI studies strongly suggest that humans also have a mirror neuron system. What has been contested by some is whether there are specific neurons that "mirror" or whether this is a function that is carried out by neurons that also do other things. The discussion from which this comment is transcribed was predicated on the existence of a mirror neuron system in humans.
31 Gallese's comments are transcribed from www.youtube.com/watch?v=loB-Lg0X1qo&feature=PlayList&p=E42C219FA01A9888&index=0, accessed 21 December 2009.
32 Gallese and Lakoff 2005: 455.
33 ibid: 456, my italics.
34 Buckner and Carroll 2007: 49.

35 Gallese and Lakoff 2005: 456.
36 Aziz-Zadeh et al 2006.
37 Iacoboni 2008: 94–5, my italics.
38 ibid: 91.
39 Wexler et al 1998; Grush 2004; Simons et al 2002; Wexler and Klam 2001.
40 Lecoq 2006: 89–91.
41 I am grateful to Lecoq graduates and actor/creator/educators Mark McKenna and Jennie Gilrain for refreshing my memory and sharing their notation of the scale with me. The minor differences between the notation and Lecoq's text reflect a couple of factors; the development over time of the way in which Lecoq taught this, and the studio experience of the student receiving the exercise.
42 Donald 2006: 15.
43 ibid: 15.
44 This connection is described by Lakoff in "The Neuroscience of Form in Art," in Mark Turner (ed.) *The Artful Mind*. Lakoff summarizes Sri Narayanan's hypothesis that the neural circuitry involved in controlling phases of motor action can also work to define "aspect" in abstract concepts.
45 These comments are transcribed from a video of the discussion: www.youtube.com/watch?v=loB-Lg0X1qo&feature=PlayList&p=E42C219FA01A9888&index=0, accessed 21 December 2009.
46 Chekhov's biography is compiled from the Fall 1983 edition of *The Drama Review*, 27(3): 3; Chamberlain 2004; Marowitz 2004; and www.michaelchekhov.org.
47 Chekhov 1963: 49.
48 ibid: 58.
49 Fauconnier and Turner 2002: 108.
50 ibid: 266.
51 This information has many implications for theories of reception in theatre audiences, addressed in McConachie 2008.
52 Fauconnier and Turner 2002: 266.
53 Originally called *Burlesque*, by George Manker Watters and Arthur Hopkins.
54 Chekhov 2005: 145.
55 ibid: 145.
56 ibid: 147.
57 ibid: 147.
58 Chekhov 1985: 86–7.
59 ibid: 87–8.
60 Chekhov 2005: 216.
61 Chekhov 1985: 59.
62 ibid: 82.
63 ibid: 65.
64 ibid: 2.
65 ibid: 3.
66 ibid: 1.

5 How does the actor identify with the character?

1 http://query.nytimes.com/gst/fullpage.html?res=9E02E2D91639F934A25750C0A960958260&paewanted=2, accessed 15 March 2011.

2 My focus is on the process of an actor in creating character, but this approach could have significant benefits for the comparison of existing performances. For example, a patient analyst could identify the range of types of actions used by Olivier/Hamlet, and compare them to those used by Gibson/Hamlet, and consequently specify how each actor's conception of the character's personality is communicated to the audience.
3 Smith, A.D. 1993: xxx.
4 ibid: xxxii.
5 In Martin 1993: 55–6.
6 Smith, A.D. 2000: 37.
7 In Martin 1993: 57.
8 ibid: 57.
9 ibid: 57.
10 ibid: 56.
11 Smith, A.D. 1993: xxix.
12 In Martin 1993: 51.
13 ibid: 51.
14 http://bigthink.com/ideas/5428, accessed 15 January 2010.
15 Gallagher and Meltzoff: 211–12.
16 ibid: 216.
17 ibid: 216.
18 ibid: 216.
19 American football, that is. Apologies to all fans of the beautiful game.
20 Balslev et al 2007.
21 Gallese et al 2004: 397.
22 Calvo-Merino et al 2005.
23 Gallese's comments are transcribed from www.youtube.com/watch?v=loB-Lg0X1qo&feature=PlayList&p=E42C219FA01A9888&index=0, accessed 21 December 2009.
24 Iacoboni et al 1999.
25 Schroeder and Matheson 2006: 28.
26 ibid: 33.
27 Schooler and Engstler-Schooler 1990.
28 British director Max Stafford-Clark is well known for starting his rehearsals with long sessions of table work in which actors "action" their scripts.
29 Benedetti, J. 2007: xvi.
30 In Carnicke 1984: 60.
31 Benedetti, J. 2007: xx.
32 "Inner Impulses and Inner Action; Creative Objectives" (1916–20) quoted in Drain 1995: 253.
33 McConachie 2003: 99.
34 Carnicke 2000: 32.
35 ibid: 32.
36 Toporkov 2004: 17.
37 ibid: 17.
38 ibid: 85, my italics.
39 ibid: 50.
40 Carnicke 2000: 33.
41 Bruner 2002: 64.

42 www.guardian.co.uk/film/2008/jan/13/awardsandprizes.danieldaylewis, accessed 12 March 2011.
43 ibid.
44 www.guardian.co.uk/film/2009/dec/10/daniel-day-lewis-nine-interview, accessed 6 March 2011.
45 ibid.
46 www.guardian.co.uk/film/2008/jan/13/awardsandprizes.danieldaylewis, accessed 12 March 2011.
47 ibid.

6 How does the actor embody emotion in fictional circumstances?

 1 Carnicke 1998: 133.
 2 ibid: 133.
 3 As in previous chapters, I quote from Jean Benedetti's translation, believing it to be more accurate than Hapgood's.
 4 Stanislavski 2008: 195.
 5 ibid: 197.
 6 Carnicke 1998: 111.
 7 Strasberg 1987: 113.
 8 Strasberg 1964: 131.
 9 ibid: 132.
10 Smith, W. 1990: 38.
11 Krasner 2000: 137.
12 Hogan 2003: 182.
13 ibid: 161.
14 LeDoux 2003: 221.
15 Ekman 2003: 33.
16 ibid: 33.
17 LeDoux 2003: 222.
18 ibid: 222.
19 ibid: 222.
20 Ekman 2003: 32.
21 LeDoux 2003: 222.
22 In Benedetti, J. 1988: 271.
23 Interview with Antonio Damasio. *Scientific American Mind*, 16 (1).
24 Damasio 1999: 48.
25 ibid: 51–2.
26 ibid: 51.
27 ibid: 342.
28 ibid: 341.
29 ibid: 52.
30 LeDoux 2003: 69.
31 ibid: 69.
32 ibid: 70.
33 Levenson et al 1990: 363.
34 Adolphs 2003.
35 Carr et al 2003.
36 Levenson et al 1990.
37 Ekman 2003: 389.

38 ibid: 389.
39 Damasio 1999: 47.
40 ibid: 48.
41 Ekman 2003.
42 ibid: 31.
43 Nichols 2006: 8.
44 Gallese et al 2004: 399, my italics.
45 Canessa et al 2009.
46 ibid: 1.
47 Benedetti, J. 1988: xv.
48 Toporkov 2004: 160.
49 A full account of these can be found in Wolford and Schechner 2001.
50 Drain 1995: 278.
51 Kolankiewicz, quoted in Wolford and Schechner 2001: 210.
52 Wolford and Schechner 2001: 326–7.
53 ibid: 287.
54 ibid: 381.
55 www.grotowski-institute.art.pl, accessed 2 September 2011.
56 Wangh 2000: xx, emphasis in original.
57 Wolford and Schechner 2001: 203.
58 In Richards 1995: 76.
59 In Drain 1995: 279.
60 Richards 1995: 6.
61 ibid: 13.
62 ibid: 12–13.
63 Grotowski, quoted in Hodge 2000: 203.
64 Wangh 2000: xxi.
65 ibid: xxi.
66 Wolford and Schechner 2001: 376.
67 Bloch et al 1994.
68 ibid: 221.
69 ibid: 221.
70 ibid: 220.
71 ibid: 223.
72 ibid: 221.
73 Chabora 2000: 239.
74 ibid: 241.
75 Corbetta et al 1998.
76 ibid: 13.
77 For example, Bebko et al 2011; Budimir and Palmović 2011; Riggs et al 2010.

Conclusion

1 www.guardian.co.uk/books/2004/sep/25/featuresreviews.guardianreview24, accessed 3 October 2011.
2 ibid.
3 Mitchell 2009: 154–5.
4 www.guardian.co.uk/books/2004/sep/25/featuresreviews.guardianreview24, accessed 3 October 2011.

5 Michael Billington, the *Guardian*, 23 June 2004.
6 Patrick Marmion, the *Daily Mail*, 23 June 2004.
7 Benedict Nightingale, *The Times*, 24 June 2004.
8 Mitchell 2009: 232.
9 Quoted on the cover of Alfreds 2007.
10 Alfreds 2007: 99.
11 www.independent.co.uk/arts-entertainment/alfreds-way-more-method-less-madness-1349648.html, accessed 12 December 2011.
12 Alfreds 2007: 6.
13 ibid: xi.
14 Allen 2000: 197.
15 ibid: 197.
16 ibid: 164.
17 ibid: 66.
18 ibid: 164.
19 ibid: 164–5.
20 Alfreds 2007: 166.
21 ibid: 197.
22 www.independent.co.uk/arts-entertainment/alfreds-way-more-method-less-madness-1349648.html, accessed 12 December 2011.
23 Ratcliffe, quoted in Allen 2000: 202.
24 Alfreds 2007: 97.
25 Unless otherwise cited, Jemmett's comments are from a conversation with the author, 29 December 2011.
26 Audience member Mark Staley.
27 Bob Hoover, *Pittsburgh Post-Gazette*, 23 July 2010.
28 Bill O'Driscoll, *City Paper*, 9 September 2009.
29 Alice T. Carter, *Pittsburgh Tribune-Review*, 23 July 2010.
30 Audience member Mary-Jo Dorsey.
31 *Twelfth Night*, Act V, I, 2590.
32 ibid: Act V, I, 2592.

Bibliography

Adolphs, R. (2003) "Cognitive Neuroscience of Human Social Behavior." *Nature Reviews Neuroscience*, 4: 165–78.

Alfreds, M. (2007) *Different Every Night*. London: Nick Hern Books.

Allen, D. (2000) *Performing Chekhov*. London: Routledge.

Argyle, M., Salter, V., Nicholson, H., Williams, M. and Burgess, P. (1970) "The Communication of Inferior and Superior Attitudes by Verbal and Non-verbal Signals." *British Journal of Social and Clinical Psychology*, 9: 222–31.

Argyle, M., Trower, P. and Bryant, B. (1978) *Social Skills and Mental Health*. London: Methuen and Co.

Aziz-Zadeh, L., Wilson, S.M., Rizzolatti, G. and Iacoboni, M. (2006) "Congruent Embodied Representations for Visually Presented Actions and Linguistic Phrases Describing Actions." *Current Biology*, 16: 1818–23.

Balslev, D., Cole, J. and Miall, R.C. (2007) "Proprioception Contributes to the Sense of Agency during Visual Observation of Hand Movements: Evidence from Temporal Judgments of Action." *Journal of Cognitive Neuroscience*, 9(9): 1535–41.

Beattie, G. (2004) *Visible Thought: The New Psychology of Body Language*. Hove: Routledge.

Bebko, G.M., Franconeri, S.L., Ochsner, K.N. and Chiao, J.Y. (2011) "Look Before You Regulate: Differential Perceptual Strategies Underlying Expressive Suppression and Cognitive Reappraisal." *Emotion*, 11(4): 732–42.

Benedetti, J. (1988) *Stanislavski*. London: Methuen.

—— (2007) *The Art of the Actor*. London: Routledge.

Benedetti, R. (2005) *The Actor at Work* (9th edn). Boston: Pearson.

Birdwhistell, R.L. (1970) *Kinesics and Context*. Philadelphia: University of Pennsylvania Press.

Bloch, S., Lemeignan, M. and Aguilera, N. (1991) "Specific Respiratory Patterns Distinguish Among Human Basic Emotions." *International Journal of Psychophysiology*, 11(2): 141–54.

Bloch, S., Orthous, P. and Santibanez, G. (1994) "Effector Patterns of Basic Emotions: A Psychophysiological Method for Training Actors," in Philip B. Zarilli (ed.) *Acting [Re]Considered: Theories and Practice*. London and New York: Routledge, 219–38.

Bogart, A. and Landau, T. (2005) *The Viewpoints Book: A Practical Guide to Viewpoints and Composition*. New York: Theatre Communications Group.

Briñol, P., Petty, R.E. and Wagner, B. (2009) "Body Postures Effects on Self-evaluation: A Self-validation Approach." *European Journal of Social Psychology*, 39: 1–12.

Brook, P. (1977) *The Empty Space*. Harmondsworth: Pelican.

Bruner, J. (2002) *Making Stories: Law, Literature, Life*. New York: Farrar, Straus and Giroux.

Buckner, R. and Carroll, D.C. (2007) "Self Projection and the Brain." *Trends in Cognitive Sciences*, 11(2): 49–57.

Budimir, S. and Palmović, M. (2011) "Gaze Differences in Processing Pictures with Emotional Content." *Collegium Antropologicum*, 35(Sup.1): 17–23.

Caggiano, V., Fogassi, L., Rizzolatti, G., Thier, P. and Casile, A. (2009) "Mirror Neurons Differentially Encode the Peripersonal and Extrapersonal Space of Monkeys." *Science*, 324(5925): 403–6.

Calvo-Merino, B., Glaser, D.E., Grèzes, J., Passingham, R.E. and Haggard, P. (2005) "Action Observation and Acquired Motor Skills: An fMRI Study with Expert Dancers." *Cerebral Cortex*, 15(8): 1243–9.

Canessa, N., Motterlini, M., Di Dio, C., Perani, D., Scifo, P., Cappa, S.F. and Rizzolatti, G. (2009) "Understanding Others' Regret: A fMRI Study." *PLoS ONE*, 4(10): e7402. doi:10.1371/journal.pone.0007402, www.plosone.org/article/info:doi%2F10.1371%2Fjournal.pone.0007402, accessed 11 May 2010.

Carnicke, S.M. (1984) "*An Actor Prepares*: A Comparison of the English with the Russian Stanislavsky." *Theatre Journal*, 36(4): 480–95.

(1998) *Stanislavsky in Focus*. Overseas Publishers Association N.V. Amsterdam: Harwood Academic Publishers.

(2000) "Stanislavsky's System," in Alison Hodge (ed.) *Twentieth Century Actor Training*. London: Routledge.

Carr, L., Iacoboni, M., Dubeau, M-C., Mazziotta, J.C. and Lenzi, J.L. (2003) "Neural Mechanisms of Empathy in Humans: A Relay from Neural Systems for Imitation to Limbic Areas." *Proceedings of the National Academy of Sciences USA*, 100: 5497–502.

Chabora, P.D. (2000) "Emotion Training and the Mind/Body Connection," in David Krasner (ed.) *Method Acting Reconsidered*. New York: St Martin's Press, 229–43.

Chamberlain, F. (2004) *Michael Chekhov*. London: Routledge.

Chekhov, M. (1963) *To the Director and Playwright*. Charles Leonard (ed.). New York: Harper and Row.

(1985) *To the Actor*. New York: Harper and Row.

(1991) *On the Technique of Acting*. New York: Harper.

(2005) *The Path of The Actor*. New York: Routledge.

Churchland, P. (2000) "Neurobiology of the Moral Virtues," in Joa Branquinho (ed.) *The Foundations of Cognitive Science*. Oxford: Clarendon Press, 77–98.

Cole, T. and Krich Chinoy, H. (eds) (1970) *Actors on Acting*. New York: Three Rivers Press.

Corbetta, M., Akbudak, E., Conturo, T.E., Snyder, A.Z., Ollinger, J.M., Drury, H.A., Linenweber, M.R., Petersen, S.E., Raichle, M.E., Van Essen, D.C. and Shulman, G.L. (1998) "A Common Network of Functional Areas for Attention and Eye Movements." *Neuron*, October.

Damasio, A. (1999) *The Feeling of What Happens*. New York: Harcourt.

Derakshan, N. and Koster, E.H. (2010) "Processing Efficiency in Anxiety: Evidence from Eye-movements During Visual Search." *Behaviour Research and Therapy*, 48(12): 1180–5.

Diderot, D. (1830) *Paradoxe sur le Comédien*.

Donald, M. (2006) "Art and Cognitive Evolution," in Mark Turner (ed.) *The Artful Mind*. Oxford: Oxford University Press, 3–20.

Drain, R. (ed.) (1995) *Twentieth Century Theatre, A Sourcebook*. London: Routledge.

Ekman, P. (1999) "Basic Emotions," in T. Dalgleish and M. Power (eds) *Handbook of Cognition and Emotion*. New York: John Wiley and Sons Ltd, 46–60.

(2003) *Emotions Revealed: Recognizing Faces and Feelings to Improve Communication and Emotional Life*. New York: Henry Holt and Company.

Ekman, P., Davidson, R.J. and Friesne, W.V. (1990) "The Duchenne Smile: Emotional Expression and Brain Physiology II." *The Journal of Personality and Social Psychology*, 58: 342–53.

Fauconnier, G. and Turner, M. (2002) *The Way We Think: Conceptual Blending and the Mind's Hidden Complexities*. New York: Basic Books.

Gallagher, S. and Meltzoff, A.N. (1996) "The Earliest Sense of Self and Others: Merleau-Ponty and Recent Developmental Studies." *Philosophical Psychology*, 9(2): 211–33.

Gallese, V. (2005) "Embodied Simulation: From Neurons to Phenomenal Experience." *Phenomenology and Cognitive Science*, 4(1): 23–48.

Gallese, V. and Lakoff, G. (2005) "The Brain's Concepts: The Role of the Sensory Motor System in Conceptual Knowledge." *Cognitive Neuropsychology*, 22(3): 455–79.

Gallese, V., Keysers, C. and Rizzolatti, G. (2004) "A Unifying View of the Basis of Social Cognition." *Trends in Cognitive Sciences*, 8(9): 396–403.

Gordon, R. (2006) *The Purpose of Playing: Modern Acting Theories in Perspective*. Ann Arbor, MI: University of Michigan Press.

Gordon, R.M. (1995) "Sympathy, Simulation, and the Impartial Spectator." *Ethics*, 105(4): 727–43.

Grotowski, J. (1978) *Towards a Poor Theatre*. London: Methuen & Co.

Grush, R. (2004) "The Emulation Theory of Representation: Motor Control, Imagery and Perception." *Behavioral and Brain Sciences*, 27: 377–96.

Hagen, U. (1973) *Respect for Acting*. Hoboken, NJ: John Wiley & Sons.

Hill, A. (1746) *The Art of Acting*. London.

Hodge, A. (ed.) (2000) *Twentieth Century Actor Training*. London: Routledge.

Hogan, P.C. (2003) *Cognitive Science, Literature, and the Arts: A Guide for Humanists.* London: Routledge.

Iacoboni, M. (2008) *Mirroring People.* New York: Farrar Strauss and Giroux.

Iacoboni, M., Woods, R.P., Brass, M., Bekkering, H., Mazziotta, J.C. and Rizzolatti, G. (1999) "Cortical Mechanisms of Human Imitation." *Science,* 286: 2526–8.

Johnson, M. (1987) *The Body in the Mind.* Chicago: University of Chicago Press.
(2008) *The Meaning of the Body.* Chicago: University of Chicago Press.

Kendon, A. (2004) *Gesture: Visible Action as Utterance.* Cambridge: Cambridge University Press.

Kirillov, A. (2004) "Teartral'naya sistema Mikhaila Chekhova" ("The Theatre System of Michael Chekhov") in *Mnemozina,* Issue 3. Moscow: Artist, Rezhisser, Teatr.

Krasner, D. (2000) "Strasberg, Adler and Meisner: Method Acting," in Alison Hodge (ed.) *Twentieth Century Actor Training.* London: Routledge, 129–50.

Lakoff, G. and Johnson, M. (1999) *Philosophy in the Flesh: The Embodied Mind and its Challenge to Western Thought.* New York: Basic Books.

Leathers, D. (1997) *Successful Nonverbal Communication.* Boston: Allyn and Bacon.

Lecoq, J. (2001) *The Moving Body.* Trans. D. Bradby. New York: Routledge.
(2006) *Theatre of Movement and Gesture.* New York: Routledge.

LeDoux, J. (2002) *Synaptic Self: How Our Brains Become Who We Are.* New York: Penguin.
(2003) *The Emotional Brain: The Mysterious Underpinnings of Emotional Life.* New York: Touchstone.

Levenson, R.W., Ekman, P. and Friesen, W.V. (1990) "Voluntary Facial Action Generates Emotion – Specific Autonomic Nervous System Activity." *Psychophysiology,* 27: 363–84.

Lewis, B. (1993) "The Circle of Confusion: A Conversation with Anna Deavere Smith." *Kenyon Review,* 15(4): 54–64.

Makkreel, R.A. (1999) "From Simulation to Structural Transposition: A Diltheyan Critique of Empathy and Defense of *Verstehen,*" in H.H. Kögler and K.R. Stueber (eds) *Empathy and Agency: The Problem of Understanding in the Human Sciences.* Boulder, CO: Westview Press, 181–93.

Marowitz, C. (2004) *The Other Chekhov: A Biography of Michael Chekhov.* New York: Applause Books.

Martin, C. (1993) "Anna Deavere Smith: The Word Becomes You." *Drama Review,* 37(4) (T140): 45–62.

McConachie, B. (2003) *American Theater in the Culture of the Cold War: Producing and Contesting Containment, 1947–1962.* Iowa City: University of Iowa Press.
(2008) *Engaging Audiences: A Cognitive Approach to Spectating in the Theatre.* New York: Palgrave Macmillan.

McConachie, B. and Hart, F.E. (2006) *Performance and Cognition: Theatre Studies and the Cognitive Turn.* London: Routledge.

McNeill, D. (1992) *Hand and Mind: What Gestures tell us about Thought.* Chicago: University of Chicago Press.

(2000) *Language and Gesture.* Cambridge and New York: Cambridge University Press.

(2005) *Gesture and Thought.* Chicago: University of Chicago Press.

http://mcneilllab.uchicago.edu/writing/growth_points.html, accessed 29 May 2009.

Mehrabian, A. (1968) "Communication Without Words." *Psychology Today,* 2: 51–2.

Mitchell, K. (2009) *The Director's Craft.* London: Routledge.

Murray, S. (2003) *Lecoq.* London: Routledge.

Nichols, S. (ed.) (2006) *The Architecture of the Imagination: New Essays on Pretence, Possibility and Fiction.* Oxford: Oxford University Press.

Noice, T. and Noice, H. (1997) *The Nature of Expertise in Professional Acting: A Cognitive View.* New Jersey: Lawrence Erlbaum Associates Inc.

Philpott, J.S. (1983) *The Relative Contribution to Meaning of Verbal and Nonverbal Channels of Communication ... A Metaanalysis.* Unpublished Master's thesis, University of Nebraska.

Richards, T. (1995) *At Work with Grotowski on Physical Actions.* London: Routledge.

Richardson, D.C., Dale, R. and Spivey, M.J. (undated) *Eye Movements in Language and Cognition: A Brief Introduction.* www.eyethink.org/publications_assets/ EMCL_RichardsonDaleSpivey.pdf, accessed 24 May 2010.

Riggs, L., McQuiggan, D.A., Anderson, A.K. and Ryan, J.D. (2010) "Eye Movement Monitoring Reveals Differential Influences of Emotion on Memory." *Frontiers in Psychology,* 1(205): 1–9.

Schooler, J.W. and Engstler-Schooler, T.Y. (1990) "Verbal Overshadowing of Visual Memories: Some Things Are Better Left Unsaid." *Cognitive Psychology,* 22(1): 36–71.

Schroeder, T. and Matheson, C. (2006) "Imagination and Emotion," in Shaun Nichols (ed.) *The Architecture of the Imagination: New Essays on Pretence, Possibility and Fiction.* New York: Oxford University Press.

Sher, A. (2003) *I.D.* London: Nick Hern Books.

Simons, D. J., Wang, R.F. and Rodenberry, D. (2002) "Object Recognition is Mediated by Extraretinal Information." *Perception and Psychophysics,* 64: 521–30.

Smith, A.D. (1993) *Fires in the Mirror: Crown Heights, Brooklyn and Other Identities.* New York: Doubleday.

(2000) *Talk To Me: Listening Between the Lines.* New York: Random House.

Smith, W. (1990) *Real Life Drama: The Group Theatre and America 1931–1940.* New York: Alfred A. Knopf.

Stanislavski, K. (1967) *My Life in Art.* Trans. J.J. Robbins. Harmondsworth: Penguin Books.

(1995) "Inner Impulses and Inner Action; Creative Objectives," in Richard Drain (ed.) *Twentieth Century Theatre: A Sourcebook.* London: Routledge, 253–7.

(2008) An Actor's Work: A Student's Diary. Trans. Jean Benedetti (ed.). London: Routledge.

Strack, F., Martin, L. and Stepper, S. (1988) "Inhibiting and Facilitating Conditions of the Human Smile: A Nonobtrusive Test of the Facial Feedback Hypothesis." Journal of Personality and Social Psychology, 54: 768–77.

Strasberg, L. (1964) "Working with Live Material." Interview by R. Schechner, Drama Review, 9(1): 117–35.

(1987) A Dream of Passion: The Development of the Method. New York: Plume.

Toporkov, V. (2004) Stanislavski in Rehearsal. Trans. Jean Benedetti. London: Routledge.

Vielmetter, G. (1999) "The Theory of Holistic Simulation: Beyond Interpretivism and Postempiricism," in H.H. Kögler and K.R. Stueber (eds) Empathy and Agency: The Problem of Understanding in the Human Sciences. Boulder, CO: Westview Press, 83–102.

Wangh, S. (2000) An Acrobat of the Heart. New York: Vintage Books.

Wexler, M. and Klam, F. (2001) "Movement Prediction and Movement Production." Journal of Experimental Psychology: Human Perception and Performance, 27: 48–64.

Wexler, M., Kosslyn, S.M. and Berthoz, A. (1998) "Motor Processes in Mental Rotation." Cognition, 68: 77–94.

Wilde, O. (1895) The Importance of Being Earnest.

Wolford, L. and Schechner, R. (eds) (2001) The Grotowski Sourcebook. London: Routledge.

Video

Les deux voyages de Jacques Lecoq (1999). Roy, Jean-Noel and Carasso, Jean-Gabriel Paris: La Septe ARTE – On Line production – ANRAT.

The Importance of Being Earnest (1988). Dir: Anthony Asquith. Perf: Michael Redgrave, Michael Denison, Margaret Rutherford, Edith Evans, Dorothy Tutin, Joan Greenwood. Paramount Pictures.

The Importance of Being Earnest (2002). Dir: Oliver Parker. Perf: Judi Dench, Rupert Everett, Colin Firth, Frances O'Connor, Reese Witherspoon. Miramax Films.

Index

Made in United States
Orlando, FL
09 February 2022

14628374R00141